English
Party
Politics

VOLUME I

READINGS IN POLITICS AND SOCIETY

GENERAL EDITOR: Bernard Crick
*Professor of Political Theory and Institutions,
University of Sheffield*

PREVIOUSLY PUBLISHED
W. L. Guttsman, *The English Ruling Class*

FORTHCOMING VOLUMES
F. W. Bealey, *The Social and Political Thought of the British Labour
Party*
Maurice Bruce, *The Rise of the Welfare State*
Nicholas Deakin, *Race in British Politics*
Edmund Ions, *Political and Social Thought in America 1870–1970*
J. K. Kumar, *Revolution*
J. P. Mackintosh, *The Growth of the Cabinet System*
William Thornhill, *The Growth and Reform of Local Government*

Previously published in this series by Routledge and Kegan Paul

David Nicholls, *Church and State in Britain Since 1820*

English Party Politics

VOLUME I 1600–1906

Edited by

ALAN BEATTIE

Lecturer in Political Science,
London School of Economics

WEIDENFELD AND NICOLSON
5 Winsley Street London W1

Editorial text © 1970 by Alan Beattie

SBN 297 17991 8 Case Bound
SBN 297 17993 4 Paper Back

Made and Printed in Great Britain by Cox & Wyman Ltd.,
London, Fakenham and Reading

To my father, John Beattie,
and in memory
of my mother, Amy Beattie

Contents

General Editor's Introduction.

The purpose of this series is to introduce students of society to a number of important problems through the study of sources and contemporary documents. It should be part of every student's education to have some contact with the materials from which the judgements of authors of secondary works are reached, or the grounds of social action determined. Students may actually find this more interesting than relying exclusively on the pre-digested diet of textbooks. The readings will be drawn from as great a variety of documents as is possible within each book: Royal Commission reports, Parliamentary debates, letters to the Press, newspaper editorials, letters and diaries both published and unpublished, sermons and literary sources, etc., will all be drawn upon. For the aim is both to introduce the student to carefully selected extracts from the principal books and documents on a subject (the things he always hears about but never reads), and to show him the great range of subsidiary and secondary source materials available (the memorials of actors in the actual events).

The prejudice of this series is that the social sciences need to be taught and developed in an historical context. Those of us who wish to be relevant and topical (and this is no bad wish) sometimes need reminding that the most usual explanation of why a thing is as it is, is that things happened in the past to make it so. These things might not have happened. They might have happened differently.

And nothing in the present is, strictly speaking, *determined* from the past; but everything is limited by what went before. Every present problem, whether of understanding or of action, will always have a variety of relevant antecedent factors, all of which must be understood before it is sensible to commit ourselves to an explanatory theory or to some course of practical action. No present problem is completely novel and there is never any single cause for it, but always a variety of conditioning factors, arising through time, whose relative importance is a matter of critical judgement as well as of objective knowledge.

The aim of this series is, then, to give the student the opportunity to examine with care an avowedly selective body of source materials. The topics have been chosen both because they are of contemporary importance and because they cut across established pedagogic boundaries between the various disciplines and between courses of professional instruction. We hope that these books will supplement, not replace, other forms of introductory reading; so both the length and the character of the Introductions will vary according to whether the particular editor has already written on the subject or not. Some Introductions will summarize what is already to be found elsewhere at greater length, but some will be original contributions to knowledge or even, on occasions, reasoned advocacies. Above all, however, I hope that this series will help to develop a method of introductory teaching that can show how and from where we come to reach the judgements that are to be found in secondary accounts and textbooks.

University of Sheffield   Bernard Crick

Preface

My studies in the history of English party politics were first stimu-
lated and guided by the late Professor Reginald Bassett, and in this
sense these volumes owe a great deal to his unrivalled knowledge of
the English political past. More immediately, Professor Bernard
Crick encouraged me to produce these volumes, and in his capacity
as Editor of the series has guided and assisted me in a manner
deserving my most sincere gratitude. My secretary, Miss Elizabeth
Schnadhorst, has done sterling work in deciphering an enormous
mass of my near-illegible handwriting, and has rivalled her Birmingham ancestor in speed and efficiency. Finally, a debt of a more
general kind: it will be obvious to the reader that the historical
period covered by this work goes beyond that with which any one
historian could be intimately acquainted. Consequently, I have
leaned heavily on the works of those scholars whose knowledge
(especially of the period before the mid-nineteenth century) is
infinitely greater than mine: I hope that the footnote references in
the Introductory sections are sufficient evidence of my debt.

The Introductions to each of the six sections of documents may
be read consecutively as a single essay in party history.

A.J.B.

Acknowledgements

The author and publishers would like to thank the following for permission to quote from copyright sources:

The Labour Party for *Labour Party Annual Conference Reports, Parliament and Revolution* and *Socialism and Government* by J. R. MacDonald and *The Game of Party Politics* by Philip Snowden; George Allen & Unwin Ltd for *Fabian Essays in Socialism* (1889), *Peace and Goodwill in Industry* by Stanley Baldwin and *Equality* by R. H. Tawney; Ernest Benn Ltd for *The Governance of England* by Sir Sidney Low and *Conservatism* by Lord Hugh Cecil; the London School of Economics and Political Science for 'Cabinet and Party, 1914–1921' by Herman Finer in *Economica* and *The Essentials of Parliamentary Democracy* by R. Bassett; the *Contemporary Review* for 'The War and the Parties' by H. Spender; the *Spectator* for 'The Purpose of an Opposition' by J. R. MacDonald; the *New Statesman* for 'Should Liberals Vote Tory?', 'Liberalism and Labour' by J. M. Keynes and 'Reflections on Party Loyalty' by R. H. S. Crossman; Methuen & Co. Ltd for *Politics and Progress* by Ramsay Muir; Cassell & Co. Ltd for *Fifty Years of Parliament* by the Earl of Oxford and *The Memoirs of the Earl of Woolton*; the Clarendon Press, Oxford for *Parliament, Its History, Constitution and Practice* by Sir Courtney Ilbert; Hodder & Stoughton Ltd for *Sometimes I Think* by Sir G. Rentoul; the Conservative and Unionist Central Office for speech by Capt. Pretyman in *Gleanings and Memoranda*, 'The Political Divide' by Ian Macleod in *The Future of the Welfare State* and 'The Maxwell-Fyfe Report'; Macmillan & Co. Ltd for *Industry and the State* by R. Boothby, H. Macmillan *et al*; Sir Keith Feiling for *What is Conservatism*; Julian Amery for *Empire and Prosperity* by L. S. Amery; *The Times*

xiii

for 'The New Europe' and 'Nuffield Inquest on the Election' by David Wood; William Heinemann Ltd for *Conservatism and the Future* by E. T. Cook; Oxford University Press for *Thoughts on the Constitution* by L. S. Amery; *Crossbow* for 'The Limits of Laissez-Faire' by Enoch Powell; Victor Montagu for *Full Speed Ahead, Essays in Tory Reform*; John Murray Ltd for *The Game of Politics* by P. G. Cambray; the Fabian Society for *The Mechanics of Victory, Labour in the Affluent Society* by R. H. S. Crossman and 'Put Policy on the Agenda' by W. Fienburgh; Lord Redmayne for 'The Commons in Action' in the *Listener*; the Estate of Lord Morrison of Lambeth for *An Autobiography* by Lord Morrison; the *Political Quarterly* for 'The Technique of Opposition' by Sir Ivor Jennings, 'Social Change, Peaceful or Violent' by Herbert Morrison and 'The Choice before the Labour Party' by R. H. Tawney.

List of Documentary Sources

3.2.13 *The Church of England Quarterly Review*, January 1837: Tithes.

3.2.14 *The Edinburgh Review*, January 1848, 'The Ministry and the New Parliament': The strength of Whiggism.

3.2.15 J. S. Mill, *On Liberty* (1859).

3.2.16 W. E. Gladstone, *The Course of Commercial Policy at Home and Abroad* (1843): Free Trade.

3.2.17 Lord Acton, *Political Thought on the Church* (1858): Politics and Christianity.

3.2.18 *Cobbett's Weekly Political Register*, December 1830 and June 1833: Parliamentary Reform.

3.2.19 *The Poor Man's Guardian*, 24 September 1831: Parliamentary Reform.

3.2.20 A Speech by Richard Cobden at Manchester, 24 October 1844: Free trade.

3.2.21 R. Gammage, *The History of the Chartist Movement* (1854).

3.2.22 Joseph Parkes to Francis Place, early 1836: Whigs and Radicals.

3.3 PARTY IN PARLIAMENT

3.3.1 Sir James Graham to F. R. Bonham, 6 January 1841: Party organization.

3.3.2 *The Greville Memoirs*, 10 February 1839: State of the parties.

3.3.3 *The Edinburgh Review*, January 1846: 'Legislation for the Working Classes'.

3.3.4 *Report on the Organisation of the Permanent Civil Service* ('The 'Northcote-Trevelyan Report'), 1854.

3.3.5 A. Symonds, *Practical Suggestions for the Internal Reform of the House of Commons* (1832): The scope of government.

3.3.6 Sir Robert Peel to J. W. Croker, 5 March 1833: Strong government.

3.3.7 *The Parliamentary Debates*, 8 February 1855: Speech by Lord Derby on strong government.

3.3.8 An exchange of letters between Disraeli and Peel, February 1844: The Whip.

3.3.9 W. Bagehot, *The English Constitution* (1867): Party feeling.

3.3.10 The Duke of Newcastle to Sidney Herbert, 27 October 1851: Party leadership.

General
Introduction

A collection of documents intended to illustrate the character of party politics over a period of approximately three centuries can only be assembled and made intelligible by specifying the area to be covered, and organizing the material in terms of particular aspects and chronological divisions. The documents which make up the major part of these volumes are intended to illustrate, within each chronological division, the activities of parties in Parliament and in the country, the rhetoric which accompanied their activities, contemporary attitudes to their place within the general political landscape, and contemporary attitudes to the general character of the constitution.

Parties and the Constitution

Contemporary interest in the working of political parties arises in part from a dissatisfaction with older modes of inquiry into political activity. Such older modes often invoked the idea of 'the constitution', understood as a set of procedural rules within which particular differences of interest or principle were reconciled or adjusted. Scepticism about 'constitutions' has taken one of two forms. Firstly, it is sometimes argued that politics is not a rule-governed activity at all: politics is about 'power', or 'class', or 'interest'. Politics cannot, on this view, involve constitutional (procedural) rules, since such rules imply the possibility of a reconciliation or adjustment of differences, and the possibility of general agreement on the distribution of authority (as opposed to agreement about particular issues or ends). To those to whom such adjustment or agreement is impossible, constitutional rules appear as the mere manifestations of the 'interests' of the dominant 'power' groups in society. The confusions inherent in this view are outlined below in the considerations of party rhetoric, and it is the second source of scepticism about which more needs to be said here. On this second view, the importance of procedural rules is accepted, but it is argued that ideas such as 'parliamentary government', 'the rule of law' and so on are incorrect or outdated descriptions of the prevailing rules. Party becomes essential to the constitution; indeed, to some recent writers, the organization and character of political parties *is* the constitution.[1] The introductions and documents in these volumes have been constructed on the belief that in Britain political parties have worked *within* the framework of the constitutional rules implicit in such ideas as 'mixed government' and 'parliamentary government'. British parties have developed in subordination to and in accordance with these rules, they have not replaced them or rendered them 'out of date'.[2] It is for this reason that each chronological section of these volumes includes an account of and documents relevant to the constitutional context *within which* party activity has occurred.

A further reason for not ignoring or taking for granted the general character of the constitution in any particular historical period is that in this way the temptations to 'read the past backwards'[3] are more firmly resisted. One of the consequences of the current attempts to reduce all British political activity to the idea of party is that any historical period which is obviously not patient of even plausible explanation in modern party terms (that is to say, any period before the 1880s) is regarded not as something to be studied in its own right and on its own terms, but as a past which is to be ransacked for clues as to the antecedents or forerunners of modern party politics. Those sections of the documents dealing with the constitution and with contemporary attitudes to party are included to enable the reader to see political parties in their contemporary

[1] See, for example, M. Duverger, *Political Parties* (1954), *passim*.
[2] For an expanded defence of this view see A. J. Beattie, 'Coalition Government in Britain', *Government and Opposition*, November 1966.
[3] M. J. Oakeshott, *Rationalism in Politics* (1962), p. 147.

context, and not as mere preludes to a predetermined state of 'party government' in the twentieth century.

Party Rhetoric

Of all the questions which arise in the literature devoted to the study of British party politics, the question of the importance to be attached to political ideas has perhaps caused most dissension and difficulty. At one extreme, there is the view that British parties have been from the time of their emergence based on coherent and articulate principles or programmes; at the other extreme is the view based on the philosophical belief that since all political action is determined by 'objective' factors such as class or self-interest, all expressions of 'principle' are either rationalizations of economic or psychological necessity, or attempts to disguise the existence of these necessities. The documents in this book are assembled in the belief that the latter view is untenable: to reduce all arguments to mere expressions of objective and necessary self-interest or class-interest is either to deny the possibility of rational discussion itself, or to elevate those who attempt such reductions (and present them as 'truths') to a position where they alone are unaffected by those factors which determine the conduct of others. On the other hand, the rejection of these crude forms of Marxism or utilitarianism need not present us with the sole alternative of believing that articulate and explicit 'principles' are the sole clues to an understanding of party activity. The important thing is to distinguish between the different kinds of argument used in politics, and to clarify the relationship between these varieties and the activities of political parties.

In the first place, to describe the everyday utterances of politicians as 'philosophy' is to obliterate all relevant distinctions. Politicians are men of action; their aim is seldom to explain, usually to persuade. For this reason, their language is frequently employed to disguise their real intentions, or to win support for their actions by presenting their case in a manner calculated to secure the widest possible support. Again, living in a world where time is short, politicians do not attempt to explore the foundations of their actions in a manner or with an articulateness expected in a university seminar or of a political philosopher. No one who had examined the career of most politicians could believe that the language they used was designed solely to explain their actions, or that, for

xxvii

example, a party pamphlet discussing the merits of family allowances could be regarded as employing the same kind of arguments
as Plato when the latter was reflecting upon the nature of justice.
The reasons for political action are important; politicians have
choices, they may do one thing or they may do another: they are
not 'determined' in their behaviour. But to describe the language of
politics as 'philosophical' is to endow it with a degree of abstraction
and articulate coherence, as well as an explanatory motive, the lack
of which is its most obvious characteristic. Moreover, whether a
politician's own account of his behaviour may be taken as sufficient
is a matter to be judged in the light of the circumstances: Peel's
own accounts of his purpose in transforming the Conservative
party after 1832 would appear to be of more value than those of
Disraeli as an explanation of what happened in those years. There is
no general formula which obviates the need to examine each case in
relation to the circumstantial evidence.

Secondly, it is quite possible to hold both that the writings and
speeches of some politicians provide a satisfactory account of their
actions, and that there are certain general principles or guides to
action according to which men have at particular times been divided (and which can be described by using labels such as 'Conservative', 'Liberal' and so on) without admitting that such principles are *always* very useful guides to particular political disputes
or coincide with the divisions of organized party. Even if it could
be shown (to take an example from an age over which much
controversy reigns) that the Whig opposition to George III was
composed solely of high-minded men indifferent to their own self-
interest, whose own statements could be taken at face-value, it
would still be true that not all who bore the Whig party label
accepted the principles of 'constitutional Whiggism', and that many
of those who bore that party label had different (and often incompatible) reasons for their opposition. There is a very great difference between the proposition that 'principles' are important and
the proposition that party politicians not only always possess such
principles but that they possess the *same ones* as their party colleagues. Again, the truth will emerge only from an examination of
the circumstances, and not from any *a priori* view about the relation
between principles and practice: parties are sometimes united upon
principles or programmes, sometimes they are not, and sometimes
there is very little 'principle' to be discovered. All this means that

the documents included under the heading of 'Party Rhetoric' are more varied and more open to misinterpretation than those in other sections of the book. Some (as in the case of Disraeli) have almost no *explanatory* value; others (as in the case of Peel) a great deal. Some are related to specific disputes, others are in the form of more general attempts to establish the existence of long standing principles.

A third difficulty is that the disputes between and within political parties are usually more transient than the constitutional and party framework within which they occur. It is reasonable to discuss the character of the constitution even between the first two Reform Acts because the constitution possessed a degree of permanence and generality which the disputes over particular legislative or administrative proposals lacked: the difference between a consideration of the constitution and a consideration of a particular party dispute is approximately analogous to a consideration of the rules of cricket and the results of particular cricket matches. To include both sorts of consideration within the same collection of documents is thus to deal with two rather different subjects, and for this reason the reader must approach the sections on party rhetoric aware of these reservations; the many different kinds of argument included within this section, and the important differences between this section and the others must always be borne in mind. It is hoped that none the less the reader will gain some appreciation of the varieties of argument in party politics, and some knowledge of those issues which are an indispensable part of the history of party.

Chronology

The documents have been arranged in six historical periods, and here again a note of caution must be introduced. The choice of significant events as convenient starting-points for an historical inquiry always possesses an element of the arbitrary. This element is magnified when, as is the case with the present volumes, the scope of the work is such as to embrace a number of rather different themes for which no one date or event would be equally significant. The years 1832 and 1867, for example, are obviously significant from the standpoint of increasing electoral participation in politics; on the other hand, they do not necessarily indicate developments of equal importance in the activities of the parliamentary parties or of party organization in the country, which might respectively require significance to be attached to, say, Peel's success in building up a fairly coherent parliamentary majority by 1841, or the foundation of the National Liberal Federation in 1877. Since all of these developments are of relevance to the history of party, the sub-divisions used can be no more than a very rough and ready means of dividing a chronological story into more manageable parts; different chronological divisions might be equally appropriate, and the ones used in this volume are merely matters of convenience.

I   1660–1760

Introduction

THE CONSTITUTION

Most of the constitutional commentaries written after 1715 had in common the view that constitutional arrangements could be presented as an intelligible and coherent whole; much importance was attached to demonstrating that, whatever difficulties might beset English politics, the absence of an agreed set of constitutional procedures was not among them. Such self-congratulation is understandable in the light of the earlier difficulties experienced by the English (after the beginning of the seventeenth century) in reaching agreement upon a set of constitutional arrangements within which the bitter divisions of economic and religious interest could be reconciled. The English Civil War was the violent manifestation of these difficulties, and was followed by a series of novel constitutional experiments, including the abolition of the Monarchy and the House of Lords, the exercise of executive power by the House of Commons, and rule by the army under Oliver Cromwell.

The Restoration of 1660 involved the recognition that none of these experiments had provided an acceptable constitutional framework, and the English returned once more to the traditional institutions of King, Lords and Commons. By the middle of the eighteenth century the success of the Restoration was generally acclaimed, and the theme of a stable 'balance' between the three institutions was established as a central category of constitutional thought. The basis of this balance was seen to lie in the general acceptance of Monarch and Parliament as permanent parts of the constitution, and in the possession by each of sufficient checks to resist dangerous concentrations of power in the hands of the others [1.1.1–2]. The Monarch's executive powers under the prerogative had been fully restored in 1660, and the Revolution Settlement of 1689 left intact his right to choose his own ministerial advisers. The political importance of Parliament had been demonstrated by its successful opposition to the Monarch both in 1641 and in the Revolution of 1688, an importance given more formal recognition by the Septennial Convention after 1716, by which the Septennial Act, enjoining parliamentary elections at least once every seven years, became an understanding that elections would be held not *more than* once every seven years.[4] This guarantee of parliamentary existence was buttressed by the need of monarchs after 1688 to raise an increased proportion of their revenue from sources involving parliamentary consent. The Monarch's right to choose his ministers was thus balanced by the need to choose ministers not wholly unacceptable to Parliament. The defeat of even so apparently dominant a Minister as Walpole in 1742 showed the reality of parliamentary power, as did the fact that the important 'First Ministers' of the period (Walpole and Pelham for example) were members of the House of Commons.[5] The fall of Walpole is of further significance in that it was not accompanied by serious or acceptable demands for his impeachment. This is some indication of the extent to which loss of political office was coming to be regarded as both normal and tolerable, rather than as evidence of fundamental constitutional differences requiring resolution by force. Finally, the danger that two such independent and powerful institutions as Monarch and Parliament might reach a position of deadlock was seen to have been avoided through the recognition by each side of the importance of the other, and by the system of influence or patronage, by which the Monarch could offer to members of Parliament rewards such as ministerial office, administrative appointments and electoral assistance, and thus safeguard himself against too obstructive a Parliament.[6] [1.1.3.]

There was little place in these views for the idea of an electorate possessing an influence independent of the House of Commons.

[4] B. Kemp, *King and Commons, 1660–1832* (1959), p. 43 et seq.
[5] A. S. Foord, *His Majesty's Opposition, 1740–1830* (Oxford, 1964), p. 214.
[6] Kemp, p. 66.

The Monarch's right to choose ministers and the electoral patronage exercised by both the Crown and the aristocracy, together with the small size of the electorate, meant that elections were seldom directly connected with changes of Ministry.[7] Even those whose sympathies lay with Lockean notions of the social contract were at great pains to emphasize the undesirability of direct electoral control over the activities of Parliament [1.1.4]; indeed, the very idea of balance implied an opposition to direct influence on the part of the electors, since this could only tilt the balance too far towards the House of Commons.

On the other hand, it is important not to underestimate the extent to which rather different interpretations of the Constitution existed within this general picture, and the extent to which even the acceptance of the idea of balance might lead to different views of constitutional propriety. The existence of even a rather vague agreement as to the nature of the constitution was not established before the 1720s; the question of the succession to the Throne was an important source of constitutional conflict before the accession of George I, and the depths of bitterness which party politics could reach before the Hanoverian accession is evidenced by the frequent fear of impeachment as a consequence of loss of ministerial office.[8] It was only the success of the Whigs in virtually abolishing the Tory Party as a serious political force by the 1720s, and the gradual erosion of what had been a large and important electorate (through local party arrangements to regulate competition and the increased cost of elections) which made possible the calm edifice of constitutional theory under the first two Hanoverians.[9] Both the Exclusion Crisis of 1679 and the Revolution of 1688 had demonstrated the extent to which the Restoration had not settled fundamental constitutional difficulties,[10] and the former crisis in particular showed the difficulties of distinguishing between 'party' issues and questions affecting the very basis of the constitution, since the Whig position was essentially the defence of the *institution* of Parliament against the claims of Monarchy.[11]

[7] Ibid., p. 79.

[8] R. Pares, *Limited Monarchy in Great Britain in the Eighteenth Century* (1957), p. 15.

[9] J. H. Plumb, *The Growth of Political Stability in England, 1675–1725* (Oxford, 1967), *passim*.

[10] J. R. Jones, *The First Whigs* (Durham, 1961), pp. 4, 212.

[11] Ibid., p. 6.

Even under the relative stability of the first two Hanoverians, differences of interpretation within the general idea of 'balance' could still occur. To some writers, the important distinction between Monarch and Parliament was one of function: the Monarch took the initiative in the formation of national policy and administration, while Parliament's role was as a controller rather than a governor [1.1.5]. The balance could also be seen as a matter of the mixed representation of certain social interests and views (aristocracy, Monarchy and democracy) whose coexistence depended not upon formal institutional arrangements such as elections and the royal prerogative, but upon a 'natural' and hidden balance of social forces [1.1.6]. Even those who attached significance to institutional arrangements could differ about the source of threats to the balance. To the independents in the House of Commons (that is to say, to those members who were independent both of Crown influence [1.1.7] and the politicians since their interests were local, their seats in most cases secure and ministerial office held no appeal for them), the balance ought to be achieved by a tension between Monarchy and Parliament *as a whole*. Control was the business of *all* Members of Parliament and not of a mere section of them [1.1.8]. So to them the presence in the House of Commons of the Monarch's ministerial and administrative nominees could be seen as a serious threat to parliamentary independence and to the constitutional balance[12] [1.1.9]. To Hume, on the other hand, it was the system of influence alone which prevented the balance from degenerating into deadlock and obstruction [1.1.10]: it was the essential lubricant of the whole system.[13]

The important consequences for party activity of these constitutional differences can be illustrated by the dilemma faced by independent members of the House of Commons. The 'country' or independent programme of the eighteenth century assumed that 'the redress of grievances' was a matter for Parliament as a whole; yet the very existence of ministers chosen by the Monarch and supported by a group of Members of Parliament who owed their seats to the Crown (the 'placemen') meant that opposition could only be effected through a sectional group of office-seeking politicians, whose aim was to replace the incumbents. It was in an

[12] Foord, p. 19.
[13] For a survey of different conceptions of balance and separation see M. J. C. Vile, *Constitutionalism and the Separation of Powers* (Oxford, 1967), Chs I–V.

attempt to remove this tension between 'party' opposition and 'institutional' opposition (that is, the opposition of the House of Commons as a whole) that the independents tried so frequently (and unsuccessfully) to abolish the system of influence and place.[14]

It was within this limited area of constitutional uncertainty that the politicians of the period acted. Strength in any eighteenth-century Ministry arose from the possession of the confidence of both the Monarch and the House of Commons, and the withdrawal of either of these supports would place a Ministry in serious difficulty.[15] Crown influence in parliamentary elections was important and indispensable, but never decisive; the Parliaments of the period contained on average only two hundred placemen, of whom no more than forty would be, from the standpoint of the incumbent Ministry, wholly reliable.[16] It was therefore important to possess, in addition, the support of at least some of the active politicians and office-seekers within the House, together with at least the tolerance of some of the independents. The tolerance of the latter was seldom very difficult to secure provided that the Ministry did not outrage their interests, but it was also from the independents that the greatest suspicion of 'influence' and threats to the balance tended to come.

'Party' activity after 1715 was confined to those members of the House of Commons who were neither strict placemen nor independents, but whose quest for office was undertaken within the limited but still significant uncertainties of the idea of 'balance'.

ATTITUDES TO PARTY

The extent to which men attached importance to party labels varied during this period: under Queen Anne, it was thought to be of the first importance to identify a politician according to his Whig or Tory inclinations. (The labels 'Whig' and 'Tory' were first used to identify the protagonists in the Exclusion Crisis of 1679–80, during which Charles II successfully resisted Parliamentary attempts to exclude his brother James, Duke of York, from the succession to the throne in view of the latter's Catholicism.) Party views were seen

[14] Foord, p. 105.
[15] J. B. Owen, *The Rise of the Pelhams* (1957), pp. 39–42.
[16] Kemp, p. 97.

as a basic means of identification, and two main sets of views were identified.[17] While by the 1720s party passions had abated, the labels of Whig and Tory were still in use, though with very different contents and with much less importance attached to them.[18]

The idea of party was often inextricably linked (indeed sometimes identified with) the idea of opposition, and attitudes to the latter were associated with attitudes to the former. The idea of politics as involving a recognition of the dispersal of political power was well-established; the absence of any one group or institution strong enough to successfully impose its will upon the rest was too obvious to ignore, and the existence of 'opposition' was thus equally obvious [1.2.1]. On the other hand, the words 'party' and 'opposition' could be used to stand for a variety of different political arrangements and attitudes. 'Party' might refer either to one side in a dispute of opinion (in something like the legal sense of a 'party to a dispute') or to a particular body of men, who might or might not have opinions in common or as the basis of their association (as in 'the country party'). In a similar manner, 'opposition' might refer simply to the *act* of opposing a particular measure, or (a significant development by the 1730s) to that section of Parliament not involved in supporting the incumbent Ministry; in the latter case, the institutionalization of an opposition section of the Commons would be evidenced by referring to '*The* Opposition'.[19] This latter usage was often put in other terms – 'court and country' – signifying those supporting the King and his Ministry as against the rest, but even here the terms could be used in various ways. The term 'court' was often used to identify those individuals who supported the Monarch and his Ministers, as distinct from the 'country' group who either actively opposed the 'court' or adopted an 'independent' position with respect to it. Under Anne, this usage was narrowed to the extent that the 'court' party were those whose loyalties lay with the Monarch in person rather than with her Ministers.[20] Again, 'country' (as was the case with 'opposition') could refer not to individuals but to the *function* of the Commons as a check upon the executive. This variety of terms,

---

[17] G. Holmes, *British Politics in the Age of Anne* (1967), pp. 16–20.

[18] C. Robbins, 'Discordant Parties: A Study of the Acceptance of Party by Englishmen', *Political Science Quarterly*, 1958, 73, p. 510.

[19] Foord, p. 154.

[20] Holmes, Ch. 11.

and the different meanings which could be attached to each of them, reflected the complicated variety of political relationships possible in a period when the constitution was subject to the different interpretations discussed above.[21]

Beside this rather confused set of attitudes, however, three factors stand out with relative clarity. In the first place, the use of two party labels (Whig and Tory) survived the demise of party passions after the 1720s (however insignificant and insincere their usage, and however changed the contents they described).[22] Secondly, the recognition of the existence of 'opposition' was firmly established by the 1730s. The extent to which opposition was regarded as *desirable* is a rather different matter. The independents saw opposition as the constitutional function of the House as a whole, and thus criticized as 'faction' the attempts of any section of the Commons to either replace or offer exclusive support for incumbent Ministers [1.2.2]. A similar criticism was likely to come from those who saw such action as encroaching upon the rights of the Monarch or as being based [1.2.3] upon mere greed for office as opposed to a genuine pursuit of principle [1.2.4]. None the less, it is clear from contemporary references to the fall of Walpole in 1742 that while some forms of opposition and party were more acceptable than others, the existence in the Commons of a group of 'outs' whose aim was to replace the 'ins' was recognized as a fact, and was extended more toleration and occasional defence than had been the case before the 1720s.[23] Finally, it is clear that none of this implies a recognition of the existence of a 'party system'. The rights of the Monarch and the presence of the independents in the Commons prevented too much importance being attached to the activities of the 'outs', and opposition politicians themselves did not conceive of politics as the regular alternation in power of parliamentary groups. The most articulate defences of the rights of oppositions were couched rather in 'once and for all' terms: They were defended as attempts to replace the incumbent Ministers by a group which would then remain *permanently* in office. It was domination and the removal of future opposition – a hauling-up of the ladder once the current opposition was aboard – which was pursued, not the prospect of alternation [1.2.3].

21 See pp. 3–5.
22 See below, pp. 10–12.
23 Foord, p. 154.

PARTIES IN PARLIAMENT

The place of party in the parliamentary politics of this period is one of the most keenly debated questions in modern constitutional history. In 1959 Professor R. Walcott argued forcefully against the then prevailing view that politics in the early eighteenth century could be described in terms of party. The power of the Monarch and the presence of the independents were, he argued, the basic facts of the age, and political activity among the parliamentary groups other than the placemen and the independents was based not upon party but upon family 'connexion' and specific interest.[24] This view has recently been strongly criticized,[25] and it is now clear that the history of parliamentary parties between the Restoration of 1660 and the accession of George III in 1760 must sharply distinguish between politics before and after the accession of George I.

In the age of Anne, party was a vital aspect of political life. The use of Whig and Tory labels to classify politicians was widespread, as was the adoption of these labels by members of the Commons. The labels reflected important differences of general principle and particular programme, and the correlation between party labels and voting in the House of Commons was extremely high.[26] There was an ebb and flow in party passions between 1660 and the 1720s, but there is no doubt that the unstable state of constitutional opinion in this period produced party bitterness and internal cohesion not confined to the reign of Anne[27] [1.3.1]. The importance of party politics was based partly on the presence of fundamental disagree-agreements about particular policies and general constitutional arrangements. It was enhanced by the presence of a large and party-minded electorate and frequent parliamentary elections, to which the parliamentary parties responded with fairly articulate and national electoral organizations, meeting before parliamentary sessions and, on the Tory side, possessing a sophisticated system of regional Whips.[28]

[24] R. Walcott, *British Politics in the Early Eighteenth Century* (Oxford, 1956).
[25] See Plumb and Holmes.
[26] Holmes, p. 35.
[27] For the Exclusion Crisis see Jones, *passim*.
[28] Holmes, p. 346.

Economic interests were clearly involved in this conflict, but it is impossible to force party divisions into the mould of land against commerce, or rich against poor. The Whigs under Anne were composed of both large landowners and commercial men, while the Tories, although more nearly a single-class party in their representation of small landowners, were never without representatives from other economic interests, and were significantly unable to match the cohesion of the Whigs. By superior unity and skilful use of patronage, and by taking advantage of the Tories' associations with Jacobitism, the Whigs had succeeded, by the 1720s, in removing the Tory Party as a serious political force.[29] Before this, the importance of parties was demonstrated by their cohesion in Parliament, their relatively sophisticated electoral organization, and the ease with which, in comparison with the later eighteenth century, mere office-seeking could be distinguished from action on the basis of principle.[30]

By the time of Walpole's ascendancy and the accession of George I, the passion of party had abated; party labels were less ubiquitous, the independents could be more easily identified, and the former parliamentary and electoral cohesion of the parties had melted into the atomic complexities and cross-voting of family and other connexions and the smaller, more easily-managed, and more locally-orientated electorate [1.3.2].

In these more placid circumstances, 'party organization' in the House of Commons was confined to that group of politicians interested in achieving ministerial office. The ministerial supporters were of course much more easy to organize than the 'opposition': the Ministry had Crown patronage and the authority of the Monarch at its disposal [1.3.3–5]. For the opposition groups organization was much more difficult. Recognition of the opposition as an institution was evidenced by the understanding (established in the 1730s) that its members sat on the left of the Speaker,[31] but its composition was seldom constant for any length of time. A connexion was usually eager for office, and thus its more competent and important members might be detached by a Ministry seeking to widen its support. The fact that a number of groups co-existed in opposition did not in itself imply or produce any cohesion in voting or policy: The

[29] Plumb, p. 172.
[30] Holmes, p. 403.
[31] Foord, p. 155.

longevity of Walpole's reign, for example, while giving the opposition some sense of unity, and contributing something to its establishment as a recognized institution, produced no single recognized opposition leader.[32] In a Parliament in which the independents were of great numerical importance, and in an age in which great policy or constitutional issues were absent, continuous and formed opposition was difficult to achieve [1.3.6]. In these circumstances, the typical tactics of the groups out of office included intrigue at court (with royal mistresses or with the successor to the throne) and attempts to weaken the Ministry by detaching some of its more important and able members or supporters. Not until the reign of George III did opposition groups seriously consider extending their efforts outside Parliament.

Thus the period as a whole represents a transition from a situation of party politics before the 1720s to the more confused and shifting balance of connexions within the context of relatively stable ministries and the importance of the independents, a situation which prevailed without serious challenge until the reign of George III.

PARTY RHETORIC

The labels of Whig and Tory originated during the Exclusion Crisis of 1679 [1.4.1–2]. The Whigs were those who, led by the Earl of Shaftesbury, wished to exclude the Catholic successor to the throne. Also involved was the place of Parliament in the constitution, and the conflict was basically between the Monarch and the Whigs (or Parliament) with the Tories playing a merely auxiliary role.[33] The conflict between the Monarch (supported by the Tories) and the Whigs took the form of a conflict between belief in Divine Right, the dominance of the prerogative power, and the persistent concern with the preservation of the ascendancy of the Church of England against Whig beliefs in the Lockean notion of social contract, limited government, Parliament as the representatives of the people, and freedom of worship (especially for Protestant dissenters).

The Revolution of 1688 blurred these differences to some extent [1.4.3]; the debates about the right to disobey the King and the

[32] Owen, p. 47.
[33] Jones, p. 6.

scope of the prerogative power were made irrelevant by the victory of Whig views on these questions, and in any case the Revolution was an all-party affair: of the seven signatories who invited William of Orange to assume the English throne, three were self-styled Tories.[34] But the old conflict was by no means entirely in abeyance. Under Anne, the frequency of elections and the accompanying outbreak of party politics revived some of the older questions. The Whigs firmly and unanimously supported the Protestant succession and the 1701 Act of Settlement which was designed to preserve it, while the Tories exhibited less enthusiasm: not from any love of Roman Catholicism so much as a traditional reluctance to impose limitations on the position of the Monarch.[35] To these established divisions were added new ones such as those on foreign policy, where the Tories took a strongly 'isolationist' position.

Whenever such conflicts arose (which, under Anne, was most of the time[36]) party labels represented real and heartfelt differences of views. Party passions, however, had cooled by the accession of George I, and the party labels were beginning to represent rather different divisions. The Whigs' commitment to the Protestant succession after 1694 put them in the somewhat novel position of appearing as the most vociferous supporters of the incumbent Monarch [1.4.4–5]. The use of Crown patronage which followed from this, together with their success in exploiting the presence of that numerically small and politically inept section of the Tories who were still flirting with the Pretender and with Roman Catholicism [1.4.6], enabled Walpole to establish the Whigs as the only significant political party.[37] The importance of patronage in this Whig victory is shown by the number of Tories who went over to the Whigs rather than lose all hope of holding office[38] [1.4.7].

The party labels were, however, kept alive under Walpole, partly because Walpole desired to consolidate his position by identifying the Tories with Jacobitism, and partly because the labels underwent something of a redefinition appropriate to changed circumstances. By the 1720s the great constitutional disputes had abated, and the Tory label began to be attached to those members of the

[34] Walcott, p. 75.
[35] Holmes, Ch. II.
[36] Ibid., p. 130.
[37] Plumb, especially p. 135.
[38] Ibid., p. 172.

Commons who were not, or did not wish to be, in the Ministry; Whiggism became, by contrast, an emblem of those in office, or those who wished to be in office. This gradual identification of Toryism with the 'country' was gradual, however, and was not fully completed until the reign of George III.[39] Thus, after the 1720s, the labels were not only less ubiquitous – contemporaries were frequently sceptical of their relevance [1.4.8] – but also became less and less evidence of divisions on constitutional or policy issues, and more and more the coinage of the pursuit of office. The identification of Whiggism with mere constitutional respectability [1.4.9] was exemplified in Lord Perceval's remark that the opposition to Walpole was 'carried on Whig principles'.[40] Whiggism had become for the mid-eighteenth century what 'democracy' was to become for the twentieth.

[39] Owen, p. 56.
[40] Foord, p. 231.

I 1660–1760

Documents

1.1 THE CONSTITUTION

1.1.1 From Sir William Blackstone, Commentaries on the Laws of England (second edition, Oxford, 1766), Vol. I, pp. 141 and 146–7.
The Lectures were first delivered in 1758.

The limitation of the King's prerogative, by bounds so certain and notorious [means] that it is impossible he should exceed them without the consent of the people . . . The former of these keeps the legislative power in due health and vigour, so as to make it improbable that laws should be enacted destructive of general liberty: the latter is a guard upon the executive power, by restraining it from acting either beyond or in contradiction to the laws, that are framed and established by the other . . . In all tyrannical governments the supreme magistracy, or the right of *making* and *enforcing* the laws, is vested in one and the same body of men; and wherever these two powers are united together, there can be no public liberty. The magistrate may enact tyrannical laws, and execute them in a tyrannical manner, since he is possessed, in quality of dispenser of justice, with all the power which he as legislator thinks proper to give himself. But, where the legislative and executive authority are in distinct hands, the former will take care not to entrust the latter with so large a power, as may tend to the subversion of its own independence, and therewith of the liberty of the subject. With us, therefore, in England, this supreme power is divided into two branches; the one legislative, to wit, the parliament, consisting of King, Lords and Commons; the other executive, consisting of the King alone.

1.1.2 From John Toland, The State Anatomy of Great Britain (*1716*), *pp. 38–9*.

The Constitution of our Parliament [has] nothing in common with other assemblies so-called elsewhere; these being courts of Judicature, and our three Estates of King, Lords and Commons, making up the supreme Legislative power of the nation.

. . . In the equilibrium of this body, and the unanimity of their deliberations, consists our greatest happiness; while, to our further comfort, the nature of their proceedings is such, that none of the Estates can scarce be surprised or reduced into any pernicious measures, but that the other two may reasonably interpose, and the people also have sufficient time to petition or remonstrate, as the matter shall most properly require.

1.1.3 From The Life of Edward, Earl of Clarendon, Written by Himself (*second edition, Oxford, 1759*), *pp. 343–4.*
The original manuscript was completed in 1670, but was first published in 1759.

The Parliament assembled together [in February 1664]. They brought the same affection and duty with them towards the King, which they had formerly . . . They had the same fidelity for the King's service, but not the same alacrity in it . . . The truth is; the House of Commons was upon the matter not the same; three years sitting . . . had consumed many of their Members; and in the place of those who died, great pains were taken to have some of the King's menial servants chosen; so that there was a very great number of men in all stations in the Court, as well below stairs as above, who were Members of the House of Commons. And there were very few of them, who did not think themselves qualified to reform whatever was amiss in Church or State, and to procure whatever Supply the King would require . . . They brought those, who appeared to them most zealous for his Service, because they professed to be ready to do anything he pleased to prescribe, to receive his majesty's thanks, and from himself his immediate directions how to behave themselves on the House . . .

1.1.4 From Algernon Sydney, 'Discourses on Government' (in Life, Memoirs Etc. of Algernon Sydney (1794), Vol. II, pp. 592–4. First edition of The Discourses : 1698.

The great treasurer Burleigh said, that parliament could do anything but turn a man into a woman . . . But if [this power] be in Parliament, it must be in those who give to Parliament-men the powers by which they act . . . The most certain testimony that can be given of [the people's] unlimited power, is, that they rely on the wisdom and fidelity of their deputies, so as to lay no restrictions upon them: they may do what they please, if they take care . . . that 'the commonwealth receive no detriment'. This is a commission, fit to be granted by wise and good men, to those they may choose through an opinion, that they are so also, and that they cannot bring any prejudice upon the nation, that will not fall upon themselves, and their posterity. This is also fit to be received by those, who seeking nothing, but that which is just in itself . . . cannot foresee what will be proposed when they are all together; much less, resolve how to vote, till they hear the reasons on both sides. The electors must necessarily be in the same ignorance; and the law which should oblige them to give those particular orders to their knights and burgesses, in relation to every vote, would make the decisions of the most important affairs to depend upon the judgement of those, who know nothing of the matters in question, and by that means cast the nation into the utmost danger of the most inextricable confusion.

1.1.5 From Henry St John (Viscount Bolingbroke), The Spirit of Patriotism (1742), p. 37.

Parliaments are not only, what they always were, essential parts of our constitution, but essential parts of our administration too. They do not claim the executive power: No. But the executive power cannot be exercised without their annual concurrence.

1.1.6 From Henry St John (Viscount Bolingbroke), A Dissertation on Parties (1735), pp. 158, 159 and 161.

It is by [a] mixture of Monarchy, Aristocracy and Democratical power, blended together in one system, and by [the] three Estates balancing one another, that our free constitution of government hath been preserved for so long inviolate . . . Absolute monarchy is Tyranny;

15

but absolute Democracy is Tyranny and anarchy both. If aristocracy be placed between these two extremes, it is placed on a slippery ridge, and must fall into one or the other ... From such observations ... it hath been concluded very reasonably that the best Form of government must be one compounded of all these three, and in which they are *all* so tempered, that *each* may produce the good effects, and be restrained by the counter-working of the other two, from producing the bad effects, that are natural to it.

1.1.7 From a letter from Francis, Lord Hastings, to his father Theophilus, ninth Earl of Huntington. Written in 1745, printed in The Hastings MSS (Historical Manuscripts Commission, *1934), p. 49.*

The King has been very generous with his offers of peerages, which have all been refused. Sir Watkin was amongst the offered: his answer was that as long as his Majesty's Ministers acted for the good of their country, he was willing to consent to anything; that he thanked his Majesty for the Earldom he had sent him, but that he was very well content with the honours he had and was resolved to live and die Sir Watkin.

1.1.8 From Henry St John (Viscount Bolingbroke), The Spirit of Patriotism *(1742), p. 61.*

According to the present form of our constitution, every member of either house of Parliament is a member of a national standing council, born, or appointed by the people, to promote good, and to oppose bad, government; and if not vested with the power of a minister of state, yet vested with the superior power of controlling those who are appointed such by the crown. It follows from hence, that they who engage in opposition, are under as great obligations to prepare themselves to control, as they who serve the crown are under to prepare themselves to carry on, the administration: and that a party, formed for this purpose, do not act like good citizens, nor honest men, unless they propose *true*, as well as *oppose false* measures of government.

1.1.9 From Charles Mordaunt, Earl of Peterborough, Remarks on a Pamphlet, etc. *(1719), pp. 20–1.*

Without enlarging upon the nature of our Constitution ... it would suffice to say, it would be better in all respects, that it consisted but of one Branch or Authority than of many; unless the different parts of the Government were calculated to be a proper balance one against the other; if there were not force enough for a regular sufficient . . . Opposition in the several parts of this Compound Government it would be liable to many objections . . . Is not [Royal] influence a force in either House of Parliament for the Dissolution of Government? Is it not a Violation of the Rights of one House, . . . destroying the very nature of Parliaments?

1.1.10 From David Hume, 'On the Independency of Parliament' (1742). Printed in The Philosophical Works of David Hume *(1878, edited by T. H. Green and T. Grose), Vol. 2, pp. 119, 120, 121 and 122.*

When there offers, therefore, to our censure and examination, any plan of government, real or imaginary, where the power is distributed among several courts, and several orders of men, we should always consider the separate interest of each court, and each order; and, if we find that, by the skilful division of power, this interest must necessarily, in its operation, concur with public, we may pronounce that government to be wise and happy. If, on the contrary, separate interest be not checked, and be not directed to the public, we ought to look for nothing but faction, disorder, and tyranny from such a government . . .

How much, therefore, would it have surprised such a genius as Cicero, or Tacitus, to have been told, that, in a future age, there should arise a very regular system of *mixed* government, where the authority was so distributed, that one rank, whenever it pleased, might swallow up all the rest, and engross the whole power of the constitution. Such a government, they would say, will not be a mixed government. For so great is the natural ambition of men, that they are never satisfied with power; and if one order of men, by pursuing its own interest, can usurp upon every other order, it will certainly do so, and render itself, as far as possible, absolute and uncontroulable.

But, in this opinion, experience shews they would have been mistaken. For this is actually the case with the British constitution. The share of power, allotted by our constitution to the house of commons, is so great, that it absolutely commands all the other parts of the government. The king's legislative power is plainly no proper check to it. For though the king has a negative in framing laws; yet this, in fact, is esteemed of so little moment, that whatever is voted by the two houses, is always sure to pass into a law, and the royal assent is little better than a form. The principal weight of the crown lies in the executive power. But besides that the executive power in every government is altogether subordinate to the legislative; besides this, I say, the exercise of this power requires an immense expence; and the commons have assumed to themselves the sole right of granting money. How easy, therefore, would it be for that house to wrest from the crown all these powers, one after another; by making every grant conditional, and choosing their time so well, that their refusal of supply should only distress the government, without giving foreign powers any advantage over us? Did the house of commons depend in the same manner on the king, and had none of the members any property but from his gift, would not he command all their resolutions, and be from that moment absolute? As to the house of lords, they are a very powerful support to the Crown, so long as they are, in their turn, supported by it; but both experience and reason shew, that they have no force or authority sufficient to maintain themselves alone, without such support.

How, therefore, shall we solve this paradox? And by what means is this member of our constitution confined within the proper limits; since, from our very constitution, it must necessarily have as much power as it demands, and can only be confined by itself? How is this consistent with our experience of human nature? I answer, that the interest of the body is here restrained by that of the individuals, and that the house of commons stretches not its power, because such an usurpation would be contrary to the interest of the majority of its members. The crown has so many offices at its disposal, that, when assisted by the honest and disinterested part of the house, it will always command the resolutions of the whole so far, at least, as to preserve the antient constitution from danger. We may, therefore, give to this influence what name we please; we may call it by the invidious appellations of *corruption* and *dependence*; but some degree and some kind of it are inseparable from the very nature of the constitution, and necessary to the preservation of our mixed government . . .

All questions concerning the proper medium between extremes are difficult to be decided; both because it is not easy to find *words* proper to fix this medium, and because the good and ill, in such cases, run so gradually into each other, as even to render our *sentiments* doubtful and uncertain. But there is a peculiar difficulty in the present case, which would embarrass the most knowing and most impartial examiner. The power of the crown is always lodged in a single person, either king or minister; and as this person may have either a greater or less degree of ambition, capacity, courage, popularity, or fortune, the power, which is too great in one hand, may become too little in another. In pure republics, where the authority is distributed among several assemblies or senates, the checks and controuls are more regular in their operation; because the members of such numerous assemblies may be presumed to be always nearly equal in capacity and virtue; and it is only their number, riches, or authority, which enter into consideration. But a limited monarchy admits not of any such stability; nor is it possible to assign to the crown such a determinate degree of power, as will, in every hand, form a proper counterbalance to the other parts of the constitution. This is an unavoidable disadvantage, among the many advantages, attending that species of government.

1.2 ATTITUDES TO PARTY

1.2.1 From John Perceval, Faction Detected by Evidence of the Facts *(1743), pp. 3, 4 and 5.*

Opposition to the Measures of Government, whether good or bad, is no new thing in this or any other country, where the People have any share in the Legislature . . . The natural Tendency in all mankind to expect more favour than they merit, provokes unjust resentments against government . . . the discontented parties of all denominations consist *in general* of men of no principle . . . its Root is always the same; – but indeed its effects are very different. It becomes in some conjunctures of very beneficial consequence, when it is led by men of honest views; and equally pernicious in others, when conducted by men of a different character. In the first case it is an Opposition; in the second it is a faction . . . Faction is of two kinds in this country – opposition led by Republicans, and opposition led by Jacobites . . . whereas the Republicans, who are the Leaders of the first faction, are in this country little more than Whigs over-heated by oppression, and an extravagant abuse of power . . . (and) . . . may be easily brought to moderate their views by what it is in the power of every honest government to apply: But the leaders of the second faction set out with Expectations that no government, without being *felo de se,* can gratify. For they set out upon the view of changing the Princes upon the Throne, and in necessary consequence to transform the Constitution and the Religion of the Kingdom . . . It is visible from hence, that it is a much less danger from a Republican than from a Jacobite; or, in softer terms, from a Whig than from a Tory opposition.

1.2.2 From John Toland, The Art of Governing by Parties *(1701), pp. 7–8, 31, 32 and 34.*

. . . of all the Plagues which have infested this nation since the death of

19

Queen Elizabeth, none has spread the contagion wider, or brought us nearer to utter ruin, than the implacable animosity of contending Parties . . . it is the most wicked masterpiece of tyranny purposely to divide the sentiments, affections, and interests of a people . . . till the accession of the Stuarts to the Imperial throne of this Realm, we never knew the *art of governing by parties*. It was set on foot among us by the first of that race . . . [later] . . . as King Charles II deluded the Clergy into his measures by the fear of Presbytery, his next trick was to divide the laity in their Politics, and to possess the Royalists with apprehensions of a Commonwealth . . . Everybody was afraid of relapsing into the former Confusions; and he dexterously insinuated by his Instruments, that nothing but the increase of his Prerogative could possibly prevent it.

1.2.3 From Henry St John (Viscount Bolingbroke), The Idea of a Patriot King *(1742), pp. 168–9.*

When parties are divided by different notions and principles concerning some particular ecclesiastical or civil institutions, the constitution, which should be *their* rule, must be that of the prince . . . as every new modification in a scheme of government and of national policy is of great importance, and requires more and deeper consideration than the warmth, and hurry, and rashness of party conduct admit, the duty of a prince seems to require that he should render by his influence the proceedings more orderly and more deliberate . . . far from forming or espousing a party he will defeat party in defence of the constitution, on some occasions; and lead men, from acting with a party spirit, to act with a national spirit, in others. When the division is about *particular measures* of government, and the conduct of the administration is alone concerned, a Patriot King will stand in want of party as little as in any other case. Under his reign, the opportunities of forming an opposition of this sort will be rare, and the pretences generally weak.

1.2.4 From Henry St John (Viscount Bolingbroke), A Dissertation upon Parties *(1735), p. xiv.*

Whilst a real difference of principles and designs supported the distinction [between Whig and Tory], we were divided into national parties; and this was misfortune enough . . . But if the distinction should remain when the difference subsists no longer, the misfortune would be still greater; because they, who maintained the distinction, in this case, would cease to be a party, and would become a faction.

1.3 PARTY IN PARLIAMENT

1.3.1 From Andrew Marvell, 'The Last Instructions to a Painter' (The poem was published in 1689). Printed in The Works of Andrew Marvell *(edited Grosart, 1872), p. 257.*

Draw next a pair of tables opening, then
The House of Commons clattering like the men,
Describe the Court and Country both set right,
On opposite points, the Black against the White,
Those having lost the nation at Tick-tack,
These now adventuring how to win it back.

1.3.2 From a Letter from Horace Walpole to Robert Trevor, 1 February 1740. Printed in The Trevor MSS *(Historical Manuscripts Commission, Report 14, Appendix 9), pp. 38–9.*

We were mistaken in our computation of members on occasion of the Place Bill, which was strongly debated till 11 o'clock tonight . . . with as much strength of argument as ever I heard against it by the gentlemen for rejecting the motion, the negatives carried it by 222 against 206, so that our majority calculated at about 40 was no more than 16; but I must observe to you, that this was occasioned by there being 26 absent that are actually in town; for we computed that the opposite party might be 208; and although some Whigs, who in other matters are constantly with us, voted for the question, there were some that we did not expect would do so.

1.3.3. From Lord Hervey's Memoirs (edited R. Sedgewick, 1952, written in May 1735), pp. 452–3.

The reason Sir R. [Walpole] gave for putting Lord Cholmondely [in the Treasury] . . . was that his Lordship was so uneasy in the Prince's service, and had so long pressed him to be removed out of it, that it was impossible for him longer to withstand that solicitation . . . nor could he, with any decency to the Prince, take Lord Cholmondely out of his service upon any pretence but that of putting him into a place of business . . . Lord Hervey remonstrated to Sir R. Walpole against this step, . . . adding that Sir R. was always feeling the weight of all the young men in the House of Commons taking a part against him, and yet on every occasion showed that they could get nothing by being attached to him . . . it was a fault not only to his friends, but even to himself if he did not make

21

the best disposition he could of those favours that were in his power; and added further, that, let him be ever so able a Minister, it was impossible for him to alter human nature, and the fundamental inducements of mankind not only to serve one another but even to serve Heaven itself; that the strength of all government . . . was rewards and punishments; and that the one was as necessary to encourage one's friends and keep them firm, as the other was to intimidate one's enemies and keep them quiet.

1.3.4 From Lord Hervey's Memoirs (*edited R. Sedgewick, 1952, written in 1727*), *pp. 65-6.*

As soon as (the King's) Civil List was settled, the old Parliament was dismissed, and soon after a new one called. The choice of this new Parliament was consigned entirely to the care of Sir R. Walpole, which confirmed the whole world in the opinion of the King's being determined to continue him First Minister, everybody being capable, without much penetration or refinement, to reason, that a man who was to have his friends, followers and adherents removed from Court would never have Court money given him to bring them into Parliament.

1.3.5 From a letter from the Duke of Newcastle to the Earl of Stanhope, 14 October 1719. Printed in Basil Williams, Stanhope (*1932*), *p. 460.*

Upon the whole My Dear Lord, I am of opinion and have long been so that we shall not fail of a better Parliament than this is at present . . . I think when I have the happiness and pleasure of seeing you, I can convince you on the many alterations that must be made for the better; almost all [the supporters of the Prince of Wales] will be turned out; Most of those that had the chief hand in choosing the Parliament brought in their own creatures, most of whom I believe we shall be able to deal with. I will take the liberty to say that I myself will make the difference of 16 votes, many others will and can do the same, and if the Court would upon such an occasion use one proper method . . . I should think we cannot fail.

1.3.6 From a letter from the Earl of Chesterfield to George Dodington, 8 September 1741. Printed in William Coxe, Memoirs of Walpole *(1798),* Vol. III, pp. 580–1.

I entirely agree with you, that we ought to have meetings to concert measures some time before the meeting of the parliament; but that I likewise know will not happen. I have been these seven years endeavouring to bring it about, and have not been able. Fox-hunting, gardening, planting, or indifference, having always kept our people in the country, till the very day before the meeting of the parliament. Besides, would it be easy to settle who should be at those meetings? If Pulteney and his people were to be chose, it would be only informing them beforehand, what they should either oppose or defeat; and if they were not there, their own exclusion would in some degree justify, or at least colour their conduct . . . These are difficulties, the insurmountable difficulties, that I foresee; and which makes me absolutely despair of seeing any good done.

1.4 PARTY RHETORIC

1.4 From John Withers, The Whigs Vindicated *(1715), pp. 4–5.*

As for the beginning of these Invidious Names, they were not so much as heard of, amongst the Englishmen, till the Discovery of *Oates'* Plot in 1678. The Detection of that black Design occasioned a mighty ferment in the Nation . . . The Duke of *York* was at that Time presumptive heir to the English Crown: But a professed and known Roman Catholic. This created a great uneasiness in the minds of the major part of the House of Commons, as well as many Lords. They concluded, that a Protestant Church could not possibly be safe under the Influence of a Popish head . . . In order to obviate so great a mischief, a Bill was brought into the lower House, to exclude the said Duke from the throne of these Kingdoms . . . They who were against the Bill of Exclusion, began about this time to be Nick-Named Tories, and they who were for it to be distinguished by the name of Whigs. The Principles which the latter proceeded on are such as these: That the supremest ruler was set up for the good of society . . . *Salus Populi Suprema Lex* was a Maxim they were no more ashamed of then than they are now . . . They thought that the Exclusion of a Popish and the advancing of a Protestant Prince to the Throne, to be fairly consistent with the Laws both of God and the Kingdom. These were, and still are, the distinguishing principles of a

23

Whig. On the other hand, the Tories preached up an indefeasible hereditary Right in the next successor to the Crown . . . and that it was a sin against God to hinder or oppose him . . . The Patrons of this doctrine, had the modesty to set themselves as the only true and genuine sons of the Church of England, and to rail against others as false brethren.

1.4.2 From David Hume, 'Of the Parties of Great Britain' (1742). Printed in The Philosophical Works of David Hume (edited T. H. Green and T. Grose, 1878), Vol. 2, 137–43.

. . . After many confusions and revolutions, the royal family was at last restored, and the ancient government re-established. CHARLES II was not made wiser by the example of his father; but prosecuted the same measures, though at first, with more secrecy and caution. New parties arose, under the appellation of *Whig* and *Tory*, which have continued ever since to confound and distract our government. To determine the nature of these parties is, perhaps, one of the most difficult problems, that can be met with, and is a proof that history may contain questions, as uncertain as any to be found in the most abstract sciences. We have seen the conduct of the two parties, during the course of seventy years, in a vast variety of circumstances, possessed of power, and deprived of it, during peace, and during war: Persons, who profess themselves of one side or other, we meet with every hour, in company, in our pleasures, in our serious occupations: We ourselves are constrained, in a manner, to take party; and living in a country of the highest liberty, every one may openly declare all his sentiments and opinions; Yet are we at a loss to tell the nature, pretensions, and principles of the different factions.

When we compare the parties of WHIG and TORY with those of ROUND-HEAD and CAVALIER, the most obvious difference, that appears between them, consists in the principles of *passive obedience*, and *indefeasible right*, which were but little heard of among the CAVALIERS, but became the universal doctrine, and were esteemed the true characteristic of a TORY. Were these principles pushed into their most obvious consequences, they imply a formal renunciation of all our liberties, and an avowal of absolute monarchy; since nothing can be a greater absurdity than a limited power, which must not be resisted, even when it exceeds its limitations. But as the most rational principles are often but a weak counterpoise to passion; it is no wonder that these absurd principles were found too weak for that effect. The TORIES, as men, were enemies to oppression; and also as ENGLISHMEN, they were enemies to arbitrary power. Their zeal for liberty, was, perhaps, less fervent than that of their antagonists; but was sufficient to make them forget all their general principles, when they saw themselves openly threatened with a subversion of the ancient government. From these sentiments arose the revolution; an event of mighty consequence, and the firmest foundation of British liberty. The conduct of the TORIES, during that event, and after it, will afford us a true insight into the nature of that party.

In the *first* place, they appear to have had the genuine sentiments of BRITONS in their affection for liberty, and in their determined resolution not to sacrifice it to any abstract principle whatsoever, or to any imaginary rights of princes. This part of their character might justly have been doubted of before the *revolution*, from the obvious tendency of their avowed principles, and from their compliances with a court, which seemed to make little secret of its arbitrary designs. The *revolution* shewed them to have been, in this respect, nothing, but a genuine *court-party*, such as might be expected in a BRITISH government: That is, *Lovers of liberty, but greater lovers of monarchy*. It must, however, be confessed, that they carried their monarchical principles farther, even in practice, but more so in theory, than was, in any degree, consistent with a limited government.

Secondly, Neither their principles nor affections concurred, entirely or heartily, with the settlement made at the *revolution*, or with that which has since taken place. This part of their character may seem opposite to the former; since any other settlement, in those circumstances of the nation, must probably have been dangerous, if not fatal to liberty. But the heart of man is made to reconcile contradictions: and this contradiction is not greater than that between *passive obedience*, and the *resistance* employed at the *revolution*. A TORY, therefore, since the *revolution*, may be defined in a few words, to be *a lover of monarchy, though without abandoning liberty; and a partizan of the family of* STUART. As, a WHIG may be defined to be *a lover of liberty though without renouncing monarchy; and a friend to the settlement in the* PROTESTANT *line*.

These different views, with regard to the settlement of the crown, were accidental, but natural additions to the principles of the *court* and *country* parties, which are the genuine divisions in the BRITISH government. A passionate lover of monarchy is apt to be displeased at any change of the succession; as savouring too much of a commonwealth: A passionate lover of liberty is apt to think that every part of the government ought to be subordinate to the interests of liberty.

Some, who will not venture to assert, that the *real* difference between WHIG and TORY was lost at the *revolution*, seem inclined to think, that the difference is now abolished, and that affairs are so far returned to their natural state, that there are present no other parties among us but *court* and *country*; that is, men, who, by interest or principles, are

25

attached either to monarchy or liberty. The TORIES have been so long obliged to talk in the republican stile, that they seem to have made converts of themselves by their hypocrisy, and to have embraced the sentiments, as well as language of their adversaries. There are, however, very considerable remains of that party in ENGLAND, with all their old prejudices; and a proof that *court* and *country* are not our only parties, is, that almost all the dissenters side with the court, and the lower clergy, at least, of the church of ENGLAND, with the opposition. This may convince us, that some biass still hangs upon our constitution, some extrinsic weight, which turns it from its natural course, and causes a confusion in our parties.

[So the Essay concludes in Editions Q and R. In place of the last paragraph, the preceding Editions read as follows:]

'Tis however remarkable, that tho' the principles of WHIG and TORY were both of them of a compound nature; yet the ingredients, which predominated in both, were not correspondent to each other. A TORY loved monarchy, and bore an affection to the family of STUART; but the latter affection was the predominant inclination of the party. A WHIG loved liberty, and was a friend to the settlement in the PROTESTANT line; but the love of liberty was professedly his predominant inclination. The TORIES have frequently acted as republicans, where either policy or revenge has engaged them to that conduct; and there was no one of that party, who, upon the supposition, that he was to be disappointed in his views with regard to the succession, would not have desired to impose the strictest limitations on the crown, and to bring our form of government as near republican as possible, in order to depress the family, which, according to his apprehension, succeeded without any just title. The WHIGS, 'tis true, have also taken steps dangerous to liberty, under colour of securing the succession and settlement of the crown, according to their views: But as the body of the party had no passion for that succession, otherwise than as the means of securing liberty, they have been betrayed into these steps by ignorance, or frailty, or the interests of their leaders. The succession of the crown was, therefore, the chief point with the TORIES; the security of our liberties with the WHIGS.

Some, who will not venture to assert, that the *real* difference between WHIG and TORY was lost at the *revolution*, seem inclined to think, that the difference is now abolished, and that affairs are so far returned to their natural state, that there are at present no other parties amongst us but *court* and *country*: that is, men, who by interest or principles, are attached either to monarchy or to liberty. It must, indeed, be confest, that the TORY party seem, of late, to have decayed much in their numbers; still more in their zeal; and I may venture to say, still more in their credit and authority. There are few men of knowledge or learning, at least, few philosophers, since MR LOCKE has wrote, who would not be ashamed to be thought of that party; and in almost all companies the name of OLD WHIG is mentioned as an uncontestable appellation of honour and dignity. Accordingly, the enemies of the ministry, as a reproach, call the courtiers the true TORIES; and as an honour, denominate the gentlemen in the *opposition* the true WHIGS. The TORIES have been so long obliged to talk in the republican stile, that they seem to have made converts of themselves by their hypocrisy, and to have embraced the sentiments, as well as language of their adversaries. There are, however, very considerable remains of that party in England, with all their old prejudices; and a proof that *court* and *country* are not our only parties, is, that almost all the dissenters side with the court, and the lower clergy, at least, of the church of ENGLAND, with the opposition. This may convince us, that some biass still hangs upon our constitution, some intrinsic weight, which turns it from its natural course, and causes a confusion in our parties.

1.4.3 From Henry St John (Viscount Bolingbroke), The Idea of a Patriot King (*1742*), *p. 129*.

The good of the people is the ultimate and true end of government, Governors are, therefore, appointed for this end, and the civil constitution which appoints them, and invests them with their power, is determined to do so by that law of nature and reason, which has determined the end of government, and which admits this form of government as the proper mean of arriving at it. Now, the greatest good of a people is their liberty ... without liberty no happiness can be enjoyed by society. The obligation, therefore, to defend and maintain the freedom of such constitutions, will appear most sacred to a PATRIOT KING.

1.4.4 From a letter from Lord Hervey to the Queen, 1734. Printed in Lord Hervey's Memoirs (*edited R. Sedgewick, 1952*).

... if Your Majesty thinks that the Tories either would or could do more than the Whigs have done to support you, all I can say is, to repeat what my Lord Sunderland answered to King William when His Majesty told him he would take the Tories in because their principles were more proper to support a King than those of the Whigs. My Lord Sunderland answered: 'That is very true, Sir, but you are not their King.'

1.4.5 From a letter from J. Menzies (the Pretender's Agent in London) to L. Inese (the Spanish Ambassador), 16 April 1716. Printed in The Stuart Papers *(The Historical Manuscripts Commission, Vol. II, 1904).*

On Saturday came on the Second Reading of the Bill in the House of Lords for taking away Triennial Parliaments . . . The most remarkable, thing was that the Tories talked like Old Whigs and Republicans, against monarchy and ministers, etc., and the Whigs magnified the advantages of unlimited absolute power, and prerogative, vilified the mob, ridiculed the people, and exalted the Crown. But, since both Whigs and Tories had made this Triennial Act, in King William's time, the reasons that were then given being repeated, and many more new ones added . . . the Whigs had very little to say but to press the question and to turn to the Book of Numbers, so the division was, 77 for the Court, 43 against it. In which shaking of the bag, the Duke of Somerset, the Duke of Rutland, the Earl of Burlington and some other Whigs left the Court, and the Earls of Yarmouth, Clarendon, and Jersey voted for the Court. A new strange jumble.

1.4.6 From the Onslow MSS *(Historical Manuscripts Commission), p. 465.*
After Atterbury's Jacobite Plot to enthrone the Pretender, it was proposed that all swear an oath of allegiance to the Government. The way in which Sir Robert Walpole made use of this is illustrated by an extract from the Onslow MSS. *Onslow was the Speaker of the House of Commons (1754–61); his papers were edited by his son in 1769.*

. . . he always aimed at the uniting of the Whigs against the Tories as Jacobites . . . as parties are generally factions, and the chief business of factions is to annoy one another, those men have always most merit with their party who contribute most to this humour, and to that, as this was designed to affect the Tories, must this silly zeal of the Whigs then in Parliament be imputed . . . Mr Walpole enjoyed and encouraged it all, as pursuing of his plan of having everybody to be deemed a Jacobite who was not a professed and known Whig.

1.4.7 From the Onslow MSS *(written in 1769, printed by Historical Manuscripts Commission, 14th Report, Appendix 9), p. 467.*

Another person who acted a very considerable part in [the opposition to Sir Robert Walpole] was Sir William Wyndham as a leader of the Tories . . . he became from a very disagreeable speaker and little knowing in business to be one of the most pleasing and able speakers of his time, wore out all the prejudices of party, grew moderate towards the dissenters, against whom he once bore a most implacable hatred . . . and formed such a new set of principles . . . that he lost all confidence in the Jacobites and the most rigid of the Tories, and it is thought would have left them entirely if he could have stood the reproach of that in his own county or could have maintained a prevailing interest there without them; and upon that footing would willingly have come into a new Whig Administration upon the exclusion of Sir Robert Walpole, with whom he would never have acted, and with the admission of some few of his Tory friends who in company with him would willingly also have left their party for such a change, swayed not a little perhaps in this by observing that no other road would lead them to those honours and preferments in the State which it was just for men of abilities to expect and a folly to exclude themselves and their families from, when they could take them as they thought without hurt to their principles and their character.

1.4.8 From Henry St John (Viscount Bolingbroke), A Dissertation Upon Parties *(1735), pp. 9 and 87.*

[A] division of parties, on the [old] principles, subsists no longer; . . . there be in truth neither a Tory, nor a Whig . . . but a Court and Country Party in being . . . the civil faith of the Old Whigs [is] assented and consented to by the Country party . . . How different the case is, on the other side, will appear not only from the actions, but from the principles of the Court party, as we find them avowed in their writings...

[After 1688] The Tories had no longer any pretence of fearing the designs of the Whigs; since the Whigs had sufficiently purged themselves from all suspicion of Republican views, by their zeal to continue monarchical government . . . [and] . . . by their ready concurrence in preserving our Ecclesiastical establishment . . . The Whigs had as little pretence of fearing the Tories; since the Tories had purged themselves, in the most signal manner, from all suspicion of favouring Popery, or arbitrary power, by the vigorous resistance they made to both. They had engaged, they had taken the lead in the Revolution, and they were fully

29

determined against the return of King James. The real essences of Whig and Tory were thus destroyed; but the nominal were preserved, and have done since that time a good part of the mischief, which the real did before.

1.4.9 From Baron Hervey, Memoirs of the Reign of King George II (*edited R. Sedgewick, 1931*), *Vol. 1, pp. 3–7. Extract written between 1727 and 1734.*

Whig and Tory had been the denominations by which men opposed in their political views had distinguished themselves for many years and through many reigns. Those who were called Whigs had been in power from the first accession of the Hanover family to the Crown; but the original principles on which both these parties were said to act altered so insensibly in the persons who bore the names, by the long prosperity of the one, and the adversity of the other, that those who called themselves Whigs arbitrarily gave the title of Tory to everyone who opposed the measures of the administration or whom they had a mind to make disagreeable at Court . . . the chief struggle now lay not between Jacobites and Hanoverians, or Tories and Whigs, but between Whigs and Whigs, who, conquerors in the common cause, were now split into civil contest among themselves, and had no considerable opponents but one another.

I 1760—1832

Introduction

THE CONSTITUTION

Politics at the accession of George III could still be described in terms of the activities of the Monarch and a Parliament whose House of Commons was divided into the placemen, the independent country gentry and the political connexions.[1] Constitutional theorists remained wedded to the idea of balance, and many of the constitutional commentaries repeated the common assumptions of writers under the first two Hanoverians [2.1.1]. On the other hand, the reign of George III provoked a constitutional debate about the limits of the royal prerogative more widespread and significant than anything in the previous period[2] [2.1.2].

The defence of George III centred around the arguments that the King was exercising a royal right to choose his own ministers which had ever been recognized as proper, and/or that his attempt to govern without the aid of the established connexions was a praiseworthy attempt to institute the factionless reign of the Patriot King [2.1.3]. From this standpoint, the opposition of the Whig connexions (centred around Newcastle and Rockingham) to George III's exercise of his prerogative of ministerial choice could be represented as the mere and insincere outrage of those who had enjoyed ascendancy under the first two Hanoverians and who were now,

[1] A classic brief account is Sir L. B. Namier, *Monarchy and the Party System* (Oxford, 1952).
[2] See H. Butterfield, *George III and the Historians* (1957).

through a proper exercise of the prerogative, out of office. The Whig defence of the opposition to George III was based on the arguments that not only was this firm exercise of the prerogative a novelty, but that it involved a freedom of choice not merely *between* connexions, but also a freedom to choose Ministers (such as Bute)[3] from outside the connexions altogether, and thus necessarily raised the whole question of the need to choose Ministers whose support was firmly established in the House of Commons [2.1.5].

The eighteenth-century debate has been continued by recent historians. 'Whig' writers such as Trevelyan[4] have defended both the importance of ideas in politics and the accuracy of the 'Rocking-hamite' interpretation of the constitution. Sir Lewis Namier,[5] on the other hand, has led a considerable body of recent writing to the view that the importance of ideas has been misconceived and/or exaggerated, and that the eighteenth-century Whig view of the constitution does not fit the facts. Such a debate involves questions of fact and interpretation. The reasons for rejecting the view that political ideas are irrelevant were outlined in the General Intro-duction, but questions of historical evidence remain. Namier suc-ceeded in showing that analysis of the Commons' division lists does not reveal the existence of a two-party system. Voting was correlated not with one of two political principles or party labels but with interest and family ties. Yet the arguments of the 'Whig' historians do not rest solely on assumptions about voting in the Commons. The division lists may reveal that party labels did not embrace a considerable section of the House, and that even those professing the Whig label differed from each other in a variety of ways. None the less, this is not to discount the place of Whiggism as an agent of political change; the Whigs were not academic inter-preters of the constitution but a set of people who to some extent wished to change it. The changes that did in fact occur towards the end of the eighteenth century cannot be accounted for without a consideration of the ideas of the Whigs. Nor need the historian be too confident of the inaccuracy of the Whig account of the consti-tution. As we have seen, the eighteenth-century constitution was

---

[3] R. Pares, *George III and the Politicians* (Oxford, 1951–2), p. 100.

[4] See G. M. Trevelyan, *History of England* (1926), and *The Two-Party System in English Constitutional History*, Romanes Lecture (Oxford, 1926).

[5] See Sir L. B. Namier, *The Structure of Politics at the Accession of George III* (1929), and *England in the Age of the American Revolution* (1930).

32

flexible enough to accommodate both the above views, and precedent alone could support both the defenders of the royal prerogative and the defenders of Parliament's control over ministries (and thus, indirectly, over the King). Indeed, it was precisely this (limited) elasticity of the constitution which made possible a debate in which both sides could claim a monopoly of precedent and propriety[6] [2.1.9]. Whatever the 'constitutionality' of George III's choice of ministers, there seems little doubt that he used his rights of ministerial choice more forcefully than did George II, that he despised 'faction' and attempted to rule without its support, and that the relations between George II and Pelham were not the same as those between George III and Lord North (at least in the earlier years of the latter's office).[7] The formation of the Chatham Ministry was a clear attempt to by-pass the connexions and to avoid the inconstancy of ministerial personnel associated with them.[8] It had been George II's apparent acceptance of Whig constitutional views which made George III appear a constitutional novelty, and enabled Fox (however insincerely) to represent himself as leader of the opposition to a tyrannical monarch.[9] Thus, whatever the facts of the case, the activities of George III provoked a constitutional debate of a kind which had been dormant since the reign of Anne.

It was becoming clear towards the end of this period, moreover, that Whig views had triumphed, and this for a number of reasons. After the 1780s, there was a decline in Crown influence [2.1.6–7], caused by a combination of 'economical reforms' (some, such as Rockingham's, designed precisely to diminish the power of the Crown, others, such as those of the younger Pitt, motivated primarily by a desire to introduce commercial principles into such areas as tendering for Government contracts), the later madness of George III and the personality of George IV, and the growth of a 'public opinion' outside the House of Commons. The significance of this latter factor lay in the development, by the 1780s, of a 'public opinion' in the provinces (as opposed to London). In so far as the theme of parliamentary reform was associated with this growth of opinion, the emphasis on elections essential to reform threw a correspondingly sceptical light on the institution of monarchy. The significant change which had occurred by the end of this period is shown in the fact that by the 1820s Canning and

[6] Pares, pp. 35, 182.   [7] Ibid., p. 183.
[8] Ibid., p. 116.   [9] Ibid., p. 183.

33

Huskisson could engage on the hitherto unknown activity of 'stumping the country'.[10] Although this decline in the influence of the Crown was not regarded as a significant topic of debate until after 1818[11] its cumulative effects made the House of Commons progressively more difficult to 'manage', and was of crucial importance to the course of party politics.[12] The failure of the incumbent Government in the election of 1830 clearly showed the limits of Crown patronage.[13]

These gradual developments were confused, however, by the short-run successes of George III in enforcing his will against the Whig opposition groups. The placemen remained a vitally important force in the House for most of the period, the Commons sat for no more than six months of the year, and the ability of the opposition groups to coerce the Monarch was limited by their inability to organize themselves in any coherent and continuous manner.[14] In 1784 George III could dismiss the Fox Ministry, which he had earlier been obliged to accept, and could break the Septennial Convention by holding elections to return a House of Commons likely to support the Ministry of Lord North. Later, he could successfully resist attempts by his Ministers to introduce a measure of Catholic Emancipation. On the other hand, actions such as these increased constitutional debate and left a legacy of Whig bitterness, and were in any case accompanied by events pointing in a rather different direction. George III's policy on American independence fell in ruins amid a House of Commons determined to remove Lord North [2.1.10], created a crisis of such magnitude that even offers of office were insufficient to still the opposition,[15] and enabled the Rockingham opposition groups to force their way into office and (significantly enough) to make stipulations about policy as a condition of coming in.[16]

Thus, Whig and monarchical views alternated in a dialectic of success and failure with the latter view, for most of George III's reign, the more successful; but by the end of the period the tendency was clear: by 1812 the Liverpool Ministry, whatever its

[10] Ibid., p. 200.

[11] A. S. Foord, 'The Waning of the Influence of the Crown', *English Historical Review* (1947), **62**, 487.

[12] B. Kemp, *King and Commons*, p. 108.   [13] Foord, p. 505.

[14] Pares, p. 94.   [15] Ibid., p. 119.

[16] Ibid., p. 100.

public rhetoric, was, in the matter of the position of the Monarch, acting upon Whig assumptions.[17] By the late 1820s even Wellington could admit that while governments might suffer particular parliamentary defeats without resigning, a systematic and successful opposition to the general policy of a Ministry must result in its eventual fall[18] [2.1.8].

The arguments about the actions of George III were essentially constitutional arguments, involving few serious disputes concerning particular legislative or policy questions.[19] On the other hand, the development towards the end of this period of an increased concern with Parliament as a *legislative body* constituted one of the most important distinctions between the late and early eighteenth century. By the first decades of the nineteenth century, back-benchers were increasingly demanding legislative activity, demands which were facilitated by the use of Select Committees as fact-finding devices.[20] The years between 1760 and 1820 saw a five-fold increase in parliamentary public business, and a distinction was drawn for the first time between government and other business.[21] Indeed, the increased volume of legislative and administrative activity, and the increased role of the Government in this activity,[22] had provoked by the 1830s a further decline in the power of the Monarch, since administrative competence played a more important part than hitherto in the choice of ministers.[23] The relationship between these developments and party organization in the House of Commons is discussed below.

To see the period 1760–1832 in terms of a gradual and uneven decline in the power of the Monarch and a parallel growth of a 'public opinion' outside the House of Commons, which together greatly modified the established picture of the balanced constitution is not, however, to say that the balance had tilted towards the House of Commons. The most significant constitutional development associated with the decline of the Monarch was not the domination of the House of Commons but the emergence of the

[17] Ibid., p. 183.
[18] A. Mitchell, *The Whigs in Opposition, 1815–1830* (Oxford, 1967), p. 80(n).
[19] Foord, *Opposition*, p. 361.
[20] Pares, p. 203.
[21] P. Fraser, *The Conduct of Public Business in the House of Commons, 1812–1827* (Unpublished Ph.D. Thesis, University of London, 1957), p. 20.
[22] Pares, p. 195.
[23] Fraser, p. 45.

c

Cabinet as the vital element in the Executive [2.1.11–13]. For most of the eighteenth century, the position of Ministers as links between the Crown and the House of Commons had given them a potential ability to play one institution against the other, and thus to achieve a degree of independence from both: the decline of the Monarch and the weakening of the idea that Ministers were responsible only to the Monarch, enabled them to emerge, especially after 1784, as executive authorities in their own right.[24] The balanced constitution was being replaced not by assembly government, but by cabinet government.

ATTITUDES TO PARTY

The debate on the royal prerogative raised once again the whole question of the respectability of 'opposition'. Formed and continuous opposition, with the object of limiting the Monarch's freedom of choice by confronting him with a pre-fabricated parliamentary majority, was clearly incompatible with George III's idea of the Patriot King, which emphasized on the contrary the idea of '*institutional* opposition' (that the limitation of Monarchy was the business of the House of Commons as a whole, and not that of a particular section of the House). The Whig position, on the other hand, clearly involved the recognition of such sectional activities as perfectly respectable. The Whig case in part rested on the well-known argument that institutional opposition was rendered impossible by the existence of the placemen – that patronage itself made sectional opposition inevitable and that 'when bad men conspire good men must associate' [2.5.5].

But in the hands of Burke, the Whig case went much further; organized opposition in the House of Commons was seen to be not merely necessary but positively desirable. The particular case of opposition to George III was generalized into an argument in favour of governments which rested almost entirely on the support of the House of Commons and of the (unreformed) electorate. The fact that this would necessarily result in the alternation of governments according to the shifts of opinion within the Commons was generally accepted by the 1820s: the idea of the opposition as the

[24] A. A. Aspinall, 'The Cabinet Council, 1783–1835', *Proceedings of the British Academy*, 1952, pp. 38, 246.

alternative government had arrived.[25] It was this idea, indeed, which was the significant contribution of reflections on party in the early nineteenth century. Opposition was no longer conceived, as had been the case with Bolingbroke, as an attempt to replace the incumbent government and thereafter to institute a permanent and irreplaceable reign of virtue; loss of office as an inevitable and desirable fact of political life was established [2.2.1–4].

Along with this went an increasing tendency to identify 'party' and 'opposition' [2.2.5]. By the 1830s the language of politics often assumed (with more or less descriptive accuracy) that the opposition could be collectively described by the use of one of the two party labels (usually Whig) and that it was not implausible to think of the opposition as 'collectively standing for' a set of particular nostrums or a number of general principles.[26] Indeed, the extent to which the 1820s saw an increasing proportion of divisions in the House of Commons which could be described as 'party questions', and the general importance attached to party by contemporaries enabled the politicians of the 1830s and 1840s to look back on the Liverpool era as a vanished golden age of party coherence.[27]

PARTY RHETORIC

During this period politics was still for many politicians the pursuit of local and personal interests, rather than a matter of 'standing upon' major political issues.[28] Politics on this view involved administration and the preservation of law and order rather than legislation: 'party divisions were primarily over the question of who was to be Government, not what Government was to do'.[29] The extent to which what had first appeared as deeply-felt principles could be cast aside in the interests of holding office was demonstrated by the formation of the Fox–North coalition in 1783, a union which Fox had earlier declared to be impossible, given the deep divisions of

[25] H. C. Mansfield, *Statesmanship and Party Government* (Chicago, 1965), especially p. 16.
[26] Foord, *Opposition*, pp. 439–50.
[27] Mitchell, pp. 5–8.
[28] Pares, p. 2.
[29] J. Brooke, 'Party in the Eighteenth Century' in A. Natan (Ed.), *Silver Renaissance* (1961), p. 21.

principle between North and the Whig opposition.[30] Even the debate over the French Revolution and the revolutionary wars was for many politicians a battle between 'ins' and 'outs', with 'principles' as the main ammunition.

On the other hand, even if the presence of such 'sham fights' is accepted, it is by no means clear that sham was all, or that all was sham. Even in an age when principles were often ladders to be climbed on the way to office, the particular ladders chosen and the need to use them at all are not without significance. It is true that the attempts of the Whigs to demonstrate their unbroken descent from the Revolution and the purity of their principles in opposition to George III were, respectively, poor genealogy and shaky constitutional law [2.3.1–2]; but belief in these things was never entirely absent, and these things were not chosen at random.[31] The sheer repetition of language could have repercussions perhaps unintended by its perpetrators: Fox's use of party labels in opposition after 1784 to distinguish him from the Pittites had resulted by the end of the French Wars [2.3.3] in a general use of the label 'Whig' to describe the opposition, in spite of the fact that the Pittites themselves refused to accept this usage and that some of them were insistent upon their own Whiggism.[32] Both the American War and the Revolutionary Wars led to a more widespread use of labels (largely due to the prosecution of the 'Whig myth' by Rockingham and Fox respectively), although in neither case (especially the first) did the division between Government and Opposition entirely correspond with the division between self-styled Whigs and Tories.

The revival of party labels was associated, during[33] the American War, with the revival of a more far-reaching debate about the constitutional position of the Monarch than had occurred since the early years of the century, although it is the *constitutional* nature of the debate – as opposed to the particular content of the administration's policy towards the American colonies – which must be emphasized [2.3.4–5]. Of the opposition groups, only the Chatham connexion disagreed with the assumption of absolute British supremacy over the colonies which moved the administration; the real opposition was to come not to the policy itself, but to the

---

[30] Foord, *Opposition*, pp. 377–91.
[31] H. Butterfield, *George III*, p. 227.
[32] Foord, *Opposition*, p. 441.
[33] Ibid., pp. 312, 328.

consequences (particularly with respect to taxation) of its failure.[34]
The opposition took advantage of these consequences, and invoked
the Whig doctrine of the constitution in support of their cause. This
constitutional cause involved, for most Whigs, the assertion of the
rights of Parliament rather than the rights of 'the people' (although
here again their willingness to invoke the support of opinion outside
the Commons was to have unforeseen consequences); even the issue
of parliamentary reform remained, until the 1820s, a Whig attempt
to control the Executive rather than a campaign to turn the House
of Commons into a machine dispensing legislative benefits for the
democracy.[35]

The debate over the American War was one of the steps by
which the language of English politics became dependent, by the
1830s, on the vocabulary of party labels and the rhetoric of reform.
The presence of the reform issue in the 1820s and 1830s involved
the Whigs in an attempt to demonstrate once again the purity of
their Revolutionary descent [2.3.6], an attempt made plausible by
the presence in their ranks of some of the great family names of the
seventeenth-century opposition such as Russell, Cavendish, and
Holland. But the difference between the Whigs of the early nineteenth century and those of the age of Anne (or even of the age of
Rockingham and Fox) was evidenced by the presence of new issues
dividing the parties (Catholic emancipation and the need for repression to deal with social unrest after the French wars, for example),
and the extent to which the new labels 'Liberal' and 'Conservative'
were emerging to supplant or reinforce those of Whig and Tory.

PARTY IN THE COUNTRY

The Whig opposition to the prosecution of the American War
involved them in a relationship with the associations and movements which grew up in the country in the 1780s as instruments of
opposition to the war and to its domestic consequences. The Whig
attitude to them was essentially one of temptation combined with
apprehension. The Whig opposition to George III and the American War was prosecuted in the House of Commons by an aristocratic clique centring around Newcastle and Rockingham, whose

[34] B. Donoughue, *British Politics and the American Revolution* (1964), pp. 288–90.
[35] Fraser, p. 6.

39

interests lay in the achievement of office and the rights of Parliament rather than in the rights of the people [2.4.1]. The activities of John Wilkes had earlier demonstrated the firmness with which the House of Commons was determined to resist any possibility of direct electoral influence, and the parliamentary reform movement in the 1780s began as a House of Commons attempt to restrict the powers of the Crown [2.4.2]; Pitt's reform scheme of 1783, for example, was designed to *increase* the representation of counties rather than urban areas.[36] The Whigs were torn between the obvious usefulness of extra-parliamentary opinion to an opposition bent on office and the desire to avoid encouraging the associations and the movements to a point at which the possibility of dictation by such bodies might arise [2.4.3–4]. The extra-parliamentary reform movements were themselves far from instruments of democratic ideas. The early unrest associated with John Wilkes revolved mainly around commercial elements in London [2.4.5], had little practical effect,[37] and was soon overtaken by the county associations led by the gentry. These bodies, such as the Yorkshire Association formed in 1780 and led by Christopher Wyvill, were, with respect to the American War and its consequences, basically in the old 'country' tradition of concern for the balance of the constitution,[38] and relatively uninterested in such questions as the increased representation of non-landed interests.

They arose partly to defend the interests of those who felt particularly vulnerable to the financial consequences of the American War, and partly from the fact that the American bid for independence itself raised questions of political representation and the extent of the prerogative power.[39] The extra-parliamentary movements of the 1780s were thus inextricably associated with the course of the American War, and with the defeat of Lord North their momentum could not be maintained.[40] The French Revolution to some extent revived the debate in the country and – in contrast to the situation during the American War – introduced what were to be basic themes in nineteenth-century Radicalism: the political participation of emerging middle-class interests, and working-class unrest[41]

[36] E. C. Black, *The Association* (Harvard, 1963), p. 8.
[37] J. Brooke, *The Chatham Administration* (1956), p. 230.
[38] I. Christie, *Wilkes, Wyvill and Reform* (1962), p. 226.
[39] G. S. Veitch, *The Genesis of Parliamentary Reform* (1913), p. 43.
[40] Christie, p. 222.   [41] Ibid., pp. 230–1.

[2.4.6]. This revival was dampened by the repression which followed upon Government fears of sedition during the French Wars, but re-emerged when, after 1815, attentions were once more focused upon the domestic scene; Whiggism then came to enshrine the principle of the expedient representation of newer forms of property in the Reform Act of 1832.

The constitutional debates during the reign of George III, while involving little democratic sentiment outside Parliament and none at all within, is none the less of significance to the history of party. In the first place, it saw a revival of interest by the opposition in the possibility of making use of extra-parliamentary opinion. The Rockingham connexion, in common with all other connexions after the 1720s, were inclined to think of opposition in terms of court and parliamentary activity. The closing years of the American War, however, saw a significant shift in the Rockinghamite attitude; the 1784 elections have been described as the first fought with anything resembling a modern electoral organization,[42] and by the 1790 elections the Whigs had a general party fund and two special election funds, as well as a central co-ordinating organization[43] [2.5.5]. This concern with electoral organization was understandable in view of the fact that whatever the immediate importance of extra-parliamentary associations and petitioning movements between the 1760s and the 1790s, the extent to which they involved both relatively sophisticated organization and an emphasis on 'programmes' could hardly escape the attention of contemporary parliamentarians.[44] Even so stout a defender of parliamentary independence as Burke, the Rockinghamite rhetorician, could consider, albeit rather hesitantly, the possibility of making an appeal to opinion outside the House of Commons, a significant indication of the extent to which thinking about electoral organization was a distinct feature of the period.[45] By the 1820s, the increased number of contested elections and the extent to which the idea of a *national* politics was emerging, were evidence enough of the persistence of the tendency[46] [2.4.7].

The second significant aspect of activity outside the Commons was that it revealed the presence of relatively novel elements,

[42] D. E. Ginter, *Whig Organisation in the General Election of 1790* (California, 1967), p. xxii.
[43] Ibid., p. xxv.
[44] Black, especially p. 14.
[45] Ginter, pp. xlviii-xlix.
[46] Fraser, p. 7.

notably the existence of a *provincial* public (novel in that for most eighteenth-century politicians, 'public opinion' had meant the opinion of the City of London) and an emergent provincial press.[47] The importance of the latter is demonstrated by the fact that by the time of Lord Liverpool's administration, Brougham (one of the Whig opposition leaders), was conscious of parliamentary debates as a means, via the provincial press, of publicizing and prosecuting issues of national importance: the reform issue itself is a case in point.[48]

Thus, apart from any changes which occurred in the techniques of parliamentary opposition, there was evidence, after the 1780s, of the existence of an extra-parliamentary opinion with a life of its own. 'The people' were beginning to replace the Monarch as a factor in the politician's life.

PARTY IN PARLIAMENT

The more widespread use of party labels, the emergence of a debate about the constitution, and the growth of opinion outside the House of Commons, affected the politicians in Parliament slowly and unevenly. The picture of the parliamentary connexions as loose groupings around a leader, based on a personal friendship, electoral patronage and the desire for office,[49] and holding together only as long as the leader had a hope of achieving office was modified only gradually; indeed, elements of it persisted well into the nineteenth century [2.5.1]. Nor did the importance attached to achieving office necessarily imply a sordid politics; it was easily compatible with an interest in administration and a belief in the public importance of good government, and was understandable in a system in which legislation was not, until the turn of the century, a significant consideration.[50]

The link between the debate on the constitution and the activities of the parties or connexions in the House of Commons lay initially in the Rockinghamite Whigs, who had to adjust themselves to the novel experience of being in opposition after years of administrative monopoly, and who slowly evolved an 'opposition

[47] Pares, p. 199.   [48] Fraser, p. 143.
[49] Pares, pp. 77–81.
[50] Ibid., pp. 30, 86.

mentality'.[51] The organization of the parliamentary parties was indistinct. There was little continuous contact between leaders and followers, and the position of 'leader of the opposition' was far from formalized. Even at times where such a leader could be identified, the indirect and quasi-collegiate nature of his leadership is illustrated by the fact that summonses to Parliament were transmitted not by 'the leader' himself, but by those of his colleagues to whom the rank-and-file owed immediate allegiance[52] [2.5.2]. On the other hand, signs of change were apparent. Fox succeeded in establishing himself as the leader of the opposition to George III and in annexing the Whig label to his actions and to his colleagues. Earlier, in 1782, the Rockingham Whigs had successfully combined to prevent the Monarch from exercising his freedom of ministerial choice, and had made stipulations about policy as a condition of taking office, activities which were to become more frequent and more successful as the years went by[53] [2.5.3]. The Rockingham opposition to George III was, indeed, a most significant step in the story of the institutionalization of opposition. In a similar manner to the opposition to Walpole in 1742, the Rockingham group had replaced an incumbent Minister and had, moreover, achieved what the former opposition had not – the removal of the Ministry as a whole, and not its 'First Minister' alone. By eighteenth-century standards the Rockingham group was reasonably well-organized, a fact not unconnected with the persistent hostility displayed toward them by George III.[54] The cohesion of the opposition in this period (1760–1832) fluctuated over time; Whig unity in particular waxed and waned, weakening greatly after the Regency crisis, and, during the French Revolution, reaching the almost complete dissolution of the groups which had been active in the opposition to the American War[55] [2.5.4]. In spite of this, a tendency to cohesion and improved organization was evident; by 1784 the Whigs had, in the Whig Club, what has been described as the first party association of a more than temporary or local character.[56]

[51] L. S. Sutherland, 'Edmund Burke and the First Rockingham Ministry', *English Historical Review* (October 1963), p. 52.
[52] Brooke, *Chatham*, p. 237.
[53] Pares, p. 112.
[54] Foord, *Opposition*, p. 305 et seq.
[55] J. W. Derry, *The Regency Crisis and the Whigs* (Cambridge, 1963), p. 1.
[56] Foord, *Opposition*, p. 406.

A tendency to increased cohesion in Government and Opposition forces was evident after the 1780s, reaching a climax during the administration of Lord Liverpool in the 1820s.[57] The increased use of party labels which accompanied this tendency was partly an attempt by party publicists to describe party divisions in terms of distinctive principles, but was much more the result of the increasing recognition of Government and Opposition as two distinct sections of the House of Commons, irrespective of whether this division coincided with divisions of principle, or even of whether principles existed at all [2.5.6]. In this 'Government and Opposition' sense, together with the gradual decline of Monarchy, a two-party situation was a recognizable tendency between the 1780s and the 1820s. After 1807 in particular, the proportion of members of Parliament bearing party labels significantly increased: 'between 1807 and 1841, the man without a party label almost disappeared from the House of Commons'.[58] The extent of the change can be seen from the fact that it has been estimated that in 1755 less than one-quarter of the House of Commons could be described as 'party men':[59] by the 1830s even the House of Lords, never the most partisan of bodies, was divided on party lines.[60]

The Liverpool Administration of 1812–27 represents the cumulative effects of these developments; the composition of the Government majority and the Opposition minority remained unusually constant throughout its existence. Nearly three-quarters of the members of the Parliaments of the Liverpool administration voted consistently in support of the Government or the Opposition.[61] By the early decades of the nineteenth century, meetings of members of the parliamentary parties were becoming both more inclusive and more frequent, and were (at least in the case of the Whig opposition in the 1820s) genuinely consultative occasions,[62] although such developments did not entirely supplant the conception (particularly on the ministerial side) of party meetings as occasions where the rank and file were merely informed of the Government's general position, and urged to give their support.[63] The reality of

[57] Ibid., p. 445. [58] Pares, pp. 191–2.

[59] Brook, *Chatham*, p. 386.

[60] D. Large, 'The Decline of the "Party of the Crown" and the Rise of Parties in the House of Lords', *English Historical Reviews*, October 1963, *passim*.

[61] Fraser, pp. 11–12. [62] Mitchell, pp. 42, 254.

[63] A. A. Aspinall, 'English Party Organisation in the early Nineteenth Century', *English Historical Review*, XLI (1926), *passim*.

the opposition as an institution in the 1820s was demonstrated by the degree to which the Whigs held together in spite of the fact that not until 1830 did they have any real hope of attaining office.[64]

This clear dichotomy between Government and Opposition was described by contemporaries in party terms, a description appropriate in the sense that while such issues as tithes, poor law reform and the game laws could not be assimilated to party lines, the proportion of divisions in the House of Commons which could be so assimilated reached an average of nearly 50 per cent in the 1820s.[65] By 1830, the party confusion which followed the end of the Liverpool Ministry had settled once again into a clear dichotomy, although this time with the Whigs as the ministerial party and the 1832 Reform Act as its consequence.

The basis of this relative stability under Lord Liverpool included the presence of the reform issue, the Whig prosecution of which gave a defensive cohesion to Liverpool's majority,[66] and the fact that the decline of the Monarch had left governments very much dependent on the Commons for their existence.[67] When to this is added the willingness of back-benchers to leave party arrangements in the hands of the leaders, and their recognition of the need for consistent legislative and administrative measures by the executive to regulate an emergent industrial society,[68] the relative stability of party politics in these years is easily understood. The extent to which this stability was based on considerations of 'strong government', is illustrated by the absence of any strong feeling of party obligation, the difficulty of achieving an exact correlation between Government and Opposition and the party labels, and the lack of both sanctions and the will to use them on the part of the Ministry [2.5.7].[69] The new considerations governing the life of nineteenth-century Ministries were recognized by Liverpool when he successfully attempted to secure the inclusion of the last genuinely independent connexion, the Grenville group, within his fold in 1820.[70]

Divisions based on 'class interest' seem to have played even less of a part than rigid divisions of party principle in the establishment of this relatively stable dichotomy of Government and Opposition;

[64] Mitchell, pp. 22–4.
[65] Ibid., p. 3 (n).
[66] Ibid., p. 19.
[67] Foord, *Opposition*, p. 466.
[68] Fraser, p. 32.
[69] W. Brock, *Lord Liverpool and Liberal Toryism* (Cambridge, 1941), p. 101.
[70] Fraser, p. 29.

in so far as party labels bore some relation to the division between Government and Opposition, the Whig/Tory division was clearly not a straightforward matter of commerce against land. The Liverpool administration received support from a number of the great landowners, but its foreign and economic policies were certainly not to their liking;[71] nor could the Liverpool 'Tories' be said to possess a monopoly of landed support. The Whigs were no more the party of commerce than the Tories,[72] and the element of land versus commerce implicit in the conflict over the 1815 Corn Law cut right across party lines.[73] The Whigs' prosecution of the Reform Bill in 1832 was far from a class act (save, perhaps, in the sense that it appealed to middle-class votes in the country): Grey's Cabinet of 1830 was an aristocratic combination *par excellence*, and Whig reform meant not the pursuit of a middle-class interest seen as their own, but the preservation of the basis of the old constitution by the extension of representation to kinds of property which, though new, might least upset the equilibrium of the old.

The period 1760–1832 thus saw within Parliament the slow and uneven development of a recognized dichotomy between Government and Opposition which was associated with the divisions of party labels, not so much because members of either side of the House would shelter under the umbrella of a single label, or because of the divisive power of political principle, but because of the general tendency of politicians and political commentators to indicate and sharpen the dichotomy on the old grindstone of party nomenclature.

This relative stability of parliamentary dispositions, of which the Liverpool Administration provided the clearest example, did not survive the 1832 Reform Act. But the fact that it had occurred, the reasons why it had occurred, and the impressions it had made upon politicians who were later to be responsible for government under the reformed constitution, meant that the English attitude to parties would never be the same again.

[71] Brock, p. 81.
[72] Pares, p. 192.
[73] Fraser, p. 35.

2   1760–1832

Documents

2.1 THE CONSTITUTION

2.1.1 From William Paley, The Principles of Moral and Political Philosophy *(1786). This extract is taken from the fifth edition (1788), Vol. II, pp. 199 and 208.*

The Government of England, which has been sometimes called a mixed government, sometimes a limited Monarchy, is formed by a combination of the three regular species of government: the Monarchy, residing in the King, the aristocracy, in the House of Lords; and the republic, being represented by the House of Commons. The perfection intended by such a scheme of government is, to unite the advantages of the several simple forms, and to exclude the inconveniences . . . there is no power possessed by one part of the legislature, the abuse or excess of which is not checked by some antagonist power, residing in another part.

2.1.2 From The Annual Register of 1763, *pp. 39 and 42.*

. . . what was the end, for which they [*the supporters of Bute and George III* – Ed.] served? Undoubtedly that the King and Kingdom should be no longer governed, or rather insulted, by a Cabal; and that his majesty should, as the law intended, choose and retain his own Ministers . . . The friends of Lord Bute and of the ministry which succeeded, were for preserving to the crown the full exercise of a right, of which none disputed the validity, that of appointing its own servants. Those of the opposition did not deny this power in the crown, but they contended that

47

the spirit of the constitution required, that the crown should be directed in the exercise of this public duty by public motives, and not by private liking or friendship . . . the observation of this rule would, and, they were of opinion, nothing else could, in any degree, counterbalance that immense power, which the crown has acquired by the gift of such an infinite number of profitable places. Nothing but the very popular use of the prerogative can be sufficient to reconcile the nation to the extent of it . . . What has now been said, we think sufficient to afford the ready a very tolerable general idea of the principles, real or pretended, which have for some time unhappily divided the nation.

2.1.3 From letters from Lord Melcombe to the Earl of Bute. Printed in John Adolphus, The History of England from the Accession of George III *(1802), Vol. 1, pp. 27 (n) and 547.*

November 1760:
During the last two reigns, a set of undertakers have farmed the power of the Crown at a price certain; and under colour of making themselves responsible for the whole, have taken the sole direction of the royal interest and influence into their own hands, and applied it to their own creatures, without consulting the Crown, or leaving any room for the royal nomination or direction. This should be prevented before any pretence of promise can be made . . .

December 1760:
Remember, my noble and generous friend, that to recover Monarchy from the inveterate usurpation of oligarchy is a part too arduous and important to be achieved without much difficulty, and some degree of danger; though none but what attentive moderation and unalterable firmness will surmount.

2.1.4 From The Auditor (a weekly magazine), *No. 3, 17 June 1762, p. 18.*

. . . the executive part of the government is lodged in the crown, together with a fiduciary power from the laws to make war or peace, and to name the statesmen, who shall form the Cabinet council . . . the present Minister is appointed by his Majesty, and . . . he possesses property enough to put him above temptation . . .

From The Auditor, *No. 7, 22 July 1762, p. 42.*

... we live in better times, under a King, who does not desire to strain the prerogative; who founds the glories of his reign in virtue; and under an administration who seek no treasonable popularity, who have no interests separate from the welfare of the Kingdom, and the honour of the Crown.

2.1.5 From Edmund Burke, Thoughts on the Cause of the Present Discontents (*1770*), *pp. 58, 59–61.*

The power of the crown, almost dead and rotten as Prerogative, has grown up anew, with much more strength, and far less odium, under the name of Influence. An influence, which operated without noise and without violence; an influence which converted the very antagonist, into the instrument, of power; which contained in itself a perpetual principle of growth and renovation; and which the distresses and the prosperity of the country equally tended to augment, was an admirable substitute for a prerogative, that, being only the offspring of antiquated prejudices, had moulded into its original stamina irresistible principles of decay and dissolution. The ignorance of the people is a bottom but for a temporary system; the interest of active men in the state is a foundation perpetual and infallible. However, some circumstances, arising, it must be confessed, in a great degree from accident, prevented the effects of this influence for a long time from breaking out in a manner capable of exciting any serious apprehensions. Although government was strong and flourished exceedingly, the *court* had drawn far less advantage than one would imagine from this great source of power.

At the revolution, the crown, deprived, for the ends of the revolution itself, of many prerogatives, was found too weak to struggle against all the difficulties which pressed so new and unsettled a government. The court was obliged therefore to delegate a part of its powers to men of such interest as could support, and of such fidelity as would adhere to, its establishment. Such men were able to draw in a greater number to a concurrence in the common defence. This connexion, necessary at first, continued long after convenient; and properly conducted might indeed, in all situations, be an useful instrument of government. At the same time, through the intervention of men of popular weight and character, the people possessed a security for their just proportion of importance in the state. But as the title to the crown grew stronger by long possession, and by the constant increase of its influence, these helps have of late seemed to certain persons no better than incumbrances. The

49

powerful managers for government were not sufficiently submissive to the pleasure of the possessors of immediate and personal favour, sometimes from a confidence in their own strength natural and acquired; sometimes from a fear of offending their friends, and weakening that lead in the country, which gave them a consideration independent of the court. Men acted as if the court could receive, as well as confer, an obligation. The influence of government, thus divided in appearance between the court and the leaders of parties, became in many cases an accession rather to the popular than to the royal scale; and some part of that influence, which would otherwise have been possessed as in a sort of mortmain and unalienable domain, returned again to the great ocean from whence it arose, and circulated among the people. This method, therefore, of governing by men of great natural interest or great acquired consideration was viewed in a very invidious light by the true lovers of absolute monarchy. It is the nature of despotism to abhor power held by any means but its own momentary pleasure; and to annihilate all intermediate situations between boundless strength on its own part, and total debility on the part of the people.

To get rid of all this intermediate and independent importance, and *to secure to the court the unlimited and uncontrolled use of its own vast influence, under the sole direction of its own private favour*, has for some years past been the great object of policy. If this were compassed, the influence of the crown must of course produce all the effects which the most sanguine partisans of the court could possibly desire. Government might then be carried on without any concurrence on the part of the people; without any attention to the dignity of the greater, or to the affections of the lower sorts. A new project was therefore devised by a certain set of intriguing men, totally different from the system of administration which had prevailed since the accession of the House of Brunswick. This project, I have heard, was first conceived by some persons in the court of Frederick Prince of Wales.

The earliest attempt in the execution of this design was to set up for minister, a person, in rank indeed respectable, and very ample in fortune; but who, to the moment of this vast and sudden elevation, was little known or considered in the kingdom. To him the whole nation was to yield an immediate and implicit submission. But whether it was from want of firmness to bear up against the first opposition; or that things were not yet fully ripened, or that this method was not found the most eligible; that idea was soon abandoned. The instrumental part of the project was a little altered to accommodate it to the time, and to bring things more gradually and more surely to the one great end proposed.

The first part of the reformed plan was to draw *a line which should separate the court from the ministry.* Hitherto these names had been looked upon as synonymous; but for the future, court and administration were to be considered as things totally distinct. By this operation, two systems of administration were to be formed; one which should be in the real secret and confidence; the other merely ostensible to perform the official and executory duties of government. The latter were alone to be responsible; whilst the real advisers, who enjoyed all the power, were effectually removed from all the danger.

Secondly, *A party under these leaders was to be formed in favour of the court against the ministry:* this party was to have a large share in the emoluments of government, and to hold it totally separate from, and independent of, ostensible administration.

The third point, and that on which the success of the whole scheme ultimately depended, was *to bring parliament to an acquiescence in this project.* Parliament was therefore to be taught by degrees a total indifference to the persons, rank, influence, abilities, connexions, and character of the ministers of the crown. By means of a discipline, on which I shall say more hereafter, that body was to be habituated to the most opposite interests, and the most discordant politics. All connexions and dependencies among subjects were to be entirely dissolved. As hitherto, business had gone through the hands of leaders of Whigs or Tories, men of talents to conciliate the people, and to engage their confidence; now the method was to be altered: and the lead was to be given to men of no sort of consideration or credit in the country. This want of natural importance was to be their very title to delegated power. Members of parliament were to be hardened into an insensibility to pride as well as to duty. Those high and haughty sentiments, which are the great support of independence, were to be let down gradually. Points of honour and precedence were no more to be regarded in parliamentary decorum, than in a Turkish army. It was to be avowed, as a constitutional maxim, that the king might appoint one of his footmen, or one of your footmen for minister; and that he ought to be, and that he would be, as well followed as the first name for rank or wisdom in the nation. Thus parliament was to look on, as if perfectly unconcerned, while a cabal of the closet and back-stairs was substituted in the place of a national administration.

Thus for the time were pulled down, in the persons of the Whig leaders and of Mr Pitt (in spite of the services of the one at the accession of the royal family, and the recent services of the other in the war) the *two only securities for the importance of the people; power arising from popularity; and power arising from connexion.* Here and there indeed a few individuals were left standing, who gave security for their total estrangement from the odious principles of party connexion and personal attachment; and it must be confessed that most of them have religiously kept their faith. Such a change could not however be made without a mighty shock to government.

To reconcile the minds of the people to all these movements, principles correspondent to them had been preached up with great zeal. Every one must remember that the cabal set out with the most astonishing prudery, both moral and political. Those, who in a few months after soused over head and ears into the deepest and dirtiest pits of corruption, cried out violently against the indirect practices in the electing and managing of parliaments, which had formerly prevailed. This marvellous abhorrence which the court had suddenly taken to all influence, was not only circulated in conversation through the kingdom, but pompously announced to the public, with many other extraordinary things, in a pamphlet which had all the appearance of a manifesto preparatory to some considerable enterprise. Throughout it was a satire, though in terms managed and decent enough, on the politics of the former reign. It was indeed written with no small art and address.

In this piece appeared the first dawning of the new system; there first appeared the idea (then only in speculation) of *separating the court from the administration*; of carrying every thing from national connexion to personal regards; and of forming a regular party for that purpose, under the name of *king's men*.

To recommend this system to the people, a perspective view of the court, gorgeously painted, and finely illuminated from within, was exhibited to the gaping multitude. Party was to be totally done away, with all its evil works. Corruption was to be cast down from court, as *Atè* was from heaven. Power was thenceforward to be the chosen residence of public spirit; and no one was to be supposed under any sinister influence, except those who had the misfortune to be in disgrace at court, which was to stand in lieu of all vices and all corruptions. A scheme of perfection to be realized in a monarchy far beyond the visionary republic of Plato. The whole scenery was exactly disposed to captivate those good souls, whose credulous morality is so invaluable a treasure to crafty politicians. Indeed there was wherewithal to charm every body, except those few who are not much pleased with professions of supernatural virtue, who know of what stuff such professions are made, for what purposes they are designed, and in what they are sure constantly to end. Many innocent gentlemen, who had been talking prose all their lives without knowing anything of the matter, began at last to open their eyes upon their own merits, and to attribute their not having been lords of the treasury and lords of trade many years before, merely to the prevalence of party, and to the ministerial power, which had frustrated the good intentions of the court in favour of their abilities. Now was the time to unlock the sealed fountain of royal bounty, which had been infamously monopolized and huckstered, and to let it flow at large upon the whole people. The time was come, to restore royalty to its original splendour. *Mettre le Roy hors de page*, became a sort of watchword. And it was constantly in the mouths of all the runners of the court, that nothing could preserve the balance of the constitution from being overturned by the rabble, or by a faction of the nobility, but to free the sovereign effectually from that ministerial tyranny under which the royal dignity had been oppressed in the person of his majesty's grandfather.

Party is a body of men united for promoting by their joint endeavours the national interest upon some particular principle in which they are all agreed. For my part, I find it impossible to conceive, that any one believes in his own politics, or thinks them to be of any weight, who refuses to adopt the means of having them reduced into practice. It is the business of the speculative philosopher to mark the proper ends of government. It is the business of the politician, who is the philosopher in action, to find out proper means towards those ends, and to employ them with effect. Therefore every honourable connexion will avow it is their first purpose, to pursue every just method to put the men who hold their opinions into such a condition as may enable them to carry their common plans into execution, with all the power and authority of the state. As this power is attached to certain situations, it is their duty to contend for these situations. Without a proscription of others, they are bound to give to their own party the preference in all things; and by no means, for private considerations, to accept any offers of power in which the whole body is not included; not to suffer themselves to be led, or to be controlled, or to be overbalanced, in office or in council, by those who contradict the very fundamental principles on which their party is formed, and even those upon which every fair connexion must stand. Such a generous contention for power, on such manly and honourable maxims, will easily be distinguished from the mean and interested struggle for place and emolument. The very style of such persons will serve to discriminate them from those numberless impostors, who have deluded the ignorant with professions incompatible with human practice, and have afterwards incensed them by practices below the level of vulgar rectitude.

It is an advantage to all narrow wisdom and narrow morals, that their maxims have a plausible air; and, on a cursory view, appear equal to first principles. They are light and portable. They are as current as copper coin; and about as valuable. They serve equally the first capacities and the lowest; and they are, at least, as useful to the worst men as to the best. Of this stamp is the cant of *Not men, but measures*; a sort of charm by which many people get loose from every honourable engagement. When I see a man acting this desultory and disconnected part, with as much detriment to his own fortune as prejudice to the cause of any party, I am not persuaded that he is right; but I am ready to believe he is in earnest. I respect virtue in all its situations; even when it is found in the unsuitable company of weakness. I lament to see qualities, rare and valuable, squandered away without any public utility. But when a gentleman with great visible emoluments abandons the party in which he has long acted, and tells you, it is because he proceeds upon his own judgement; that he acts on the merits of the several measures as they arise; and that he is obliged to follow his own conscience, and not that of others; he gives reasons which it is impossible to controvert, and discovers a character which it is impossible to mistake. What shall we think of him who never differed from a certain set of men until the moment they lost their power, and who never agreed with them in a single instance afterwards? Would not such a coincidence of interest and opinion be rather fortunate? Would it not be an extraordinary cast upon the dice, that a man's connexions should degenerate into faction, precisely at the critical moment when they lose their power, or he accepts a place? When people desert their connexions, the desertion is a manifest *fact*, upon which a direct simple issue lies, triable by plain men. Whether a *measure* of government be right or wrong, *is no matter of fact*, but a mere affair of opinion, on which men may, as they do, dispute and wrangle without end. But whether the individual *thinks* the measure right or wrong, is a point at still a greater distance from the reach of all human decision. It is therefore very convenient to politicians, not to put the judgement of their conduct on overt-acts, cognizable in any ordinary court, but upon such matter as can be triable only in that secret tribunal, where they are sure of being heard with favour, or where at worst the sentence will be only private whipping.

I believe the reader would wish to find no substance in a doctrine which has a tendency to destroy all test of character as deduced from conduct. He will therefore excuse my adding something more, towards the further clearing up a point, which the great convenience of obscurity to dishonesty has been able to cover with some degree of darkness and doubt.

In order to throw an odium on political connexion, these politicians suppose it a necessary incident to it, that you are blindly to follow the opinions of your party, when in direct opposition to your own clear ideas; a degree of servitude that no worthy man could bear the thought of submitting to; and such as, I believe, no connexions (except some court factions) ever could be so senselessly tyrannical as to impose. Men thinking freely, will, in particular instances, think differently. But still as the greater part of the measures which arise in the course of public business are related to, or dependent on, some great, *leading, general principles in government*, a man must be peculiarly unfortunate in the choice of his political company, if he does not agree with them at least nine times in ten. If he does not concur in these general principles upon which the party is founded, and which necessarily draw on a concurrence in their application, he ought from the beginning to have chosen some other, more conformable to his opinions. When the question is in its nature doubtful, or not very material, the modesty which becomes an individual, and (in spite of our court moralists) that partiality which becomes a well-chosen friendship, will frequently bring on an acquiescence in the general sentiment. Thus the disagreement will naturally be rare; it will be only enough to indulge freedom, without violating concord, or disturbing arrangement. And this is all that ever was required for a character of the greatest uniformity and steadiness in connexion. How men can proceed without any connexion at all, is to me utterly incomprehensible. Of what sort of materials must that man be made, how must he be tempered and put together, who can sit whole years in parliament, with five hundred and fifty of his fellow-citizens, amidst the storm of such tempestuous passions, in the sharp conflict of so many wits, and tempers, and characters, in the agitation of such mighty questions, in the discussion of such vast and ponderous interests, without seeing any one sort of men, whose character, conduct, or disposition, would lead him to associate himself with them, to aid and be aided, in any one system of public utility?

I remember an old scholastic aphorism, which says, 'that the man who lives wholly detached from others, must be either an angel or a devil'. When I see in any of these detached gentlemen of our times the angelic purity, power, and beneficence, I shall admit them to be angels. In the mean time we are born only to be men. We shall do enough if we form ourselves to be good ones. It is therefore our business carefully to cultivate in our minds, to rear to the most perfect vigour and maturity, every sort of generous and honest feeling, that belongs to our nature. To bring the dispositions that are lovely in private life into the service and conduct of the commonwealth; so to be patriots, as not to forget we are gentlemen. To cultivate friendships, and to incur enmities. To have both strong, but both selected; in the one, to be placable; in the other immovable. To model our principles to our duties and our situation. To be fully persuaded, that all virtue which is impracticable is spurious; and rather to run the risk of falling into faults in a course which leads us to act with effect and energy, than to loiter out our days without blame, and without use. Public life is a situation of power and energy; he trespasses against his duty who sleeps upon his watch, as well as he that goes over to the enemy.

There is, however, a time for all things. It is not every conjuncture which calls with equal force upon the activity of honest men; but critical exigencies now and then arise; and I am mistaken, if this be not one of them. Men will see the necessity of honest combination; but they may see it when it is too late. They may embody, when it will be ruinous to themselves, and of no advantage to the country; when, for want of such a timely union as may enable them to oppose in favour of the laws, with the laws on their side, they may at length find themselves under the necessity of conspiring, instead of consulting. The law, for which they stand, may become a weapon in the hands of its bitterest enemies; and they will be cast, at length, into that miserable alternative between slavery and civil confusion, which no good man can look upon without horror; an alternative in which it is impossible he should take either part, with a conscience perfectly at repose. To keep that situation of guilt and remorse at the utmost distance is, therefore, our first obligation. Early activity may prevent late and fruitless violence. As yet we work in the light. The scheme of the enemies of public tranquillity has disarranged, it has not destroyed us.

If the reader believes that there really exists such a faction as I have described; a faction ruling by the private inclinations of a court, against the general sense of the people; and that this faction, whilst it pursues a scheme for undermining all the foundations of our freedom, weakens (for the present at least) all the powers of executory government, rendering us abroad contemptible, and at home distracted; he will believe also, that nothing but a firm combination of public men against this body, and that, too, supported by the hearty concurrence of the people at large, can possibly get the better of it. The people will see the necessity of restoring public men to an attention to the public opinion, and of restoring the constitution to its original principles. Above all, they will endeavour to keep the House of Commons from assuming a character which does not belong to it. They will endeavour to keep that House, for its existence, for its powers, and its privileges, as independent of every other, and as dependent upon themselves, as possible. This servitude is to a House of Commons (like obedience to the divine law) 'perfect freedom'. For if they once quit this natural, rational, and liberal obedience, having deserted the only proper foundation of their power, they must seek a support in an abject and unnatural dependence somewhere else. When, through the medium of this just connexion with their constituents, the genuine dignity of the House of Commons is restored, it will begin to think of casting from it, with scorn, as badges of servility, all the false ornaments of illegal power, with which it has been, for some time, disgraced. It will begin to think of its old office of Control. It will not suffer that last of evils to predominate in the country: men without popular confidence, public opinion, natural connexion, or mutual trust, invested with all the powers of government.

When they have learned this lesson themselves, they will be willing and able to teach the court, that it is the true interest of the prince to have but one administration; and that one composed of those who recommend themselves to their sovereign through the opinion of their country, and not by their obsequiousness to a favourite. Such men will serve their sovereign with affection and fidelity; because his choice of them, upon such principles, is a compliment to their virtue. They will be able to serve him effectually; because they will add the weight of the country to the force of the executory power. They will be able to serve their king with dignity; because they will never abuse his name to the gratification of their private spleen or avarice. This, with allowances for human frailty, may probably be the general character of a ministry, which thinks itself accountable to the House of Commons; when the House of Commons thinks itself accountable to its constituents. If other ideas should prevail, things must remain in their present confusion, until they are hurried into all the rage of civil violence, or until they sink into the dead repose of despotism.

2.1.6 From the Parliamentary Debates *(New Series, Vol. VI, 8 March 1822) c.1174.*
The extract is from a Treasury Circular printed therein.

On Wednesday next . . . a motion is to be made by Lord Normanby, to abolish the office of one of the Paymaster Generals, and . . . on the day following, Mr Creevey makes a similar motion against the Board of Control. In this manner the just and necessary influence of the Crown is from day to day attacked . . . ; it will be quite impossible for any set of men to conduct the government of this country, unless practices of this kind shall be successfully resisted. It seems as if the Opposition, in despair of coming into office, had determined to break down the means of administering the affairs of the country.

2.1.7 From a letter to Lord Grenville from Thomas Grenville April 1809. Printed in the Dropmore *Papers (Historical Manuscripts Commission), Vol. IX, p. 294.*

[Some of your observations] on the practical details of government cannot afford such answers as it will be possible to afford in any public discussion, and least of all in Parliament. You cannot tell the people, when they complain of facts which establish corruption in the military department . . . you cannot tell them that the influence of what they call corruption is, for practical purposes, too small rather than too great . . .

2.1.8 From the Greville Memoirs *(edited J. L. Strachey and R. Fulford, 1938), Vol. II, pp. 61–2.*
The extract was written on 17 November 1830, and concerns the fall of Wellington's government.

Went to Downing St. yesterday morning, and found that the Duke and all the Ministers were just gone to the King. He received them with the greatest kindness, shed tears, but accepted their resignation without remonstrance . . . The King seems to have behaved perfectly through-out the whole business, no intriguing or underhand communication with anybody, with great kindness to his Ministers, anxious to support them while it was possible, and submitting at once to the necessity of parting with them . . . he is an incomparable King, and deserves all the encom-iums that are lavished on him.

2.1.9 From the Parliamentary History *(Vol. XXII, 15 March 1782), c. 1197.*
The debate concerns the fate of Lord North's Ministry.

The Lord Advocate: Suffer the present ministry to remain, and frame [a] coalition. Turn them out, and there is no coalition, but the gentlemen on the other side succeed in their room . . . The present motion . . . went immediately to the removal of all the ministers without distinction; therefore it was directly throwing the whole of the government into the hands of the other side of the House. Lord John Cavendish said, that by agreeing to the present motion, the House by no means placed the opposition in power . . . . They did no more than take the executive government from the present hands, and leave it to his Majesty to frame such a new administration as his Majesty should think most proper. This was not a new practice . . . it had been often done to the advantage of the nation . . .

2.1.10 From a letter to George III from Lord North, 18 March 1782. Printed in The Correspondence of George III *(edited Sir John Fortescue, 1927), Vol. V, p. 394.*

. . . the fate of the present Ministry is absolutely and irrecoverably decided . . . the torrent is too strong to be resisted; your Majesty is well apprized that, in this country, the Prince on the Throne, cannot, with prudence, oppose the deliberate resolution of the House of Commons: Your Royal Predecessors (particularly King William the third and his late Majesty) were obliged to yield to it much against their wish in more circumstances than one: They consented to changes in their Ministry which they disapproved because they found it necessary to sacrifice their private wishes, and even their opinions to the preservation of public order, and the prevention of those terrible mischiefs, which are the natural consequence of the clashing of two branches of the Sovereign Power in the State ... The Parliament have altered their sentiments, and as their sentiments whether just or erroneous, must ultimately prevail, Your Majesty having persevered, as long as possible, in what you thought right, can lose no honour if you yield at length ... to the opinion and wishes of the House of Commons.

2.1.11 From a report of Fox's first interview with Lord North, 14 February 1783. Printed in The Correspondence of Charles James Fox *(edited Lord John Russell, 1853), Vol. II, p. 38.*

Mr Fox having urged that the King should not be suffered to be his own Minister, Lord North replied: 'If you mean there should not be a Government by departments, I agree with you ... There should be one man, or a Cabinet, to govern the whole, and direct every measure ... The King ought to be treated with all sort of respect and attention, but the appearance of power is all that a King of this country can have ...'

2.1.12 From a letter to George III from Lord Grenville, 18 March 1807. Printed in the Dropmore Papers *(Historical Manuscripts Commission), Vol. IX, p. 119. The letter is a reply to the King's request to the Cabinet not to raise the issue of Catholic Emancipation.*

Lord Grenville has the honour most humbly to lay before your Majesty the minute of a meeting of [some of the Cabinet] ... Your Majesty's servants have considered with the most respectful and dutiful attention the answer which your Majesty has done them the honour to return to their minute of the 15th inst. They beg leave most humbly to represent to your Majesty that, at the time when your Majesty was graciously pleased to call them to your councils, no assurance was required from them inconsistent with those duties which are inseparable from that station. Had any such assurance been then demanded, they must have expressed, with all humility and duty, the absolute impossibility of their thus fettering the free exercise of their judgement. Those who are entrusted by your Majesty with the administration of your extensive Empire, are bound by every obligation to submit to your Majesty without reserve the best advice which they can frame to meet the various exigencies and dangers of the times.

> *2.1.13 From a letter to Spencer Perceval from George Canning, 5 March 1809. Printed in Spencer Walpole,* Life of Perceval *(1874) Vol. 1, p. 321.*
> *The letter is concerned with the role of the Cabinet in advising the Duke of York about the allegation that he supported his mistress's habit of promising military advancement in return for money. Its importance lies in the fact that while the arguments are concerned with the position of the Duke, they would apply equally to the King.*

What is the relation between the government and the Duke of York? Has he put his defence into our hands, and therewith the regulation of his conduct with a view to that defence also? . . . It is the essence of advice given by persons *responsible* for giving it, that it should be either accepted or rejected *in toto*. Otherwise there is no safety for the advisers, and will probably be no consistency in the conduct, which is only partially guided by their advice.

2.2 ATTITUDES TO PARTY

2.2.1 From the Parliamentary Debates *(New Series, Vol. 25, 10 April 1826), c. 135 and 145.*

Sir John Cam Hobhouse: . . . It was said to be very hard on his Majesty's ministers to raise objections to this proposition. For his own part, he thought it was more hard on his Majesty's opposition (*a laugh*) to compel them to take this course . . .

Mr Tierney: . . . An honourable friend near him had called the opposition the 'King's Opposition'. The propriety of this appellation had been recognized by the gentlemen on the other side; and indeed it could not be disputed. From his personal experience, he could bear testimony to the truth of the designation . . . For years he had opposed the measures of government, because he disapproved of their principles; but when they changed their tone he had not been backward in giving them his . . . support. My honourable friend (continued Mr Tierney) could not have invented a better phrase than that which he has adopted, for we are certainly, to all intents and purposes, a branch of his Majesty's government. Its proceedings for some time past had proved, that though the gentlemen opposite are in office, we are in power. The measures are ours, but all the emoluments are theirs (cheers, and laughter).

2.2.2 From a speech by Earl Camden on the East India Declaratory Bill, the Parliamentary History (*Vol. XXVII, 12 March 1788*), c. 243.

Though in office himself, he declared he honoured an opposition; and he had no scruple to say, that he thought an opposition of great service to the country, when conducted on public principles. An opposition awed ministers, and kept them vigilant. It checked their career, put them upon their guard, taught them where error lay, and how to correct it.

2.2.3 From John Ranby, An Inquiry into the Supposed Increase of the Influence of the Crown (*1811*), pp. 38–9.

The opposition is an exact counterpart of the ministerial party . . . with this difference, that the opposition aspire to the situation which the ministerial party possess . . . The two parties thus composed, are to be considered as the principals in that legitimate warfare of parties in parliament from which much benefit is derived to the public.

2.2.4 From James Macpherson, A Short History of the Opposition during the Last Session of Parliament (*1779*), pp. 2–3 and 47.

The Revolution . . . established a balance of influence, between the Crown and the People . . . The representatives of the latter having a great deal to bestow, as a body, thought themselves, as individuals, entitled to a share in a government, which they supported. A mutual dependence was created, by the possession of the means of conferring favours. A Prince, who stood in need of supplies, was directed, by a common prudence, where to choose his servants. But as candidates were more numerous than offices, the disappointed never failed to persecute the successful; till, by watching faults, errors, or misfortunes, they obtained their point, and they themselves became, in their turn, the objects of attack . . . An habitual jealousy of the power of the Crown, kept open the ears of the public to every alarm. Scarce any measure of Government could be so free from error, as not to be vulnerable on some

61

popular ground. Every Opposition seized this obvious advantage, and assumed or obtained the title of the 'popular party'. No distinction was made, in this respect, between Whig and Tory. Each party, when out of place, adopted the same principles; and thus both were alternately dignified with the once honourable name of Patriots . . .

In every popular government, opposition is not only natural, but, when conducted on liberal principles, useful, and even necessary. There is a kind of charm in authority, which may induce the most virtuous magistrates to extend it too far . . . The original object of a national representation, was to watch over the political rights of the people, and to check the incroachments of the executive power.

2.2.5 From 'The Opposition', The Quarterly Review (Vol. 28, October 1822), pp. 197, 198 and 219.

The inseparable attendants of freedom are party and faction . . . Our constitution affords every facility for their growth by the liberty, great in theory and almost boundless in practice, which it bestows . . . The offices of the ministers are therefore to bodies, what an elective situation of honour and emolument is to individuals, and there is as much certainty of rival competitors for the one, as for the other. As the body which is successful must be removed whenever its rival can produce a majority of votes, and as its removal constitutes in effect the election of this rival, the latter, under the name of the Opposition, daily resorts to every imaginable artifice to strengthen its interest, and procure the dismissal of its opponent. The ministry has therefore not only to transact the business of the state, but to carry on an offensive and defensive war on its own private account . . . It has to sustain the two-fold character of a government and a mere political party. The nation is of course eternally embroiled in an election contest between two bodies for the reins of power . . .

When we look into the history of any of those nations of which the name, or the shadow, only now remains, we constantly find parties, corresponding in nature with those which are known among us by the names of whig and tory . . . the nation is the chief arbiter between [these] contending bodies . . .

We have hitherto spoken of the ministry and the opposition without once remembering who at present compose them; we are now however compelled to reverse this, and to speak almost altogether of the parties which at this moment form these important bodies . . .

The necessity for the existence of an efficient opposition is . . . only secondary in degree for the existence of a ministry. Although this body is self-appointed, [and] is scarcely tolerated by the letter of the constitution

. . . it has to perform public duties of the very highest importance to the state. It has to act as the guardian and champion of the constitution and laws – as the inspector of the conduct of ministers, the denouncer of their incapacity and misdeeds – and as the leader of the nation in its opposition to their measures and in the attempts to remove them from office . . . By holding itself constantly in readiness, and duly fitted at all points for undertaking the direction of public affairs, it gives to the sovereign and nation that perfect independence and efficient control over the ministers, on which the good of the state so essentially depends.

2.3 PARTY RHETORIC

2.3.1 From a speech by the Earl of Chatham on a motion by the Duke of Richmond. Parliamentary History (Vol. XVI, 22 November 1770), c. 1107.

I cannot avoid seeing some capital errors in the distribution of the royal favour. There are men, my Lords, who, if their own services were forgotten, ought to have a hereditary merit with the House of Hanover; whose ancestors stood forth in the day of trouble, opposing their persons and fortunes to treachery and rebellion, and secured to his Majesty's family this splendid power of rewarding. There are other men, my Lords . . . who, to speak tenderly of them, were not quite so forward in their demonstrations of their zeal to the reigning family . . . I know I shall be accused of attempting to revive distinctions . . . But there are some distinctions which are inherent in the nature of things. There is a distinction between right and wrong and between Whig and Tory.

2.3.2 The Standing Toasts of the Whig Club, from The Whig Club, Instituted in May 1784, RULES.

I The glorious and immortal memory of King William III.
II The Constitution, according to the principles asserted at the Revolution.
III The Rights of the People.
IV The Friends of Freedom.
V The Cause for which Hampden bled in the field, and Sydney on the scaffold.
VI May the names of Russell and Cavendish be ever united in defence of the liberties of their country.
VII May it be the character of the Whig Club, never to slacken

63

their efforts in adversity, nor to forget their principles in prosperity.

VIII The House of Brunswick, and may they never forget the principles which seated their family upon the throne of Great Britain.

IX May the example of one Revolution prevent the necessity of another.

2.3.3 From a speech by Fox in support of a 'Motion for putting an end to the war with France' (30 May 1794). Printed in Charles James Fox: Speeches During the French Revolution (1920), pp. 203 and 218. The motion was lost by 208 votes to 55.

The House had never sanctioned the dangerous speculation that to secure England we must destroy Jacobinism in France. The experience of ages had proved it to be the will of Providence that monarchies, oligarchies, aristocracies, republics might exist in all their several varieties in different . . . parts of the world without imposing the necessity of endless wars on the rest . . . the French government had existed for two years. A powerful confederacy had been formed, numerous armies and great generals employed against it, and yet internally it appeared to be stronger than ever . . . if we chose to revert to the old maxim of state policy, that the internal anarchy of France, or of any other country, was no concern of ours, then, indeed, our success in the East and West Indies would tell in our favour . . . The settlements and islands we had taken . . . were excellent materials for negotiation, but nothing for overturning the present government of France . . . He therefore wished the House and country to consider whether we had not now the means of making peace . . .

Some sanguine men were of opinion that certain principles established in one country must necessarily disturb the peace of another – He had doubted the doctrine when he first heard it; and the more he had examined it the more he disliked it. If it was maintained that opinions held in France must contaminate the minds of Englishmen, this would lead to a revival of every species of intolerance, and to a more rigorous scrutiny of opinions than could be safe for states and individuals, more especially for this country. Had it not often been said that the French Revolution owed its origins to the American War . . . ? This was so plausible that he knew not how to doubt it. Not that the French took the American opinions as they really were; they adapted them crudely in theory and perverted them in practice. Whence did the Americans derive their opinions? . . . they carried them with them from England. He must, therefore, deprecate questioning opinions on the possible consequences to which they might lead, for then would both America and England be found guilty. Whence were derived the Rights of Man, so much abused by misapplication, so fundamentally true? . . . from Great Britain; from what philosophy, if it was still safe to use the word; that which Locke and Sydney taught and illustrated . . . He would now assume that the House was to differ from him in all he had said, and to persist in the plan for overturning Jacobinism in France as the only road to peace . . . Then every Frenchman would know what he had to expect of us.

2.3.4 From a speech by R. Hart-Davis, M.P., 22 February 1819. Parliamentary Debates, *Vol. XXXIX, c. 594.*

He was not ashamed of avowing himself a Tory, or rather he gloried in the title, but not as frequently explained in that House. The only difference he knew of between a good Old Whig and Tory was, that the Whig apprehended the more immediate danger to the constitution from the undue influence of the Crown, whereas, the Tory conceived that it was as likely to arise from the encroaching and overbearing licence of the people. He was, however, convinced, that both would be found fighting under the same banner, whenever a real attack was made upon the constitution. (Loud cheers) . . .

2.3.5 From Thomas Somerville, The History of Political Transactions and of Parties *(1792), pp. 569–70.*

If there be any fundamental and comprehensive principle, distinguishing the whigs from the tories, it is that which they avow with respect to the interfering claims of the prince and the people. The privileges of the people the whigs profess to guard with a jealous eye, and to vindicate from the encroachment of every rival interest. The tories are devoted with the supreme affections of their hearts to maintain the prerogative of the crown . . . In every question, therefore, of interference between prerogative and privilege, that is not already fixed with precision by statute or precedent, the whigs, in conformity with their principles, may be expected to adhere to the latter, and the tories to the former, and yet there is not any one part in which both parties have acted more vaguely, and so often in direct opposition to their favourite principles. If we collect and examine the long catalogue of questions, directly or indirectly referring to that subject, from the era of the revolution down to the present times, they will rather appear to have been disputes between administration and opposition, than between whig and tory, and to have

65

had for their object, not the support of principle, but the acquisition and retention of power. But however variable and contradictory the sentiments of whigs and tories may have been with respect to questions purely political, yet both of them have more uniformly adhered to those principles of religious and ecclesiastical polity, which were coeval with their existence as parties. The whigs, whether within or without the pale of the national church, have been not only professed, but generally consistent, active friends to religious liberty.

2.3.6 From a letter to Lord Grey from Viscount Lambton, 3 January 1820. Printed in Life and Letters of the First Earl of Durham (*edited S. J. Reid, 1906*), Vol. I, p. 129.

In a public view I think the preservation of the Whig party in Parliament of the utmost importance. It is really in practice the only defence for the liberties of the country. By that party the Revolution was effected, the Protestant succession maintained . . . How many unconstitutional measures have been checked, how many much mitigated in their character, by its exertions.

2.4 PARTY IN THE COUNTRY

2.4.1 From Edmund Burke, 'A Letter to Sir Hercules Langrishe, M.P.' (1792). Printed in The Works and Correspondence of Edmund Burke (*1852*), Vol. IV, p. 540.

Virtual representation is that in which there is a communion of interests, and a sympathy in feelings and desires between those who act in the name of any description of people, and the people in whose name they act, though the trustees are not actually chosen by them . . . Such a representation I think to be, in many cases, even better than the actual . . . The people may err in their choice; but common interest and common sentiment are rarely mistaken. But this sort of virtual representation cannot have a long or sure existence, if it has not a substratum in the actual. The man must have some relation to the constituent.

2.4.2 From 'Parliamentary Reform', The Edinburgh Review (*July 1809*), pp. 277–306.

The great leading evils in our actual condition . . . may be reduced perhaps to the three following heads: First the burden of our taxes; second the preponderating influence of the Crown . . . and thirdly, the monopoly of political power which the very permanency and nature of the constitution has a tendency to create in the hands of a small part of the nation, and the growing jealousy and disaffection which this is likely to breed in the body of the people. For these, and for all the other disorders which threaten our body politic, the popular prescription is parliamentary reform . . .

With us, . . . the people are getting as wise as their rulers; and ceasing already to recognize any real superiority in those to whom they had been accustomed to look up with implicit confidence, they begin to feel that distrust and dissatisfaction with the actual aristocracy which has burst out into such fatal disorders in some other countries . . . Two miserable consequences result from this evil. In the first place, affairs are administered with much less wisdom and judgement, than if the public servants were chosen, on account of their serviceable qualities, from the whole body of the nation. In the second place, there is evident danger of disorder among the people themselves . . . We have always professed to be on the whole friendly to . . . reform; and if the people be generally desirous of it, we think the time is come when it ought no longer to be withheld . . . The *only* check to the encroachments of power and the oppressions of . . . tyranny, is the spirit, the intelligence, the prepared *resistance*, of the people.

2.4.3 From 'A Letter to the Honourable Charles James Fox', from Edmund Burke. Printed in the Works *(1852), Vol. V, pp. 509–10.*
The letter was written 8 October 1777.

You are sensible, that I do not differ from you in many things . . . I have ever wished a settled plan of our own, founded in the very essence of the American business . . . I know that [Lord Rockingham] and those who are much prevalent with him, though they are not thought so much devoted to popularity as others, do very much look to the people; and more than I think is wise in them, who do so little to guide and direct public opinion . . . As to that popular humour, which is the medium we float in, if I can discern anything at all of its present state, it is far worse than I have ever known . . . The greatest number have a sort of heavy, lumpish, acquiescence in government, without much respect or esteem for those who compose it . . .

2.4.4. From a letter to the Marquis of Rockingham from Edmund Burke, 5 December 1769. Printed in The Correspondence of Edmund Burke *(edited Lucy Sutherland, 1958), Vol. II, p. 116.*

I hope the Yorkshire Petition is in forwardness, and will now be presented. Calcraft gave me the enclosed names wishing that I would get
some friends to forward their petition. That man's appearing in a cause,
though unlucky to it, does not discredit it entirely. The only effect it has,
is that, which I have long seen with infinite grief from the coldness and
dilatoriness of many of our friends in their manner of acting; bold men
take the lead, to which others are entitled; and they soon come to a
power, not natural to them, by the remissness of those who neither know
how to be effectual friends or dangerous enemies, or active champions in
a good cause. They complain of the unnatural growth of such people;
and they are the cause of it. When the Gentlemen of the County of Kent
abandoned the rights of their dependants and adherents the Freeholders
of the County, it was but natural that they should abandon them, and
look for their protectors wherever they could find them.

2.4.5 From 'A view of the present State of Public Affairs', The
Political Register (*No. XII, 1768*), *pp. 218 and 243*.

Is it . . . of no consequence, how far corruption and venality prevail?
how great the number and undue influence of the grandees? how much
the national debt may be increased? what taxes are laid on our exports?
. . . the question is not what degree of freedom *individuals* do still
possess: but whether the *state* is not in a dangerous condition; whether
the *constitution* is not unhinged; whether *government* is not become a
mere *cabal*; whether we are not on the verge of losing our liberties in
aristocracy . . . But, thank Heaven! It is not too late to propose remedies
for the disorders of our country . . . The people of property are . . . the
fountain of authority; and in all countries, and under all forms of government, there ought, in certain cases, to lie an appeal from governors, who
may be corrupted, to the people, who cannot be bribed against their
general interest. . . .

The property of the commons of Britain consists of the landed, the
monied, and the commercial interests . . . The monied interest is not
represented at all . . . The case is the same with the commercial interests
. . . While the election of representatives is thus confined to so small a
part of the people, can it be said that the house of commons *represents* the
property of the commons of Britain? May not the interest of a few
persons deputed by a twentieth part of the people, by a fiftieth part of
the property, be, by an artful and corrupt court, made to appear to them
quite *different* from part of the *nation* . . .

Were every substantial housekeeper, in every county, a voter, and all
votes of equal weight, bribery must proceed with a very slow pace.

2.4.6 From Thomas Paine, The Rights of Man (*1791*).
Everyman edition (1906), pp. 51, 53, 54, 133–4 and 135.

The Constitution of France says, *That every man who pays a tax of sixty sous per annum* (two and sixpence English) *is an elector*. What article [i.e. of the English constitution – Ed.] will Mr Burke place against this? Can anything be more limited, and at the same time more capricious, than the qualifications of electors are in England? Limited – because one man in a hundred (I speak much within compass) is admitted to the vote. Capricious – because the lowest character that can be supposed to exist, and who has not so much as the visible means of an honest livelihood, is an elector in some places. . . .

The French Constitution says, *That the number of representatives for any place shall be in a ratio to the number of taxable inhabitants or electors*. What article will Mr Burke place against this? The county of Yorkshire, which contains nearly a million souls, sends two county members; and so does the county of Rutland, which contains not one hundredth of that number. The town of Old Sarum, which contains not three houses, sends two members . . .

Much is to be learned from the French Constitution. Conquest and tyranny transplanted themselves with William the Conquerer from Normandy into England, and the country is yet disfigured with the marks. May, then, the example of all France contribute to regenerate the freedom which one province of it destroyed . . .

Many things in the English government appear to me the reverse of what they ought to be and what they are said to be . . . in the manner in which an English Parliament is constructed it is like a man being both mortgager and mortgagee, and in the case of misapplication of trust it is like the criminal sitting in judgement upon himself. If those who vote the supplies are the same persons who receive the supplies when voted and are to account for the expenditure of those supplies to those who voted them, it is *themselves accountable to themselves*; and the Comedy of Errors concludes with the Pantomime of Hush . . . They order these things better in France. . . .

When men are spoken of as Kings and subjects, or when Government is mentioned under the distinct and combined heads of Monarchy, Aristocracy and Democracy, what is it that *reasoning* man is to understand by the terms? . . . as there is but one species of man, there can be but one element of human power, and that element is man himself . . .

From the Revolutions of America and France . . . it is evident that the opinion of the world is changed with respect to systems of Government,

69

and that Revolutions are not within the compass of political calculations ... All the old Governments have received a shock from those [Revolutions] that already appear, and which were once more improbable, and are a greater subject of wonder, than a general Revolution in Europe would be now. When we survey the wretched condition of Man, under the Monarchical and hereditary systems of Government, dragged from his home by one power, or driven by another, and impoverished by taxes more than enemies, it becomes evident that those systems are bad, and that a general Revolution in the principle and construction of Government is necessary.

What is a Government more than the management of the affairs of a Nation? It is not, and from its nature cannot be, the property of any particular man or family, but of the whole community, at whose expense it is supported; though by force and contrivance it has been usurped into an inheritance, the usurpation cannot alter the right of things. Sovereignty, as a matter of right, appertains to the nation only.

2.4.7 From the Diary of Lord Ellenborough, 30 August 1830. Printed in Lord Ellenborough, A Political Diary *(edited Lord Colchester, 1881), Vol. II, p. 348.*

Wrote a long letter to Hardinge on the present position of the Government and our policy. I gave my opinion that any accession of men which destroyed the unity of the [Duke of Wellington's] Government would do harm. That we must meet our difficulties by measures ... That the question of Reform could not be made an open question. It was best for the country that parties should be decidedly separated. It might then choose which it preferred, and men would be obliged to take a side. We had better be out with character than in with a detachment of the enemy ...

2.5 PARTY IN PARLIAMENT

2.5.1 From a 'Circular' in the Braybrooke MSS (Essex County Record Office). Printed in Sir Lewis Namier's Monarchy and the Party System *(Oxford, 1953), p. 23.*
The circular illustrates, through its analysis of the state of the House of Commons in 1788, the importance of 'connexion', and the possibility of accounting for allegiances without the use of party labels.

1. Party of the Crown . . . . . . 186[1]
This party includes all those who would probably support his Majesty's Government under any Minister, not peculiarly unpopular.

2. The Party attached to Mr Pitt 52
Of this party were there a new Parliament, and Mr P. no longer Minister, not above twenty would be returned.

3. Detached Parties supporting the present Administration, viz:
    1. Mr Dundas 10
    2. Marquis of Lansdowne 9
    3. Earl of Lonsdale 9
    4. East Indians 15

4. The independent or unconnected Members of the House . . . . [108][2]
Of this body of men about forty have united together, in conjunction with some members of the House of Peers in order to form a third party for the purpose of preventing the Crown from being too much in the power of either of the two other parties who are contending for the government of the country, and who (were it really necessary) might with the assistance of the Crown, undertake to make up an administration to the exclusion both of Mr Pitt and Mr Fox, and of their adherents.

5. The Opposition to the present Administration:
    1. The Party attached to Mr Fox 138
    2. Remnants of Lord North's Party . . . 17
6. Absentees and Neutrals 14

2.5.2 From a letter to Viscount Castlereagh from Charles Arbuthnot, 14 March 1819. Printed in The Correspondence of Charles Arbuthnot (*edited A. Aspinall, 1941*), *pp. 15–16.*

For the first two days of the week ... we were sitting till very late at night with very nearly empty benches on our side of the House, and with benches crammed up to the very corners on the Opposition side ... we were told that, seeing we could not get attendance, they had signed a paper binding themselves never upon any occasion to quit the House without Tierney's leave. I know this to be a fact ... the evil of non-attendance was thought so serious that Long and Huskisson went with me to Fife House, and joined with me in declaring that the Government

---

[1] The figure as here is 185, but on the next page, in the summary, it appears as 186 which makes up the correct total of 558.

[2] The number is not given here, but lower down in a summary list of the parties.

would be broken down in a fortnight's time unless those in office would, throughout the evening, *without pairing off*, devote themselves to the House.

2.5.3 From a letter to Lord Herbert from Lady Elizabeth Pembroke, in February 1779. Printed in Henry, Elizabeth, and George (*edited Lord Herbert, 1939*).
The letter reveals the connexion between the unity of the opposition and the decline in royal power.

I fancy there is no doubt of Lord S[andwich] being moved from his place, and I believe they have offered Lord Howe to come in his room, but Party here is such a thing, that they will not suffer some to come in unless the whole Party come in at once, and all the other set go out . . . I do think it is a hard case upon our Kings, that though they should wish to take a proper man into a proper place, he [*sic* – Ed.] cannot generally do it without having out all his Ministers good as well as bad . . .

2.5.4 From a letter to F. Jeffrey from Francis Horner, on the death of Fox in 1806. Printed in The Memoirs and Correspondence of Francis Horner (*1843*), *Vol. I, pp. 374–5.*

I look upon what has been called Mr Fox's party, the remains of the old Whig faith, as extinguished entirely with him; his name alone kept the fragments together, after the party had long ago been broken to pieces. At the same time, I cannot resist the conviction, that, in spite of appearances, there is in the middling order of people in this country a broad foundation for a popular party, constituted by the opinions, interests, and habits of those numerous families who are characterized by moderate but rising incomes, a careful education of their youth, and a strict observance of the great common virtues . . . I take my hopes of there still being a chance of defending successfully the liberties of England . . .

2.5.5 From the Declaration of, and Form of Association recommended by the Whig Club (*1796*).
The statutes referred to are the Sedition Acts arising from the unrest during the French Wars.

The Whig Club, invariably adhering to the principles of the British Constitution as established at the Revolution, cannot be unconcerned spectators of the destruction of the most important securities of Public Liberty which were provided at that glorious era. The Constitution can, in our judgement, now only be restored by the exercise of that just authority which the National Opinion must ever possess over the proceedings of the legislature. We, therefore, deem it our duty, by every means which yet are legal, to appeal to the judgement of the People, and to procure a declaration of their opinion. With this view, we have invited our fellow-subjects to associate for obtaining the Repeal of the two Statutes passed in the present session of Parliament . . . The measure which we propose is unquestionably legal and constitutional; and it appears to us to be not only justified, but called for, by the exigency of the times. *When bad men conspire good men must associate.*

2.5.6 From the Parliamentary History (*Vol. XXVII, 19 March 1788*), *c. 237.*
Lord Abingdon, in the course of a speech criticizing the East India Company for changing from support to opposition over the East India Declaratory Bill, said:

And how shall we account for this? has the devil got into the herd of swine? . . . Or is it that some great political general, putting himself at the head of a scouting party of his own, is so manœuvring between the two grand armies of Whigs and Tories, as to be ready to join either whenever the strongest of the two shall afford him the opportunity of doing so?

2.5.7 From a letter to Sir Robert Peel from Lord Liverpool (then Prime Minister), 9 October 1812. Printed in C. S. Parker, Sir Robert Peel (*1899*), *Vol. I, pp. 41–2.*

I have not the least objection to Sir Charles Saxton being elected for Cashel. You may assure him from me that I only expect from my friends a generally favourable disposition, and that I shall never attempt to interfere with his right to vote as he may think consistent with his duty upon any particular question.

3   1832–1867

Introduction

THE CONSTITUTION

The constitutional tendencies which had been apparent in the last three-quarters of the reign of George III continued after the 1832 Reform Act. The Monarch was rapidly becoming that 'dignified' part of the constitution described by Bagehot (in spite of Victoria's own view of her position and the successful defence of her prerogatives on a few occasions) [3.1.1]. The formation of the Aberdeen Coalition in 1852, for instance, can be described virtually without reference to the Queen,[1] and this at a time when party cohesion in the Commons was at its lowest; after 1832 the fate of Ministers depended on the Commons [3.1.2–5].

The other constitutional tendency, the growth of a public opinion outside the Commons, had been enshrined in the 1832 Reform Act itself. Here, however, the position was by no means as clear as in the case of the Monarch. The addition to the electorate involved in the Act was numerically small – the total electorate was increased from approximately 435,000 (representing less than 5 per cent of the adult population) to approximately 650,000 – and in any case what the Whigs had wished to add was not numbers as such, but a newer kind of property. Eighteenth-century practices such as localism and electoral patronage persisted in a society in which the territorial forces of conservatism were both strong and a major part of

[1] C. H. Stuart, 'The Formation of the Coalition Cabinet of 1852', *Transactions of the Royal Historical Society*, 1954, 5, 68.

the House of Commons. 'The influence of the middle classes' was exercised not mainly through membership of the Commons but through *ad hoc* and only occasionally successful movements such as the Anti-Corn Law League. The idea of 'the electorate' was not yet established as a basic element in the constitution and arguments about the respectability of the mandate continued throughout the period [3.1.5–8]. The 'electorate' was a relatively small number of voters who still thought of politics in local terms, and the Commons was affected by outside opinion not so much through national elections recognized as the major means of choosing a government but through the activities of groups such as the League and the Chartists. Even such discontent as was manifested in these pressures was much reduced by the economic prosperity of the 1850s and early 60s.[2]

None the less the Reform Act, and the ideas which surrounded it, had influenced the context within which the House of Commons worked. The electorate was more difficult to manage by traditional practices, and the pull exerted on urban members by electors sceptical of 'virtual representation' and Whig theories of the independence of Parliament was both too great to ignore and was centripetal in its effect on the cohesion of parties in the Commons. A national electorate may not have existed in the modern sense, but electors were clearly becoming a more independent and influential force.

All this clearly made things more difficult for government; the patronage and esteem of the Crown was no longer something to which a Cabinet could turn in its hour of need, and that stable support in the Commons which patronage had facilitated was made difficult to create by other means because of the extent to which the Commons was increasingly looking over its shoulder to the electors and opinion without.[3] The Radical advocacy of an M.P.'s complete dependence upon the opinions of his electors was resisted by the other parties precisely because, given the degree of localism in elections, such dependence would immeasurably increase the difficulties of party cohesion and thus of government in the House of Commons.[4]

[2] A. Briggs, *The Age of Improvement* (1960), p. 305, et seq.
[3] N. Gash, *Politics in the Age of Peel* (1953), p. xxi.
[4] N. Gash, *Reaction and Reconstruction in English Politics, 1832–1852* (Oxford, 1964), p. 30, et seq.

In these circumstances, Ministers had two main lines of defence. First, the notion of collective responsibility, by which a Ministry could hope, by standing together, to prolong its existence by forcing the House to contemplate replacing it completely in the event of its defeat;[5] and the corresponding attempt to make the Ministry's actions appear as an indissoluble whole (through 'votes of confidence') and thus prevent back-benchers from defeating particular measures while retaining a helpless government in office.[6] Secondly, Ministers or opposition leaders could attempt to establish a stable Parliamentary support on the basis of party cohesion: the relevance of this second solution to the development of party in the period is obvious.

It is important to emphasize, however, that despite the difficulties of governing which arose from the decline of the Monarch and the growth of 'public opinion' – difficulties which have caused many to look back on the period between the first two Reform Acts as 'the golden age of the private member' – the traditional distinction between an executive which took the initiative and a Parliament which controlled rather than governed was never entirely lost. The weaknesses of the Cabinet never led to the transfer of government to the House of Commons. The Commons could, at best, obstruct rather than take the initiative,[7] and the extent to which the Cabinet in this period increased its share of the public business of the House is evidence of the unwillingness of back-benchers to create a *gouvernement d'assemblée* [3.1.9].

PARTY RHETORIC

That contemporaries often thought it reasonable to explain differences between the parties in terms of their avowed objects is clear [3.2.1]; much of the basis for these differences was laid during the debates on the Reform Bill in 1832.[8] But to the historian, the clarity of the party publicist is apt to appear misleading. In the first place, some of the more consistent pursuits of politicians between the first two Reform Acts were neither concerned with legislative policy nor a means of distinguishing between party labels. The Conservatism

[5] J. P. Mackintosh, *The British Cabinet* (1962), p. 103.
[6] Ibid., p. 85. [7] Ibid., p. 92.
[8] Gash, *Reaction*, p. 123.

of Peel, for example, was constitutional rather than legislative in the sense that it aimed to preserve government (the maintenance of law and order) in the novel constitutional framework bequeathed by the Reform Act and by broadening the electoral base of the Conservative Party, thus to establish the Reform Act itself as the maximum point of concession to the popular element [3.2.6]. To Peel, legislative issues such as the repeal of the Corn Laws were to be viewed not in terms of their intrinsic merits, but from the standpoint of their effectiveness in cementing the adherence of newly-enfranchised opinions and as obstacles to further change and to the lawlessness manifested in such movements as Chartism.[9] Government, not particular issues, was the concern, and the adherence of urban interests to the Conservative cause was to be the means of its preservation. Despite his opposition to Peel over the Corn Laws Disraeli was to sail a very similar course after the Conservative split in 1846 had, for the time being, put an end to the attempt.

Nor was Conservatism a label describing men united behind a similar creed. Much has been made of 'Tory Reform' in this period, and it is true that the rhetoric of reform was not the monopoly of Liberalism [3.2.7–8] But humanitarian reform was not the banner of all Tories: Ashley's Factory Bills were frequently defeated or crippled by Tory industrialists in the Lords[10] and 'Tory Reform' did not necessarily imply any sympathy for state action. The Tories were frequently motivated by a desire to protect local interests against centralization[11] and the humanitarian Toryism of Coleridge, Carlyle and Disraeli's 'Young England' [3.2.9–11] was characterized by its emphasis on the need for social amelioration *without* the aid of the state. Oastler and Sadler, despite their 'Tory-Radical' labels, voted against the 1833 Factory Act because it contained provisions for inspection.[12] For Peel and 'Young England' to live under the same party label shows the lack of any central bond of 'principle', unless it was the suspicion of state activity in the regulation of private conduct. The eighteenth-century view of politics as a matter of government and administration rather than legislation was common to nearly all Parliamentary politicians until after 1867.

[9] Ibid., pp. 130–9,
[10] Paul Smith, 'Tory Paternalism and Social Reform in Early Victorian England', *American Historical Review* (January 1958), p. 326.
[11] Ibid., p. 335.   [12] Ibid., p. 326.

Nor was the situation fundamentally different in the other party. What was coming to be known as the Liberal Party [3.2.14] was a parliamentary coalition of Whigs, Liberals and Radicals. The Whigs were a group defined in terms of aristocratic connexion and historical performance, more suspicious than the middle-class Liberals of the consequences of democracy but united with them in the belief that the Radicals had not suspicion enough [3.2.3–4].

With the exception of some of the Radicals, the Liberal Party was by the 1850s as emphatic on the need for 'good government' as ever Peel had been, and was conscious of a difference between itself and the Derby-Disraeli Tories not in terms of issues or legislative proposals but on precise grounds of administration: by then, the Tories were thought to be too fond of patronage and 'corruption' in a system in which fiscal prudence and incorruptibility were the proper qualifications of Ministers. Sound administration, not class or the rhetoric of popular Liberalism, was what kept Gladstone, Lowe, Palmerston and Russell together.[13]

Legislative programmes as a vehicle of social reform were a secondary concern to both Conservatives and Liberals. Even the Liberals, despite their traditional associations with 'progressive' action, were stirred by the new electoral necessities which followed 1867, rather than by conviction, to the concern for working-class conditions represented by legislation on education, drink, health, housing and the poor law.[14] The only coherent set of principles which mid-Victorian Liberalism possessed – those of the Manchester school – were neither common to the party as a whole nor favourable to State intervention [3.2.15]. In the diluted form of Gladstonian Liberalism [3.2.16] they indicated not state action or legislative programmes but almost the reverse – that peace, economy and free trade would indirectly but inevitably lead to the amelioration of social conditions.[15]

The lack of emphasis on legislative programmes even at the level of public rhetoric is, however, best evidenced by the language of Radicalism – a creed supposedly well to the 'left' of both Conservatism and Liberalism. Radicalism, although by no means a united force, was anti-aristocratic and in favour of free trade. Neither of these prejudices formed a basis for a legislative programme, nor was such a programme necessarily desired: aristocratic

[13] J. Vincent, *The Formation of the Liberal Party, 1850–1858* (1966), pp. 12–13.
[14] Ibid., p. 243.   [15] Ibid., p. 244.

government such as this period witnessed was hardly subject to Radical demands for its extension, and a modern historian has pointed to the links between Bright and the 'constitutionalist' opposition to government of the later eighteenth century[16] [3.2.18]. To most middle-class Radicals after the 1840s, 'the people' (usually middle-class 'people' [3.2.19]) were invoked not that they might indicate the ways in which legislation could improve their conditions, but as a counterweight to the power of an aristocratic system of government [3.2.20]. Only the working-class Chartist movement had elements of 'collectivism' within it, and even here they were accompanied by constitutional demands which would have been familiar to the gentry of the 1780s [3.2.21]; the Chartists were, in any case, the most unsuccessful of extra-parliamentary movements. On the whole, the recent description of Radicalism as 'a miscellany of vaguely humanitarian enthusiasms, chiefly for the relief of the individual from metaphysical rather than material distress'[17] is appropriate enough.

In essence, the real division in this period was not that indicated by party labels, but that between the established political forces of the aristocracy and the gentry and the newer elements of the working classes, middle classes and dissent [3.2.22], the latter groups working for the most part outside the formal arenas of Parliamentary politics;[18] the distance between the mood of this 'popular radicalism' and the Liberal front-bench of the 1850s was significantly great. Even 'popular radicalism', in opposition to an aristocratic system of government, was not mainly concerned with particular legislative programmes; in so far as it provided the basis of the Liberal Party's support in the country until the 1880s, it was characterized by 'the growing ability of whole new classes to stand on their own feet and lead independent lives' and 'the novelty of participation in politics, rather than attachment to a programme or doctrine'.[19]

In sum, the party rhetoric of the period does not reveal a great attachment to social reform through legislation on the part of any of the parliamentary combinations. Party rhetoric was manufactured in a situation in which the parliamentary groups had a common

[16] A. Briggs, *Victorian People* (1954).
[17] Vincent, p. 301.
[18] Kitson Clark, *The Making of Victorian England* (1962), *passim*.
[19] Vincent, pp. xiv, 258.

mistrust both of state intervention and (with the exception of some of the Radicals) of democracy.[20] The difficulty was to work out the implications of 1832, and here the urban appeals of Peelite Conservatism in the interests of sound administration were not a world apart from Gladstonian liberalism, nor was Disraeli's emphasis on the landed element in society [3.2.12] either very different from some brands of Whiggism or pursued with indifference to the importance of newer forms of property. In the end, the attachment of 'popular radical' feeling outside Parliament to the Liberal party of the late 1850s was due partly to a failure of the Conservatives to strike the necessary rhetorical balance between appeals to the old and to the new, partly to the past successes of the Whigs in annexing reform, progress and dissent [3.2.5, 3.2.13, 3.2.17] to their own banner, and to the fact that the Parliamentary Liberal Party was 'adopted' by the new opinions outside Parliament almost in spite of itself. It is not differences over issues, or principles, which impress the historian as characteristic of party in this period, since such differences as existed were the property of individuals or groups rather than the basis of party as a whole. Far more impressive is the desire of two broad parties, the majority of whose members had common assumptions and common roots in the old political order, to achieve the support both of the old entrenched interests, and the newer ones admitted in 1832, without sacrificing too much of their independence as politicians and governors.[21]

PARTY IN PARLIAMENT

Party cohesion in the parliaments of this period was conditioned by the constitutional context within which politics was pursued. The increased importance attached to party cohesion by Ministers [3.3.1] is shown by how far appeals to party 'discipline', for instance, were replacing the use of the House of Lords to resist Private Members' Bills which the government opposed; for throughout the period, the member without a party label was relatively rare[22] [3.3.4]. On the other hand, the frequency of

[20] M. Cowling, *1867 : Disraeli, Gladstone, and Revolution* (Cambridge, 1967), p. 2, et seq.
[21] Ibid., *passim*.
[22] Gash, *Reaction*, p. 59 (n).

divisions in which there was an extremely low correlation between voting and party labels is evidence of the degree of resistance to these appeals, and the extent to which that willingness to be led which was a feature of back-benchers under Liverpool[23] was neither cumulative nor reliable.[24]

The tendencies promoting party cohesion were various, and the years 1834 to 1845, in particular, saw a House of Commons in which party voting was common.[25] A recent examination of the Commons in the 1840s has shown the extent to which voting was correlated with party labels (revealing at the same time, however, a great number of issues which were not approached in a party spirit).[26] This was in large measure due to Peel's attitude to party, which consisted in the belief that any government after 1832 ought to be supported until it could not merely be replaced, but replaced by a party with sufficiently stable support to form an effective government. Party was, to Peel, an instrument of strong government, providing Ministers with coherent and lasting support[27] and thus providing for both effective executive action and that basis in opinion outside the Commons without which no Ministry was secure.[28]

The importance attached to electoral, as well as to parliamentary, activity is shown in the work of Bonham as Peel's political agent after 1832; the use of a central party agent as a means of putting potential candidates in touch with vacant seats increased parliamentary party cohesion to the extent that central recommendations enhanced the candidates' chances of adoption.[29]

Contemporary concern with the maintenance of stable and effective government arose from the extent to which the decline of royal patronage and the growth of a more independent 'public opinion' had made management of the Commons increasingly

[23] See above, pp. 42–45.

[24] Fraser, *The Conduct of Public Business*, p. 45.

[25] D. E. D. Beales, 'Parliamentary Parties and the "independent member", 1810–1860', in *Ideas and Institutions of Victorian Britain* (edited R. R. Robson, 1967), p. 12.

[26] W. O. Aydelotte, 'Voting Patterns in the British House of Commons in the 1840s', *Comparative Studies in Society and History*, 1962–1963, **5**, 151.

[27] N. Gash, 'Peel and the Party System', *Transactions of the Royal Historical Society*, 1947, **5**, 58.

[28] Gash, *Politics*, Ch. II.

[29] Ibid., p. 416.

difficult. The need for such stability was confirmed by the growth in the volume of Parliamentary business [3.3.5–7]. The general recognition of the need for ministerial leadership in this situation was manifest in procedural reforms designed to distinguish between government and private member's business, and in the tone of select Committees on Procedure.

The Committee of 1861 reported that:

'it must be remembered how large a proportion of the public business transacted is now devolved on the ministers of the Crown . . . and while they remain responsible for good government and for the safety of the state, it would seem reasonable that a preference should be yielded to them, not only in the introduction of their bills, but in the opportunities for pressing them on the consideration of the House.'[30]

Leaders on both sides of the House were united in the recognition not only of the need to preserve good government, but also of the importance of restraining those of their followers whose independence and zeal would make such government impossible.[31] This emphasis on the need for coherent executive action was an identifiable part of Conservative rhetoric between the Reform Acts [3.3.6–7]. It is seen in the fact that Peel held office by 1841 'as the leader of a party: the brute votes in the lobby which had put him into power'[32]; and it appears in the later attempts of Derby and Disraeli in the 1850s to rebuild into an instrument of government[33] the party shattered in 1846. But the Liberals also saw the need for cohesion; after 1830 they had had to accustom themselves to the novelty of being in office,[34] and never lost their sense of being a separate party.[35] By the 1850s the Liberals had a near-monopoly of administrative competence,[36] and while relatively uninterested in party popularity, their front-bench was keenly aware of the connexion between sound administration and stable parliamentary

[30] Quoted in J. Redlich, *The Procedure of the House of Commons* (1908), Vol. I, p. 115.
[31] Gash, *Reaction*, p. 122.
[32] Ibid., p. 147.
[33] W. D. Jones, *Lord Derby and Victorian Conservatism* (Oxford, 1956), p. 230.
[34] Gash, *Reaction*, p. 125.
[35] J. B. Conacher, 'Party Politics in the Age of Palmerston' in P. Appleman *et al.* (editors), *1859 : Entering an Age of Crisis* (Indiana, 1959), p. 165.
[36] Vincent, p. 19.

support. Both they and subsequent historians could regard the 1859 compact between Russell and Palmerston as a 'turning-point' in party history[37] – not so much because it represented a novel desire for Liberal unity, but rather a long-sought success in achieving it.

On the other hand, that such 'turning-points' might be viewed in this way shows the difficulty involved in translating the desire for governmental stability into concrete terms of unity in the lobbies. The decline of Crown patronage and the pulls of electoral localism and independence were factors inimical to party cohesion. Granted that the arguments of the more important leaders concerned the means of achieving party unity rather than the desirability of the end itself,[38] the very language of these arguments assumed the existence of either unreliable party men, or men not to be seen at all in a party light[39] [3.3.8–9]. All the arguments about whether an opposition could best keep its unity by opposing at all costs or by acting more 'responsibly' made sense only on the assumption that the opposition *could* defeat the government in the house – an implausible assumption had the Commons been entirely composed of two sets of cohesive partisans. Party leaders (whose own position was far from formalized) [3.3.10] had to rely upon the presence of a traditional sense of difference between the parties and upon a general reluctance to bring government to a standstill; they had few real sanctions [3.3.11–13]. In age in which neither national party labels nor an electorate voting almost solely with reference to those labels had emerged, 'control' over the actions of back-benchers was slight. Nor was the weapon of dissolution very effective; it has never been very clear why dissolution should be more of a threat to back-benchers than to Ministers, but in any case the circumstances of this period were such as to make it little of a threat: the royal consent to dissolutions was by no means automatic, and the principle that it involved – appealing to the electors 'over the heads' of the Commons – was by no means widely accepted. Only once was it used explicitly as a threat (by Derby in 1858).[40] As Peel himself recognized, it was not the Conservative

---

[37] R. Blake, *Disraeli* (1966), p. 406.

[38] Ibid., p. 354.

[39] For the slow increase in party voting, see A. L. Lowell, 'The Influence of Party upon Legislation in England and America', *Annual Report of the American Historical Association* (1901).

[40] Mackintosh, pp. 89–90.

split in 1846 which was remarkable, but his success in having held the party together for so long [3.3.15].

Party unity between the Reform Acts was a series of short-lived attempts to govern in changed circumstances by two parties which were coalitions in a very real sense. Peel's majority, built up by 1841, was shattered in 1846, and it was only painfully rebuilt by Derby and Disraeli in the 1850s[41] [3.3.15]. The 'Liberal' groups which united in the 1835 Lichfield House compact to defeat Peel were out of office by 1841, and were seldom cohesive again until the 1850s. Party unity was a front-bench aim, achieved only intermittently and only to the extent that party rhetoric and personality (such as the mutual dislike of Disraeli and Gladstone) kept alive a sense of separateness, and to the extent that the desire for stability was shared by back-benchers to whom the leaders could address few effective threats. Even on the part of the leaders, the desire for sound administration was not always accompanied by support for those techniques of party unity which might make it possible. Gladstone's reaction to the Conservative meetings called by Derby and Disraeli in 1867 to cement party unity shows the strength of older views about the privileges and status of the House of Commons [3.3.17–19].

The emphasis on party unity, and the occasional successes in achieving it, were matters of tactics and of a general recognition of the importance of stable government; the unity of 'class interests', despite the attention now lavished upon this explanation, is of limited importance. The sophisticated statistical techniques which have recently been brought to bear upon the relationship between voting in the Commons, class and party label have shown that the closeness of their correlation varied from time to time[42] and from one issue to another.[43] A clear account of the connexion between 'economic interest', party label and voting is made difficult by the extent to which Members might each possess a number of *different* interests.[44] Moreover, since 'objective' economic status cannot *determine* political opinion, and since a Parliament whose members were incapable of considerations other than personal interest could never exercise any *constitutional* function or authority, it is not

[41] Gash, *Reaction*, pp. 184–6
[42] Aydelotte, *passim.*
[43] Ibid., p. 157.
[44] See the Appendix by Aydelotte to Clark, *Making*, op. cit.

surprising that the analysis of the class composition of Parliament is of limited explanatory value. As a matter of fact, the correlation between class and party label is weak. The Liberal label covered both 'aristocratic' Whigs and 'middle-class' elements, and even the Whigs possessed an internal variety of opinion.[45] The criterion of class status yields interesting correlations not so much about parties in the House but rather about the House as a whole and the country outside it. Landed interests dominated both parties, and recent sociological writings confirm that 'classes were represented in almost the same proportion in each of the two Parliamentary groupings'.[46] On the other hand, even the fact of a class correlation between the composition of Parliament and those interests outside it requires interpretation before much can be made of it. It cannot, for example, be the sole evidence for any claim that Parliament was 'unrepresentative'; such a claim would also have to consider what Parliament *did* (as opposed to how Parliament was composed) and what the notion of representation was *seen* to involve. These limitations on class analysis are important: this period in particular is rich with examples of the fact that what is important is not the 'objective' interests of politicians, but what they *see* as their interests [3.3.16]. It is difficult to explain the 1832 Reform Act as a conflict between 'objective' economic interests when only two members of Grey's Cabinet were not substantial landowners;[47] nor, if a direct relationship between economic position and political opinion is assumed is it easy to explain how the repeal of the corn laws in 1846 managed to be accepted by the House of Commons. Indeed, the Repeal of the Corn Laws is the paradigm example of the limitations of 'class' explanations of politics between the Reform Acts. An overwhelmingly landed House of Commons, many of whose members *also* possessed commercial and industrial interests,[48] passed an Act in response to pressure from the overwhelmingly middle-class Anti-Corn Law League in a situation in which strong support for the bill came from many members whose interests were least connected with commerce and industry,[49] and in which those votes

[45] Vincent, pp. 20–2.
[46] W. Guttsman, *The British Political Elite* (1963), p. 88.
[47] Guttsman, p. 36.
[48] Kitson Clark, 'The Repeal of the Corn Laws and the Politics of the 1840s', *Economic History Review*, 1951, **2**, *passim*.
[49] Earl Fitzwilliam, for example; see D. Spring, 'Earl Fitzwilliam and the Corn Laws', *American Historical Review* (January 1954), p. 304 and especially p. 287.

85

which can be clearly correlated with economic interest cut across party lines. The explanation lies not in any 'class interest' but in a view of the political situation. The Repeal of the Corn Laws is properly explained as an Act in which the political leaders *disregarded* the claims of class in pursuit of the reconciliation of opinion outside the House in the interests of political and constitutional stability. The 'class' approach to politics in this period is misleading primarily because it diverts attention from the major content of party activity in this period: a set of *opinions* about the role of government and the advantages of party unity in the aftermath of 1832.

ATTITUDES TO PARTY

During this period, thinking about politics in terms of parties was firmly established. Not all politicians accepted party organization as desirable [3.4.1], few, if any, allowed it to obliterate the idea of the independence of Members of Parliament [3.4.2], and none held the view that the constitution could be described solely in its terms. None the less, party as a context of political action was, in various ways, taken for granted. To Peel, as has been shown, it was potentially an instrument of strong government and the preservation of the constitution; to some it was a vehicle of principle, to others an ominous Trojan horse for democracy. By the 1860s, party was an accepted institution of the political world in the sense that in spite of its real incoherence and its position as the object of some hostile attacks, to act for party advantage was a motive with meaning[50] [3.4.3]. The presence of positive defenders of political parties is significant. The occasional willingness of parliamentarians to combine was explained by Brougham on the grounds that:

'it may be expedient, and even necessary, in certain emergencies of public affairs, for men who apprehend the same peril from a policy pursued by the government of their country, to form a combination in order to resist the measures adopted or threatened, and to waive minor differences of opinion in order to act in concert and with effect, preferring, as Mr Fox says, the giving up

[50] Cowling, p. 4 and *passim*.

of something to a friend rather than surrender everything to an enemy.'[51]

The reference to Fox is illuminating since it reveals the extent to which the politicians of the period were eager to assimilate the past to the present, and the extent to which the facts of party history in the recent past had made it difficult to think of party confusion as either normal or desirable. The former factor was a particular Whig preoccupation; for they after 1832 both spoke the Foxite language and possessed the names of Foxite history, Grey, Lansdowne, Holland, Russell et al.[52] The latter factor, however, has greater significance for the history of party. The state of party cohesion under Lord Liverpool had left a memory to which those who had experienced it (and even some of those who had not) were constantly referring [3.4.4–7]. Lord Morpeth's view in 1834 that in the 1820s the Commons was 'divided into two principal parties, in whose hands the conducting of the business was vested',[53] and the unfavourable comparison which he drew with the existing confusion of party, were widely shared. When to such a memory of the recent past are added the traditional habit of representing all history since the Civil War in terms of two party labels [3.4.8–9], and the existing interest in strong government [3.4.10–11], the secure place of party in political rhetoric between the Reform Acts is easily understood. It is also interesting to note that the conception of party government as facilitating the direct *electoral* choice of Ministries was beginning to emerge in these years [3.4.12]. It might be possible to represent the facts of party in the first half of the nineteenth century as not dissimilar from those in the 1760s[54] (in spite of the situation under Liverpool and, later, under Peel), but there is a clear difference in terms of the context of *opinion*. By 1867, party was widely accepted as an established framework of action, and party confusion and incoherence, where it existed, widely deplored [3.4.13–14].

[51] Henry, Baron Brougham, *Political Philosophy* (1846), Vol. II, p. 45.
[52] Gash, *Reaction*, p. 160.
[53] Quoted in Fraser, pp. 44–5.
[54] Sir L. Namier, *Crossroads of Power* (1962), p. 231.

PARTY IN THE COUNTRY

The activities of parties in the country were pursued in the context of the general tendencies of the constitution. The effect of the 1832 Reform Act had not been to replace one political class by another, but to place limitations upon what a Parliament largely composed of and thinking about politics in a manner derived from the traditional order might do, and thus to make it more sensitive to opinions without.[55] It was in the country, rather than in Parliament, that the new order was most in evidence, and it was to the country that those political leaders who, like Peel, supported the repeal of the Corn Laws, were, in part, addressing themselves.[56] This body of opinion outside Parliament was the subject of the numerous arguments about 'the mandate', and some of its more organized manifestations (such as the Anti-Corn Law League and, to a lesser extent, the Chartists) had obvious implications for the value of party organization in the country.

The politicians, in their desire to avoid dictation by the electors, were aware of these consequences of the Reform Act, and this awareness was expressed both in their public rhetoric and their willingness to experiment with relatively new forms of political organization [3.5.1–2]. Peel's conception of politics as a matter of broadening the base of Conservatism to include the towns was aided by the growth or revival of Conservative and Constitutional local associations after 1834 [3.5.3], and bore fruit in the election of 1841, after which Peel was able to take office with a majority made possible by urban support. Local political organization and electoral appeals such as the Tamworth Manifesto [3.5.4] all played their part in a Peelite strategy designed to preserve good government and to establish the constitution in a new state of equilibrium.[57]

The technicalities, as well as the general implications of the 1832 Reform Act, provided an incentive to party organization in the constituencies in that the Act left voters themselves responsible for

[55] S. F. Woolley, 'The Personnel of the Parliament of 1833', *English Historical Review*, 1938, **53**, April, *passim*.
[56] K. Clark, 'The Electorate and the Corn Laws', *Transactions of the Royal Historical Society*, 1947, **5**, 126.
[57] Gash, *Reaction*, p. 136.

claiming a place on the electoral register. Local and central politi-cians were quick to see the possibilities in this, and Registration Societies grew up as a means of searching out qualified voters[58] [3.5.5]. Most of the local organizations which sprang up or were revived after 1832 were, as in the case of South Lancashire, locally inspired.[59] None the less, the national elements in these develop-ments were clear enough; most of the local organizations sheltered under one of the parliamentary party labels, and electioneering on national terms was often in evidence, as in 1837 when the local Conservative clubs supported Peel.[60] Contemporary fears about the implications of the clubs and local organizations for the inde-pendence of Members of Parliament was not without some founda-tion[61] [3.5.6–7].

The role of the central party institutions in this period was not so much to initiate such local action as to make attempts at guidance and co-ordination.[62] These attempts were pursued partly through London clubs such as the (Conservative) Carlton and the (Liberal) Reform, founded in 1832 and 1836 respectively. The novelty of such central clubs lay in their political (as opposed to purely social) purposes of connecting provincial politicians with their counter-parts in the metropolis and raising election funds.[63] Alongside these central party organizations grew the professional party managers, typified by Frederick Bonham, working closely with the parlia-mentary whips and leaders, with headquarters at the Carlton, and regarding electioneering as a matter in which professional expertise was possible. The division of labour between Bonham and the Whips was an organizational recognition of the legitimacy of this claim and of the presence of a new political situation.[64] After 1835, Bonham created a permanent committee to supervise Conservative election campaigns, and the increased knowledge of the state of registration in the various constituencies made possible by this kind of organization facilitated more accurate forecasts of the result of dissolutions.[65] The 1841 election result represents the first

[58] J. A. Thomas, 'The System of Registration and the Development of Party Organisation, 1832–1870', *History*, 1950, **30**.
[59] R. Hill, *Toryism and the People* (1929), p. 44.
[60] Ibid., p. 46.
[61] Gash, *Politics*, Ch. XV.
[62] Hill, p. 47.
[63] Gash, *Politics*, p. 400, et seq.
[64] Ibid., p. 412. [65] Ibid., p. 420.

planned defeat of a government using the country as the major area of combat.[66] After the 1846 split, Bonham went with Peel and Conservative central organization declined; but the tendency remained, and the revival of a professional central party organization was an important part of Disraeli's later attempts to rebuild the Conservative Party.

The importance of opinion outside the House of Commons and the degree to which it was in touch with metropolitan developments was enhanced by the rapid growth of the provincial press as a popular institution in the 1860s. This growth, facilitated by the development of railways and the telegraph and aided by the repeal of the Stamp Duty, was clearly an important vehicle for the new orders provoked by industrialization in England.[67]

On the other hand, these important developments in local party activity and the emergence of a national politics need to be seen in their proper perspective. Throughout the period, the central party organs had little direct control over the constituencies, and the constituencies themselves were subject to party organization only to a limited extent. Crown patronage was limited, but the 1832 Reform Act had by no means abolished that patronage controlled by the aristocracy and exercised in the counties and the 'corrupt' small boroughs. Deferential attitudes among the electorate were extremely strong, and in general the eighteenth-century pattern of electioneering persisted throughout and beyond the period. Moreover, not only were most contemporary politicians unwilling to elevate the electorate to a position of sovereign importance, but the electors themselves thought about politics largely in local, rather than national, terms. The communication between localities and between localities and London was increasing apace, but the result was very far from a homogeneity of opinion. The anti-aristocratic politics of Birmingham and Sheffield were very different from those of the counties, and even between the urban areas themselves major differences were apparent.[68] The full expression of 'outsider' opinion in the country came after the 1867 Reform Act rather than in this period, where the gap between even the Liberal parliamentarians and their potential allies in the urban, dissenting, middle

[66] N. Gash, 'F. R. Bonham, Conservative Political Secretary', English Historical Review, 1948, 63, 522.

[67] Vincent, pp. 58–62.

[68] Clark, The Making, pp. 129–31.

classes was extremely wide.[69] For the period between the Reform Acts, party in the country was represented by a number of limited, locally inspired experiments in political organization, loosely co-ordinated and seldom directed by the embryo central institutions, among an electorate still thinking about politics in local terms and often voting along lines familiar to earlier centuries. As such, party organization represented hesitant attempts to come to terms with the consequences of Reform by politicians who, while forced to recognize the necessity and advantage of popular support, were still suspicious of its implications and anxious to prevent such organization from becoming the instrument of democracy rather than the servant of parliamentary government.

[69] Vincent, *passim.*

3 1832–1867

Documents

3.1 THE CONSTITUTION

3.1.1 From Walter Bagehot, The English Constitution (*1867*).
World Classics edition (1928), p. 224.

If hereditary royalty had been essential to parliamentary government,
we might well have despaired of that government. But accurate investigation shows that this royalty is not essential; that, upon average, it is
not even in a high degree useful; that though a King with high courage
and fine distinction – a King with a genius for the place – is always useful, and at rare moments priceless, yet that a common King, a King such
as birth brings, is of no use at difficult crises, while in the common course
of things his aid is neither likely nor required – he will do nothing, and he
need do nothing.

3.1.2 From Alphaeus Todd, On Parliamentary Government in
England (*1866*), *Vol. I, p. 20.*
Todd is considering the consequences of the 1832 Reform Act.

... the representation of the people was placed upon a wider basis, by
the introduction of the commercial and manufacturing classes – which,
ever since the peace of 1815, had been growing in wealth and importance
– to a share of political power ... At the same time, by increasing the
weight and influence of the House of Commons in public affairs, while
it diminished the means previously at the disposal of the crown for

exercising a constitutional control over the proceedings of Parliament, it served to render Parliamentary government a more onerous undertaking.

3.1.3 From a letter to King William IV from Melbourne, 15 April 1835. Printed in Lord Melbourne's Papers (*edited L. C. Sanders, 1889*), *pp. 274–5.*
Melbourne is considering the difficulties of taking office while the Irish Church question is still unsettled.

It must be manifest that those who have borne . . . a part in these proceedings, cannot, with any regard to their own consistency, or with the least hope of effectually serving your Majesty, undertake to carry on your Majesty's government unless it is understood that they are to act without delay upon the principle [*of using the surplus revenue of the Irish Church for the purposes of education for all classes* – Ed.]; that they are to carry that principle into practical effect, and that in so doing they are to receive the sanction, approbation, and support of your Majesty . . . [Also] Viscount Melbourne must declare that, whilst he trusts he is incapable of recommending to your Majesty any individuals whose character and conduct appear to him to disqualify them from holding any situation of trust and responsibility, he can neither admit nor acquiesce in any general or particular exclusions, and that he must reserve to himself the power of recommending for employment any one of your Majesty's subjects who is qualified by law to serve your Majesty.

3.1.4 From a memorandum by Anson concerning the formation of Sir Robert Peel's Ministry in 1841. Printed in the Letters of Queen Victoria (*First Series, 1907*), *Vol. I, p. 384.*

With regard to Peel's position with the Queen, he [Melbourne] thought that circumstances must make it . . . The less personal objections the Queen took to any one the better, as any such expression is sure to come out and personal enemy is made. It was also to be recollected that Peel was in a very different position now, backed by a large majority, to when the other overture was made – He had the power *now*, to extort what he pleased, and he fancied he saw the blank faces of the party when Peel told them that he had agreed to the dismissal or resignation of only two of the Queen's ladies.

3.1.5 From a speech by Sir Robert Peel, moving a motion of 'No Confidence', 27 May 1841. Parliamentary Debates (Vol. 58, 27 May 1841), c. 803 and 814.

The resolution which I mean to propose affirms two propositions – first, that Her Majesty's Government do not sufficiently possess the confidence of the House of Commons to enable them to carry through the House measures which they deem of essential importance to the public welfare; and secondly, that their continuance in office under such circumstances is at variance with the spirit of the constitution . . . I presume I shall hardly be asked to define what I mean by 'The Spirit of the constitution' . . . I speak of that system which implies that the Ministers of the Crown shall have the confidence of the House of Commons . . . [The Prime Minister, Lord Russell] says that from the doctrine of the responsibility of Ministers it follows that they ought to enjoy the confidence of the House of Commons; and he justly describes, in powerful language, the consequences which would follow from departing from the constitutional rule . . . You cannot, in this country, restrict the influence of party . . . The noble Lord said 'From the collisions of party arise the energy and principle of the constitution of popular government' . . .

3.1.6 From a speech by Viscount Melbourne, defending the government during the debate on the Address, 24 August 1841. Parliamentary Debates (Third Series, Vol. 59, 24 August 1841), c. 70–1.

The meaning of this motion in plain English is, 'we have now a majority in the House of Commons'. To judge by some of the declarations at the hustings, I suppose there is such a majority; at the same time it must be recollected that Members are sent *ad consultandum de rebus arduis regni*. We are not, therefore, to judge, what the conduct of members may be by their declarations on the hustings.

3.1.7 From a speech by Lord Russell, reported in The Times, *26 April 1831.*

On this occasion the electors had more than a common duty to perform, for they were called upon not merely to select men the best fitted to defend their rights and interests, but to answer by their conduct this question put to the electors of the Empire by His Majesty in dissolving

Parliament: 'Do you approve – Ay or No – of the principle of a reform in the representation?'

3.1.8 From 'Sir Robert Peel's Address,' The Quarterly Review, *February 1835.*
The article is considering the 'Tamworth Manifesto'.

Sir Robert Peel's Address is – in *itself* and independently of its topics – a proof that he accepts, and will – unfettered by old customs and traditions of government – endeavour to meet the exigencies of the times. When before did a Prime Minister think it expedient to announce to the *people*, not only his acceptance of office, but the principles and even the details of the measures which he intended to produce; and to solicit – not from Parliament, but from the people – 'that they would so far maintain the prerogative of the King as to give the Ministers of his choice not, indeed, an implicit confidence, but a fair trial?' In former times such a practice would have been thought derogatory and impugned as unconstitutional, and would have been both; but the new circumstances into which the Reform Bill has placed the Crown, by making its choice of ministers immediately and absolutely dependent on the choice of the several constituencies, and in the first instance, quite independent of the concurrence of the assembled Parliament, have rendered such a course not merely expedient, but inevitable.

3.1.9 From 'The Budget', The Quarterly Review *(December 1852), p. 267*
The passage concerns arguments about manning the navy.

Mr Disraeli tells us that the Government have had a Committee sitting on this subject. We are sorry to hear it: the very appointment of such a committee is a kind of surrender – a confession that something is wrong, and made by those who ought rather – if they found public opinion running so strongly in a wrong direction as to require to a public enquiry – to have met it boldly as Ministers of the Crown, and endeavoured to correct it by their official and parliamentary authority. The Cabinet and the Board of Admiralty ought to be the only *committees* in which such *fundamental* principles should be discussed; subaltern committees and commissions are everywhere only crutches for those, who feel themselves too weak to walk alone.

3.2 PARTY RHETORIC

3.2.1 From M. D. Bulwer, M.P., The Lords, The Government and the Country *(1836), pp. 86 and 88.*

How does a wise general usually combine and cheer the forces he commands? . . . [By] favouring and promoting those who serve under [him] . . . Not that I am one of those who see no talent and no merit out of my own political circle . . . It is not that I like exaggerated and sectarian party zeal . . . But in times like the present, when two parties, professing two perfectly distinct creeds, are struggling for power, there never has been, and perhaps there cannot well be, any other policy, in order to maintain our own credit, and weight, and respectability with the public, than to favour our own friends alone.

3.2.2 From a speech by Macaulay during the Second Reading of the Reform Bill. Parliamentary Debates *(Vol. 35, 16 December 1831), c. 378 and 392.*

. . . now, when the Kingdom from one end to the other is convulsed by the question of Reform, we hear it said . . . 'would you alter the Representative system in such agitated times as these?' Half the logic of misgovernment lies in this one sophistical dilemma: If the people are turbulent, they are unfit for liberty: if they are quiet, they do not want liberty . . .

This Bill . . . admits the great body of the middle orders to a share in the government . . . great constituent bodies are quite as competent to discern merit, and quite as much disposed to reward merit, as the proprietors of boroughs . . .

I bring . . . no accusation against the working classes . . . If I would refuse to the working people that larger share of power which some of them have demanded, I would refuse it because I am convinced that, by giving it, I should only increase their distress. I admit that the end of government is their happiness. But, that they may be governed for their happiness, they must not be governed according to the doctrines which they have learned from their illiterate, incapable, low-minded flatterers . . . That the agitation of the question of Reform has enabled worthless demagogues to propagate their notions with some success, is a reason for speedily settling the question in the only way in which it can be settled . . .

There is a change in society. There must be a change in the government . . . That there is such a change, I can no more doubt than that we have more power looms, more steam-engines, more gas-lights than our ancestors . . . Therefore, be content to guide that movement which you cannot stop . . . Then will it be, as it has hitherto been, the peculiar glory of our Constitution that, though not exempt from the decay which is wrought by the vicissitudes of fortune, and the lapse of time, in all the proudest works of human power and wisdom, it yet contains within it the means of self-reparation.

3.2.3 From a remark by Sir F. Baring, First Lord Northbrook (c. 1840) Quoted in Thomas George, Earl of Northbrook *(1908), p. 33.*

[Whiggery means] the existence of a body of men connected with high rank and property, bound together by hereditary feelings, party ties, as well as higher motives, who in bad times keep alive the sacred flame of freedom, and when the people are roused stand between the constitution and revolution and go with the people, but not to extremities . . . A Whig is like a poet, born not made. It is as difficult to become a Whig as to become a Jew.

3.2.4 From a speech by Lord Hartington at Accrington, 2 December 1883 Printed in B. Holland, Life of the Eighth Duke of Devonshire *(1911), Vol. I, pp. 405–6.*

I confess I am not dissatisfied with the position that the Whig party have in former times occupied, and that I believe they occupy at the present time. I admit that the Whigs are not the leaders in popular movements, but the Whigs have been able, as I think, to the great advantage of the country, to direct, and guide, and moderate those popular movements. They have formed a connecting link between the advanced party and those classes which, possessing property, power and influence, are naturally averse to change, and I think I may claim for the Whig party that it is greatly owing to their guidance and to their action that the great and beneficial changes, which have been made in the direction of popular reform in this country, have been made not by the shock of revolutionary agitation, but by the calm and peaceful processes of constitutional acts. That is the part which the Whigs have played in the past, and which I believe the Whigs or those who represent them now, may be called upon to play with equal advantage in the future.

3.2.5 From a speech by Lord John Russell. Parliamentary Debates (*Vol. 35, 4 June 1841*), *c. 1210.*

The right honourable member for Pembroke quotes the authority of a great man, but without that authority which attaches to a real admirer of his principles, and follower of his conduct. I will also quote his words. On an occasion when the Whig party was in a state of discomfiture, and almost of despondency, Mr Fox said, that if he could entertain any hope of advancing the great cause of civil and religious freedom, which he had ever espoused, he would not slacken in his exertions . . . Espousing the principles of Mr Fox, like him we will not desert the cause on which we have embarked.

3.2.6 From a speech by Sir Robert Peel. Speeches of Sir Robert Peel, Lord Stanley and Sir James Graham *at Merchant Tailors' Hall, 12 May 1838.*

My object for some years past, that which I have most earnestly laboured to accomplish, has been to lay the foundation of a great party (cheers), which, existing in the House of Commons, and deriving its strength from the popular will, should diminish the risk, and deaden the shock of collision between the two deliberative branches of the legislature – which should enable us to check the too importunate eagerness of well-intending men, for hasty and precipitate changes in the constitution and laws of the country, and by which we should be enabled to say, with a voice of authority, to the restless spirit of revolutionary change, 'here are thy bounds, and here shall thy vibrations cease'. Gentlemen, I was deeply impressed with a conviction of the necessity of forming such a party from the period when a great change was made in the representative system of the country; I am confident that those who were the most convinced of the abstract merits of that change, who saw its absolute necessity in the progress of events, and the change of public opinion, would now admit . . . that although a necessary, still it was a fearful experiment – that there was a danger that the great shock given to prescriptive authority might lead to too hasty prescriptive [*sic* – Ed.] and irrational future changes – that those who were strongest in good intentions might, in their too sanguine hopes of reaching a species of perfection which could not be attained, forego that degree of perfection which was attainable – that there was a risk – and that those who had become possessed of a new power might think it useless if permitted to remain quiescent, and if not brought into constant and daily exercise. Gentlemen, that conviction led me to the conclusion that it was necessary, by prudence, by patience, by assuming a new position, by the rejection of the old tactics of party, suited to other times, and adapted to other circumstances – that it was desirable at that time to form a party whose bond of connexion should be the maintenance of that particular measure of reform, but determined to resist further constitutional changes – (cheers) changes having a tendency to disturb the balance of a mixed government. There were at that time in operation other causes which powerfully and mainly influenced the changes of opinion which so rapidly took place with respect to the necessity of reform. There had lately been exhibited to the empire those events which in France, in three short days, had trampled to the dust an ancient dynasty, and had shown physical power triumphant over constituted authority, and had engaged the sympathies of mankind not in favour of constituted authority, but of those who had resorted to a system of violation of all law and order . . . If you ask me what I mean by conservative principles . . . I will, in conclusion, briefly state what I mean by conservative principles. By conservative principles, I mean, and I believe you mean, the maintenance of the Peerage and the Monarchy – the continuance of the just powers and attributes of King, Lords and Commons in this country . . . By conservative principle I mean, that, coexistent with equality of civil rights and privileges, there shall be an established religion and imperishable faith, and that established religion shall maintain the doctrines of the Protestant Church . . . By conservative principles I mean . . . the maintenance, defence and continuance of those laws, those institutions, that society, and those habits and manners which have contributed to mould and form the character of Englishmen.

3.2.7 From Coningsby *(1844), a novel by Disraeli. 1948 edition, pp. 104 and 106.*

'. . . and now for our cry,' said Mr Taper.

'It is not a Cabinet for a good cry,' said Tadpole; 'but then, on the other hand, it is a Cabinet that will sow dissension in the opposite ranks, and prevent them having a good cry.'

'Ancient institutions and modern improvements, I suppose, Mr Tadpole?'

'Ameliorations is the better word; ameliorations. Nobody knows exactly what it means.'

'We go strong on the Church?' said Mr Taper.

'And no repeal of the Malt Tax; you were right, Taper. It cannot be listened to for a moment.'

'Something might be done with the prerogative,' said Mr Taper; 'the King's constitutional choice.'

'Not too much,' replied Mr Tadpole. 'It is a raw time yet for prerogative. . . . I tell you what, Mr Taper, the time is gone by when a Marquis of Monmouth was letter A, Number One.'

'Very true, Mr Tadpole. A wise man would do well now to look to the great middle class, as I said the other day to the electors of Shabbyton.'

'I had sooner be supported by the Wesleyans,' said Mr Tadpole, 'than by all the marquesses in the peerage' . . .

'That we should ever live to see a Tory government again! We have reason to be very thankful.'

'Hush!' said Mr Tadpole. 'The time has gone by for Tory governments; what the country requires is a sound Conservative government.'

'A sound Conservative government,' said Taper musingly. 'I understand: Tory men and Whig measures.'

3.2.8 From Lord Shaftesbury, 'Infant Labour', The Quarterly Review (December 1840), p. 171.

It is a monstrous thing to behold the condition, moral and physical, of the juvenile portion of our operative classes, more especially that which is found in the crowded lanes and courts of the larger towns, the charnel-houses of our race . . . Damp and unhealthy substrata, left altogether without drainage; frail tenements, low and confined, without conveniences or ventilation; close alleys and no supply of water: all these things overtopped by the *ne plus ultra* of rent, reward the contractor and devour the inhabitants. Emerging from these lairs of filth and disorder; the young workers, 'rising early, and late taking rest', go forth that they may toil through fifteen, nay, seventeen relentless hours, in sinks and abysses, oftentimes more offensive and pernicious than the holes they have quitted . . . the question is not whether the children of the poor may not with perfect propriety, with advantage to their parents and themselves, be employed to a certain extent in the labour of looms and shops. No doubt they may – But can it be pronounced necessary to our social welfare, or national prosperity, that children of the tenderest years should toil, amid every discomfort and agency of posture, and foul atmosphere, for fifteen or sixteen successive hours . . . Can it be for our honour, or our safety, that their young hearts, instead of being trained in the ways of temperance and virtue, should be acquiring knowledge of those vices which they will afterwards practise as adults? . . . We . . . know that our system begets the vast and inflammable mass which lies waiting, day by day, for the spark to explode it into mischief. We cover the land with spectacles of misery; wealth is felt only by its oppressions . . . Sickness has no claim on the capitalist; a day's absence, however necessary, is a day's loss to the workman . . .

But here comes the worst of all – these vast multitudes, ignorant and excitable in themselves, and rendered still more so by oppression and neglect, are surrendered, almost without a struggle, to the infidels and democrats . . . Let your laws, we say to Parliament, assume the proper functions of law, protect those for whom neither wealth, nor station, nor age, have raised a bulwark against tyranny; but, above all, open your treasury, erect churches, send forth the ministers of religion; reverse the conduct of the enemy of mankind, and sow wheat among the tares – all hopes are groundless, all legislation weak, all conservatism nonsense, without this alpha and omega of policy.

3.2.9 From Kenelm Digby, 'The Broadstone of Honour', (c. 1820). Quoted in C. H. Whibley, Lord John Manners and his Friends (1925), Vol. I, p. 133.

So far from intending any reproach upon the lower classes of society, I pronounce that there is ever a peculiar connection, a sympathy of feeling and affection, a kind of fellowship which is instantly recognized by both, between these and the highest order, that of gentlemen. In society, as in the atmosphere of the world, it is the middle which is the region of disorder and confusion and tempest.

3.2.10 From a letter from Lord John Manners to his brother, September 1842. Printed in C. H. Whibley, Lord John Manners and his Friends (1925), Vol. I, p. 137.

Let us show the people, that is, the lower orders, by adding to their comforts and pleasures in the only legitimate way a legislature can do so – viz., by voting money to build public baths, to keep up, or rather to restore, public games, to form public walks, that we are their real friends. Let us give them back the Church holy-days, open the Churches and Cathedrals to them, and let our men of power in their individual capacities assume a more personal and consequently a more kind intercourse with those below them. In a word, let society take a more feudal appearance than it presents now. That's my vision; it may be a wrong one; but if, as I believe, the Whig one of giving the people political power and prating to them of the rights of man, the glories of science, and the merits of political economy, is wrong, I can see no other way save the old and worn out one of 'laissez-faire, laissez-aller'.

*3.2.11 From Thomas Carlyle, 'The Gospel of Mammonism',
in* Past and Present *(1843). Edited A. M. D. Hughes (1918),
pp. 132 and 149–50.*

It must be owned, we for the present, with our Mammon-Gospel, have
come to strange conclusions. We call it a Society; and go about professing openly the totallest of separation, isolation. Our life is not a mutual
helpfulness; but rather, cloaked under due laws-of-war, named 'fair
competition' and so forth; it is a mutual hostility. We have profoundly
forgotten everywhere that *Cash payment* is not the sole relation of human
beings; we think, nothing doubting, that *it* absolves and liquidates all
engagements of man. 'My starving workers?' answers the rich Mill-
owner: 'Did I not hire them fairly in the market? . . . What have I to
do with them more?' – Verily Mammon-worship is a melancholy creed
. . .

If I were the Conservative Party of England I would not for one
hundred thousandth of an hour allow those Corn Laws to continue! . . .
When two millions of one's brother-men sit in Workhouses, and five
millions, as is insolently said, 'rejoice in potatoes', there are various
things that must be begun, let them end where they can.

*3.2.12 From Disraeli's speech at Shrewsbury, May 1843.
Printed in Moneypenney and Buckle,* Life of Disraeli *(1912),
Vol. II, pp. 140 and 143.*

You should not part with him [Peel] for what he has done; neither
should you part with him because you think he will do a certain act which
I believe that he will not [*i.e. repeal the Corn Laws* – Ed.]. If I find the
government receding really from their pledges and opinions – if I find
them, for instance, throwing over that landed interest that brought them
to power – my vote will be recorded against them . . .
I will never commit myself on this great question to petty economical
details; I will not pledge myself to miserable questions of sixpence in
seven-and-sixpence or eight shillings of duties about corn; I do not care
whether your corn sells for this sum or that, or whether it is under a
sliding scale or a fixed duty; but what I want, and what I wish to secure,
and what, as far as my energies go, I will secure, is the preponderance of
the landed interest. Gentlemen, when I talk of the preponderance of the
landed interest, do not for a moment suppose that I mean merely the
preponderance of 'squires of high degree'. My thought wanders farther
than a lordly tower or a baronial hall, I am looking in that phrase . . . to

the population of innumerable villages, to the crowds in our rural towns: I mean that estate of the poor which, in my opinion, has been already dangerously tampered with; I mean the great estate of the Church, which has before this time secured our liberty, and may, for aught I know, still secure our civilization; I mean also by the landed interest that great building up of our laws and manners, which is, in fact, the ancient polity of the realm . . .

When I hear a political economist, or an Anti-Corn Law Leaguer, or some conceited Liberal reviewer, come forward and tell us, as a grand discovery of modern science . . . that 'Property has its duties as well as its rights', my answer is that that is but a feeble plagiarism of the very principle of that feudal system which you are always reviling. Let me next tell those gentlemen who are so fond of telling us that property has its duties as well as its rights, that labour also has its rights as well as its duties; and when I see masses of property raised in this country which do not recognise that principle . . . when I hear of all this misery and all this suffering; when I know that evidence exists in our Parliament of a state of demoralisation in the once happy population of this land which is not equalled in the most barbarous countries – I cannot help suspecting that this has arisen because property has been permitted to be created and held without the performance of its duties.

3.2.13 From The Church of England Quarterly Review (*January 1837*), *Vol. I.*
The article is concerned with the attack on Tithes.

'In these latter ages (we quote Bishop Warburton) every sect, thinking itself the true church, or at least the most perfect, is naturally pushed on to advance its own scheme upon the ruins of the rest, and where argument fails, civil power is made to come in, as soon as ever a party can be formed in the public administration; and we find they have been but too successful in persuading the magistrate that his interests are much concerned in these religious differences. Now the most effectual remedy for those dangerous and strong convulsions into which states are so frequently thrown by those struggles, is an alliance which establishes one church, and gives a full toleration to the rest, only keeping sectaries out of the public administration, from a heedless admission to which these disorders have arisen.'

Do not current events exemplify the sagacious truth of this last observation? A civil right to tithes by way of state provision to the Clergy has lasted in Great Britain upwards of a thousand years. Can the houses of Russell or Landsdowne or Melbourne show a better title to their *benefices*?

3.2.14 From 'The Ministry and the New Parliament', The Edinburgh Review, *January 1848.*

When we speak of a *liberal system of government* – a phrase, we confess, which is not very precise – we mean such a system of government as is indicated by the old Whig party of England, improved and enlarged by modern speculation, particularly in questions of public economy and jurisprudence . . . Considered as a mere party combination, as resting merely on the ancient Whig connection and the support of a few, prominent and historical families, the present government [*Lord Russell's* – Ed.] stands on too narrow a basis to be able to survive the first parliamentary storm. But if we consider its position in the country, and the principles which it represents . . . and if we estimate the comparative values of the forces now opposed to it, the elements of its strength will be seen to be numerous and important.

3.2.15 From John Stuart Mill, On Liberty (*1859*). *Everyman Edition (1910), pp. 72–3.*

In England, from the peculiar circumstances of our political history, though the yoke of opinion is perhaps heavier, that of law is lighter, than in most other countries of Europe; and there is considerable jealousy of direct interference, by the legislative or executive power, with private conduct; not so much from any just regard for the independence of the individual, as from the still subsisting habit of looking on the government as representing an opposite interest to the public. The majority have not yet learnt to feel the power of the government their power, or its opinions their opinions. When they do so, individual liberty will probably be as much exposed to invasion from the government, as it already is from public opinion. But as yet, there is a considerable amount of feeling ready to be called forth against any attempt of the law to control individuals in things in which they have not hitherto been accustomed to be controlled by it; and this with very little discrimination as to whether the matter is, or is not, within the legitimate sphere of legal control . . . There is, in fact, no recognized principle by which the propriety or impropriety of government interference is customarily tested . . . The object of this Essay is to assert one very simple principle, as entitled to govern absolutely the dealings of society with the individual in the way of compulsion and control, whether the means used be physical force in the form of legal penalties, or the moral coercion of public opinion. That principle is, that the sole end for which mankind are warranted, individually or collectively, in interfering with the liberty of action of any of their number, is self-protection. That the only purpose for which power can rightfully be exercised over any member of a civilised community, against his will, is to prevent harm to others. His own good, physical or moral, is not a sufficient warrant . . . The only part of the conduct of any one, for which he is answerable to society, is that which concerns others. In the part which merely concerns himself, his independence is, of right, absolute. Over himself, over his own body and mind, the individual is sovereign.

3.2.16 From W. E. Gladstone, The Course of Commercial Policy at Home and Abroad *(1843). Reprinted by the Cobden Club, 1919.*

During the revolutionary war we became in a great degree, partly from political causes, and partly from our mechanical inventions, the manufacturers, merchants, and carriers of the world. Our trade yielded high profits, our expenditure entailed enormous burdens and very high prices; the manufacturing genius and industry of the people, and the wealth of the country, received as it were a forced and precocious development . . . But with the peace the pursuits of peace naturally revived on the Continent and our customers became our rivals . . . In the meantime we had lost any chance of saying we will contract our operations and will fall back on ourselves within our own circle of Supply and Demand. We had become immediately and, as it were, organically, dependent on our foreign trade . . . it was a main artery of the system, through which, in great part, buoyancy or depression affected our industrial life . . .

Thus it had become no matter of doctrinal optimism, but one of the most plain and proximate utility – we should rather say, of iron necessity – that we should more frankly enter into general competition in the markets of the world, and should consequently use every effort to cheapen production by relieving the materials of industry . . . from fiscal exactions, and by mitigating, with a just measure of regard to existing interests, and to the virtual pledges which grow out of established laws, all partial burdens upon trade, by which the community as a whole is laid under contribution to support the particular pursuits of certain of the classes comprised within it. If we are to flourish and if we are to live we must learn, one way or another, to compete with cheaper labour, with lighter taxes, with more fertile soils, with richer mines than our own; and if this is to be done, both the working hand, and the material upon which it is to work, must, as soon as practicable, be set free.

3.2.17 From Lord Acton, 'Political Thought on the Church'
(1858). Printed in The History of Freedom and Other Essays
(edited J. N. Figgis and R. V. Laurence, 1907), p. 208.

The political character of our own country bears hardly more resemblance to the Liberal Governments of the Continent – which have
copied only what is valueless in our institutions – than to the superstitious
despotism of the East, or to the analogous tyranny which in the Far
West is mocked with the name of freedom. Here, as elsewhere, the progress of the constitution, which it was the work of the Catholic ages to
build up, on the principles common to all the nations of the Teutonic
stock, was interrupted by the attraction which the growth of absolutism
abroad excited, and by the Reformation's transferring the ecclesiastic
power to the Crown. The Stuarts justified their abuse of power by the
same precepts and the same examples by which the Puritans justified
their resistance to it . . . The Revolution of 1688 destroyed one without
favouring the other . . . it was a restoration in some sort of the principles
of government, which had been alternately assailed by absolute monarchy, and by a fanatical democracy . . .
   The danger which menaces the continuance of our constitution proceeds simply from the oblivion of those Christian ideas by which it was
originally inspired. It should seem that it is the religious as well as the
political duty of Catholics to endeavour to avert this peril, and to defend
from the attacks of the Radicals and from the contempt of the Tories the
only constitution which bears some resemblance to those of Catholic
times.

3.2.18 From Cobbett's Weekly Political Register, *4 December*
and 22 June 1833.

The farmers . . . seeing that there was more danger to be dreaded from
the labourers than from the aristocracy, the stock-jobbers and the
parsons, have generally made, and are making, *common cause* with the
labourers . . . The tradesmen in the country-towns have the same
interest in this matter as the farmers. They know that it is better *for them*
also that the fruit of the land should be given to the labourers, who would
then be their *customers*, which the aristocracy, the Jews, the stock-
jobbers and the parsons are not. In short, all the *industrious* classes have a
common interest with the labourers.
   . . . what did we want the Reform Bill FOR? It certainly was, that it
might do us some good; that it might better our situation; that it

might cause us to be better off. And, how was it to do this? Why, by the lopping off of pensions, sinecures, grants, and other emoluments; and by suffering us to keep our earnings instead of giving them to the tax-gatherer; and thereby to be enabled to live better, to have more and better victuals and drink, more and better clothes, better lodging: that we might be enabled to lead, in short, easier and happier lives. This was what *the people* wanted the Reform Bill for, and not for the gratification of any abstract or metaphysical whim . . .

3.2.19 From The Poor Man's Guardian, *24 September 1831.*

Meetings are everywhere holden – and petitions are preparing in every quarter, to promote [the Reform Bill's] allowance – but by whom are these meetings convened, and by whom attended – by whom are such petitions signed? – why, by your hypocritical, time-serving, property-loving, 'middle-men' . . . Yes, friends, and fellow countrymen, we protest that this measure is a mere *trick* to strengthen against your rightful claims the tottering exclusiveness of our blessed constitution. It is clear, *we* GAIN nothing by it . . . why, before even they have gained their own admittance – do they not shut the doors of Parliament against you? for will they *tolerate* our *mention* even of '*universal suffrage*' etc? . . . do they not scout the very mention of equality? – and is not *property*, which you have not, the very pivot on which all their thoughts and wishes turn?

3.2.20 From a speech by Richard Cobden at Manchester, 24 October 1844. Printed in Speeches of Richard Cobden *(edited J. Bright and T. Rogers, 1870), Vol. I, p. 209.*

[Imagine] The absurdity, the mockery of bringing up men in round frocks to a dinner-table and giving them thirty shillings, because they had ploughed well, or hoed well, or harrowed well . . . what must be the concomitant order of things? It would argue, in the first place, that the prizemen who were so treated were an abject and servile class. It would argue that the trader who could condescend to be treated so would himself be little better than a slave. And if you needed such stimulants as these to make you carry on your business as you ought to do, where do you think you would fare in the race of industry as compared with other classes? Where would you be if you were so childish as to be fondled and dandled by a body of Members of Parliament? Why, there would not be a country on the face of the world that you could compete with – that is evident. You would, like them, be going to these same parliamentary men, begging them to be your dry nurses, in order that they might pass an Act of Parliament to protect you in your trade . . . the whole course of the conduct of these gentlemen [*i.e. protected landlords* – Ed.] . . . is just a gratuitous piece of impertinence to the rest of the community. What do we care what they do with their land? . . . all we say is this, 'if you do not make the most of your land, it is no reason why we should be starving that you may grow rushes' . . . it is intended to make us believe that we are indebted to them, and must wait until they choose to supply us with our food; that is something like a condescension . . . on their part, that they give us their food in exchange for our manufactures . . . when my Lord Stanley takes credit to . . . agricultural associations for having improved agriculture during the last five years, I say it is not due to these agricultural associations, but to the Anti-Corn Law League. It is owing to that that the agriculturalists and the landowners have been roused from their lethargic sleep. They are buckling on their armour to meet the coming competition, which competition will do for them what nothing else will do, and what it has done for manufactures – it will make the agriculturalists of this country capable of competing with the farmers of any part of the world.

3.2.21 From R. G. Gammage, The History of the Chartist Movement *(1854), pp. 10–11 and 14–15.*

. . . a society was established in the metropolis under the unassuming title of the Working Men's Association. Although its name gave no indication of a political tendency, its leading object was to secure for the people their fair share in the representation. So careful did the association affect to be of the influence of the working classes, that no person out of their ranks was admitted to a voice in its affairs. Persons belonging to the middle and upper classes were accepted as honorary members, but nothing more . . .

A committee had been appointed, consisting partially of M.P.s and partially of members of the association, whose office was to mould their views into the form of a bill, to be afterwards submitted to a public meeting; which bill contained six cardinal points. The six points were – Universal Manhood Suffrage, Annual Parliaments, Vote by Ballot, No Property Qualifications, Payment of Members, and Equal Voting districts. To this bill was given the title of *The People's Charter* . . .

But it was not the political question alone which engaged the attention of the radical reformers. Political reforms were certainly valued because of their abstract justice, but they were also looked upon as a means of securing a better social position for the humbler classes . . . It may be doubted whether there ever was a great political movement of a people without a social origin. The chief material object of mankind is to possess the means of social enjoyment. Secure them in the possession of these, and small is the care they have for political abstractions. It is the existence of great social wrongs which principally teaches the masses the value of political rights . . . In times of comparative prosperity there is scarcely a ripple to be observed on the ocean of politics, but let that prosperity be succeeded by a period of adversity and the waves of popular discontent will roll with such impetuous force as to threaten the existence of the political fabric . . . There might be no clear idea at the commencement of the movement for the charter as to the way in which political power worked to their disadvantage. Still less might they be aware of the nature of those social measures, which its possession in their hands would enable them to apply for the improvement of their condition. The mystery, as to the cause of social misery, the Working Men's Association endeavoured to solve.

3.2.22 From a letter to Francis Place from Joseph Parkes, early in 1836. Printed in J. K. Buckley, Joseph Parkes of Birmingham *(1926), p. 127.*

The new Town Councils are of course compounded of much local *Whiggism,* a deleterious ingredient. This is unavoidable because union alone could have defeated the Common enemy. But the Radicals will in a year or two work all the scum off . . .

You write me about parties . . . All the gangs are what they have ever been. Tories are burked, no resurrection for them. Whigs, will of course raise their bidding with the People's growing power and demand.

They are an unnatural party standing between the People and the Tory aristocracy chiefly for the pecuniary value of offices and vanity of power . . . Their hearse is ordered . . .

3.3 PARTY IN PARLIAMENT

3.3.1 From a letter to F. R. Bonham from Sir James Graham, 6 January 1841. Peel Papers (British Museum, Add. Mss. 40616), ff. 191–4.

I am very glad indeed that Peel has written to you, and that you have gone into detail on the state of Parties and of relative numbers. This after all is the cardinal Point: With a majority in the House of Commons everything is possible; without it, nothing can be done.

3.3.2 From The Greville Memoirs (*edited H. Reeve, 1874*), *First Series, Vol. I.*
The extract was written on 10 February, 1839.

A pretty correct analysis of the House of Commons presents the following result: 267 Government people, including the Irish tail; 66 Radicals, 5 doubtful, and 315 Conservatives; 4 vacant seats, and the Speaker.

3.3.3 From 'Legislation for the Working Classes', The Edinburgh Review (*January 1846*), *pp. 64 and 68.*

One of the most marked characteristics of the present time is the large amount of public attention which is given to the working classes. Up to a comparatively recent period, the Houses of Parliament, and the political writers in the newspapers, were almost exclusively occupied with questions relating to foreign policy, finance, Indian and Colonial government, Parliamentary reform, religious toleration, and other similar matters; generally involving the conduct and permanence of the existing administration. All measures concerning the state of the working classes were avoided by the Ministers of the Crown, and studiously left to the care of the country gentlemen, who, when any grievance became prominent, voluntarily undertook the trouble of devising some palliative, and of carrying the measure through Parliament. The legislation relating to this class of subjects thus consisted of detached and limited measures, not proposed on the responsibility of the government; the consent of Parliament was generally obtained by arrangement, with little or no debating; and the attention of the press, and the public at large, was in consequence but slightly attracted to the proceedings. But, after about thirty years operation of the form of poor law which was introduced at the end of the last century, the state of things which it produced became intolerable, and *some* change was seen to be absolutely necessary . . . The irritation between the agricultural labourers and the farmers – springing directly from the poor law, and showing itself in incendiarism and riot – was such, in 1830–1, as to demand a remedy from the legislature. The remedy was applied with a vigorous hand by the administration of Lord Grey . . . Since then [through the Poor Law, limitations on children in factories, etc.] . . . whatever reproaches may be cast on the legislature of this country for the sufferings of the more indigent classes, it cannot be justly accused of having treated them with indifference or neglect. . . .

3.3.4 From the 'Report on the Organisation of the Permanent Civil Service' (the 'Northcote-Trevelyan Report', 1854). Printed in British Parliamentary Papers *(1854–1855), Vol. 20, p. 449.*

It cannot be necessary to enter into any lengthened argument for the purpose of showing the high importance of the Permanent Civil Service of the country in the present day. The great and increasing accumulation of public business, and the consequent pressure upon the Government, need only to be alluded to; and the inconveniences which are inseparable from the frequent changes which take place in the responsible administration are matters of sufficient notoriety. It may safely be asserted that, as matters now stand, the Government of the country could not be carried on without the aid of an efficient body of permanent officers.

3.3.5 From Arthur Symonds, Practical Suggestions for the Internal Reform of the House of Commons *(1832), p. 5.*

The present construction of the House of Commons, as a legislative body, renders it incapable of performing even a small portion of its business; a few measures occupy almost its entire attention, to the exclusion of others equally important, though not so striking, or so pressing. It is the object of the following suggestions, to point out a remedy for an evil which, if unchecked, will neutralize many of the benefits which may be expected to flow from the proposed reform of Parliament.

3.3.6 From a letter to J. W. Croker from Peel, 5 March 1833. Printed in J. R. Thursfield, Peel *(1904), p. 125.*

I could have trampled the Bill to dust. What does this show? That there is no steadiness in the House, that it is subject to any impulse, that the force of party connections, by which alone a Government can pursue a consistent course, is quite paralysed . . . The question is not, Can you turn out a Government? but, Can you keep in any Government and stave off confusion? . . . What are we doing at this moment? We are making the Reform Bill work; we are falsifying our own predictions . . .

*3.3.7 From a speech by Lord Derby, explaining why he had
refused to form a government in 1855.* Parliamentary Debates
(*Third Series, Vol. 136, February 1855*), *c. 1336.*

To [take office] dependent for support from day to day upon precarious
and uncertain majorities, compelled to cut down this measure, to pare
off that – to consider with regard to each measure not what was for the
real welfare of the country, but what would conciliate some half-dozen
men here, or obviate the objections of some half-dozen there – to regard
it as a great triumph of Parliamentary skill and Ministerial strength to
scramble through the Session of Parliament, and to boast of having met
with few and insignificant defeats – I say this is a state of things which
cannot be satisfactory to any Minister, and which cannot be of advantage
to the Crown, or to the people of this country . . . to be a Minister on
sufferance; to hold such a position without any security for enforcing
your own views . . . would be such an intolerable and galling servitude
as no man of honour or character would voluntarily impose himself to . . .
Under all these circumstances – from all these considerations – I came to
the conclusion that with the unassisted numerical strength of those who
placed their confidence in me, it was impossible that I could feel any
assurance of forming – that which I concur . . . in deeming most desirable and necessary for the country at the present period – a strong
Government.

*3.3.8 From an exchange of letters between Disraeli and Peel,
4 February and 6 February 1844. Printed in C. S. Parker,
Sir Robert Peel (1899), Vol. III, pp. 144–6.*

Dear Sir Robert,
    I was quite unaware until Friday night, when I was generally ap-
prised of it, that the circumstance of my not having received the usual
circular [*i.e. the party whip* – Ed.] from yourself to attend Parliament was
intentional . . . I am bound to say that I look upon the fact of not having
received your summons, coupled with the ostentatious manner in which
it has been bruited about, as a painful personal procedure which the past
by no means authorised.

My Dear Sir,
    My reason for not sending you the usual circular was an honest
doubt whether I was entitled to send it – whether towards the close of

the last Session of Parliament you had not expressed opinions . . . which precluded me . . . from proffering personally an earnest request for your attendance . . . It gives me, however, great satisfaction to infer from your letter . . . that my impressions were mistaken, and my scruples unnecessary.

3.3.9 From Walter Bagehot, The English Constitution (1867) 1928 edition, p. 125.

The moment, indeed, that we distinctly conceive that the House of Commons is mainly and above all things an elective assembly, we at once perceive that party is of its essence. There never was an election without a party . . . The House of Commons lives in a state of perpetual potential choice: at any moment it can choose a ruler and dismiss a ruler. And therefore party is inherent in it, is bone of its bone, and breath of its breath.

Secondly, though the leaders of a party no longer have the vast patronage of the last century with which to bribe, they can coerce by a threat far more potent than any allurement – they can dissolve. This is the secret which keeps parties together. Mr Cobden most justly said, 'He had never been able to discover what was the proper moment, according to members of Parliament, for a dissolution. He had heard them say they were ready to vote for everything else, but he had never heard them say they were ready to vote for that.' Efficiency in an assembly requires a solid mass of steady votes; and these are *collected* by a deferential attachment to particular men, or by a belief in the principles those men represent, and they are *maintained* by fear of those men – by the fear that if you vote against them, you may yourself soon not have a vote at all.

Thirdly, it may seem odd to say so, just after inculcating that party organization is the vital principle of representative government, but that organization is permanently efficient, because it is not composed of warm partisans. . . . The body is eager, but the atoms are cool. If it were otherwise, parliamentary government would become the worst of governments – a sectarian government . . . of all modes of enforcing moderation on a party, the best is to contrive that the members of the party shall be intrinsically moderate, careful, and almost shrinking men . . . Our English system . . . makes party government permanent and possible in the sole way in which it can be so, by making it mild.

3.3.10 From a letter to Sidney Herbert from the Duke of Newcastle, 27 October 1851. Printed in Lord Stanmore, Sidney Herbert, A Memoir (1906), Vol. I, p. 145.

First, as to leadership. That Lord Aberdeen is, all things considered, our natural leader, and the *only* man who could properly assume that position, I think there can be no doubt. If he would *place himself* in that post, we should all recognize the claim. It has always appeared to me that the idea of *electing* a leader is a mistake, and an inversion of the proper constitutional view of party mechanism. A leader should become such, either because he is generally recognized as *facile princeps* in position, popularity, talent, discretion, debating power, or other qualifications necessary to balance the differences of opinion to be found in all parties, or by being selected by the Sovereign as her adviser when her Ministers have resigned . . . If, however, a leader is *elected* by his party without the claims of superiority and obvious reasons which others beside his party must recognize, it appears to me that he must be placed in a false position.

3.3.11 From The Greville Memoirs (edited H. Reeve, 1874). First Series, Vol. III.
The extract was written on 25 February 1834.

There has been a meeting at Althorp's today, numerously attended, in which he talked with some effect as it is said, the audience having gone away in a humour to support the Government . . . Althorp began by saying that unless gentlemen would more regularly and consistently support the government it could not be carried on . . .

3.3.12 From The Greville Memoirs (edited H. Reeve, 1874). First Series, Vol. III.
The extract was written on 25/26 July, 1833.

. . . the truth is that the House of Commons is in such a state that it is next to impossible to say what Ministers can or ought to do, or what the House will do. There is no such thing as a great party knit together by community of opinion . . . The government conciliate no attachment, command no esteem and respect, and have no following . . . every man is thinking of what he shall say to his constituents, and how his vote will be taken, and everything goes on . . . from hand to mouth . . . It is every day more apparent that with such a House of Commons, so elected, so acted upon, no government can feel secure; none can undertake with confidence to carry on the affairs of the country.

3.3.13 From a letter to Henry Brougham from Sir James Graham, 1831. Printed in C. S. Parker, Sir James Graham (1907), Vol. I, p. 170.

Our majority is not made up of men we can reckon upon as of old – nominees, or persons with few constituents, attached to us as members of a party . . . of 'thick and thin men' in the old sense we have not many more than are in office.

3.3.14 From a letter from Peel to his wife, 1846. Printed in C. S. Parker, Sir Robert Peel (1899), Vol. II, p. 347.
Peel is reflecting upon his experiences as Prime Minister between 1841 and 1846.

It was not an easy task – considering the diversity of views on many important subjects which prevailed both among the leading men of both parties and among their followers – to bring about a practical concurrence in a common course of action.

On reflecting on all that passed, I am much more surprised that the union was so long maintained than that it was ultimately severed.

3.3.15 From 'The Budget', The Quarterly Review, December 1852, pp. 272–3.
The article discusses the state of the administration in 1852.

What reasonable expectation can we have of their stability? As *an existing government*, chosen by the Crown in the legitimate exercise of its authority, it is entitled to a fair, and even indulgent trial; but our readers know that we have long since doubted, almost despaired, of the possibility of any effective Government to be administered subject to 'the feelings of a modern House of Commons' [*a phrase used by Disraeli in his budget speech* – Ed.] – and it is obvious that a ministry constructed on the temporary concert of three, or indeed four, distinct and widely differing parties, is in a position of very peculiar difficulty . . . We confess that we do not see how it is to obtain sufficient numerical strength in the House of Commons without such sacrifice of individual character as would deprive it of all moral support; and we must regret that a more homogeneous combination of all the political elements that are or profess to be Conservative, had not afforded the entry of a better prospect of extrication from the discredit and danger of *Government on sufferance.*

3.3.16 From a letter to J. H. Scarlett from Lord Fitzwilliam, 29 November 1845. Quoted in F. M. Thompson, The English Historical Review, *1959, p. 237.*

I should be sorry to see the Whigs entirely merged in the Conservatives. I do not like party divisions to run by classes and not by principles; all the aristocracy and the landed gentry on the one side, the democracy and town people on the other: or all church against all dissent.

3.3.17 From a letter to Disraeli from Lord Derby, 25 February 1867. The Disraeli Papers, *Hughenden Manor, B/XX/S/412. The letter concerns the discussions on Reform.*

My Dear Disraeli,
       My report of the Carlton Meeting, brought to me by Ridley and B. Stanhope, corresponds in the main with yours, but is hardly as favourable.
       According to them there were 150 present, of whom about two-thirds were in favour of . . . Residential Suffrage, with *three* years residence. They came to no distinct resolution; and the only points on which they seem to have been agreed was [*sic* – Ed.] that whatsoever we proposed we should stand by, and not accept amendments dictated by Gladstone. They would take a £5 franchise; if proposed by us – They admitted that if we proposed £6, and we were beaten, we could not, on such an issue, go to the country; and they would, in such a case, prefer our resignations to assent. If this is the general feeling (and they represented it as universal) and we cannot propose £5, I think it is a strong argument in favour of meeting our fate on the bolder line; but I am afraid . . . that our own party would not be united in our support . . .

3.3.18 A letter to Disraeli from Lord Derby, 10 March 1867. Disraeli Papers, *Hughenden Manor, B/XX/S/420. The letter makes arrangements for the announcement of the Reform Bill to the Conservative Party.*

I will summon a meeting of the party for Thursday; it is not possible to have it sooner, for the Bill is to be again before the Cabinet on

Tuesday; and we cannot withdraw all the party from the House of Commons on a Wednesday; but I think Thursday is quite soon enough, and we can give an *early notice* of the meeting.

3.3.19 From a speech by W. E. Gladstone on the First Reading of The Representation of the People Bill, 18 March 1867. Printed in Hansard, *Vol. 186, c. 26–7.*

. . . till the Bill of the right honourable gentleman [*the Chancellor of the Exchequer* – Ed.] is in our hands – and he has promised that it will be in our hands tomorrow morning – it is impossible to arrive at any conclusion, or to enter fully into the question with such an amount of knowledge as the gravity of the circumstances demand. But, Sir, having said that, I must frankly state that the impression made upon my mind by the statement of the right honourable gentleman is . . . not on the whole a pleasing one . . . When the Resolutions of the right honourable gentleman were produced we waived every question and every difficulty, except only the desire we entertained that a definite meaning should be attached to those Resolutions. When the right honourable gentleman, acceding very fairly to the general desire expressed by the House, produced the skeleton of a Bill, no difficulty was raised on this side of the House with regard to the principle of that Bill. It was never in print; but the statement which I had the honour to make . . . was that from the description given of it by the right honourable gentleman, I hoped when we saw it in print we might find that – though there might be points – which should be raised on the provisions of the Bill – yet that these points might fairly be considered in Committee. But though this is the fourth day of our progress . . . with reference to the Reform question, I am afraid, to use a homely phrase, that the right honourable gentleman has only 'led us still deeper into the wood' . . .

Many of the propositions – the main propositions – of the Bill have obtained so remarkable a publicity, that it has been our duty to apply ourselves, availing ourselves of the information we had obtained, to a consideration of the measure. With the aid of the knowledge we have thus obtained beforehand of the principles of the Bill we have now acquired a more complete – though still an incomplete view of its nature – than we could have had if we had been depending simply on the statement of the Minister. About three days ago a meeting of the more select spirits was held in Downing Street. A portion of the information imparted to that meeting found its way even to us, the mere mob of the House of the Commons (Oh! Oh!). As my observation is questioned by several honourable Members, I must add to it this remark – that, so far as I know, after an experience of thirty-four years, it is a practice entirely novel for a Minister of the Crown to gather in his house (*the reference is to Lord Derby* – Ed.) those Members of Parliament who he thinks agree with him, and state to them, days in advance of the House of Commons, the particulars of a great measure which it is his intention to submit to Parliament . . . This is an innovation, and it is an innovation which is not an improvement. I hope, therefore, that there will be much consideration before it is repeated.

3.4 ATTITUDES TO PARTY

3.4.1 From a public letter to his constituents from John Bright, July 1850. Printed in G. M. Trevelyan, The Life of John Bright (1913), p. 192.

. . . I would not, for a moment, sit in Parliament for Manchester, or for any other constituency, if it was to be understood that I am to forget my own character and long-held principles, and what I believe to be the true interests of the country, to abandon all these, and vote as the necessities of *party* may require, at the crack of the Treasury Whip.

3.4.2 From Sir Richard Vyvyan, A Letter from Sir Richard Vyvyan to his Constituents (1842), pp. 31 and 38.

The difficulties of a member resolved to act independently of party, are far greater now than they were formerly; and his attempts to engage the attention of the House of Commons, constituted as that assembly now is, unless he be a confirmed supporter or opponent of the administration, cannot conduce to the advantage of his country, his constituents, or of himself . . . One of the results of the severe struggle between the Whigs and Tories during the last twelve years, has been the annihilation of that section of the House, by whom the Minister of the day was frequently reminded, that his arbitrary will could not be allowed to prevail upon questions involving great principles of policy. Formerly, there were to be found among the representatives of the nation several independent members, who, although anxious to support the executive government, and refusing to attach themselves to a systematic opposition, never hesitated to express their disapprobation, of the minister's conduct, by speaking and voting against him . . .

The House of Commons at the beginning of the present session has only two sections – that which supported Sir Robert Peel's government, and that which adhered to the late administration . . . *parliament is virtually in abeyance*, and . . . the Ministers of the Crown can carry any measure, or change any law, not in consequence of . . . their prudence . . . but because the present government calculate upon the dread of the majority, that should they resign, their successors would be those statesmen who preceded them.

3.4.3 From a letter to Lord Stanley from Sir James Graham, 24 December 1839. Printed in C. S. Parker, Sir James Graham (1907), Vol. I, p. 289.

The possession of power in our popular form of government is the sole object of political warfare. The means used to obtain this end will vary in the circumstances, and must be guided by discretion. But it is not in human nature that a great party can be kept together by the abstract hope of checking the misconduct of a bad Administration, in the absence of the fixed purpose of displacing them . . . Let it once transpire that you are afraid to take the Government, and your party is gone . . .

3.4.4 From The Franchise, What Shall we do with it? (*Anon, 1858*).

Parties are split, broken up, or materially modified; Her Majesty's Ministers, and Her Majesty's Opposition, as our fathers knew them, two compact and always opposed bodies, are swept away, for which let us be thankful, since, besides other benefits, it increases the facilities for introducing such measure of Reform as the nation desires . . .

3.4.5 From a letter from Peel to his wife, 9 January 1828. Printed in C. S. Parker, Sir Robert Peel (1899), Vol. III, p. 150.

. . . I think we are entirely agreed upon the course to be pursued, namely that there ought to be a strong government in the House of Commons, and that it will not do to rely merely upon the violence of party spirit.

My view is to reunite the old Party, which was in existence when Lord Liverpool's calamity befell him. I cannot undertake the business of the House of Commons without more assistance than the mere Tory party, as it is called, would afford me.

ENGLISH PARTY POLITICS

*3.4.6 From Peel's reply to the King's Speech, 7 February 1833.
Printed in* The Speeches of Sir Robert Peel *(1853), Vol. II,
p. 612.*

He wished he could have said, that he reposed an increased confidence in
the present ministers; but that was not the case; he felt no disposition to
place an additional trust in them; his course therefore was determined
solely by public considerations, without one view of personal advantage.
The great change that had recently taken place in the constitution of the
House [*i.e. the 1832 Reform Act* – Ed.], justified and required from men
a different course of action. Formerly there were two great parties in the
state, each confident in the justice of its own view – each prepared to
undertake the government upon the principles which it espoused. All
the tactics of party were then resorted to, and justifiably resorted to, for
the purpose of effecting the main object – that of displacing the government. He doubted whether the old system of party tactics were applicable
to the present state of things – whether it did not become men to look
rather to the maintenance of order, of law, and of property, than to the
best mode of annoying and disquieting the government.

*3.4.7 From a letter to the King of the Belgians from Queen
Victoria, 17 March 1852. Printed in* The Letters of Queen
Victoria *(First Series, 1907), Vol. II, p. 464.*

One thing is pretty *certain* – that *out* of the *present state* of confusion and
discordancy, a *sound state* of *Parties* will be obtained, and *two parties*, as
of old, will again exist, without which it is *impossible* to have a *strong*
government. *How* these Parties will be formed it is impossible to say at
present.

3.4.8 From Alphaeus Todd, On Parliamentary Government in
England *(1866). Second edition 1887, Vol. I, p. 111.*

Party as well as parliamentary government originated with William III,
who, in 1696, constructed his first parliamentary ministry upon an
exclusively Whig basis. But the idea was unhappily abandoned by the
King in his subsequent administrations, and it was not until the House
of Hanover ascended the throne that Ministers were, as a general rule,
exclusively selected from amongst those who were of the same political
creed, or who were willing to fight under the same political banner.

3.4.9 From G. W. Cooke, The History of Party *(1837), Vol. I, p. vi.*

The conduct and revolutions of our two national parties occur but incidentally, even in the most comprehensive Histories of England: it is the object of the following work to separate from the mass of circumstances with which they are mingled, and weave them into a connected and detailed narrative . . .

In a recent number of the *Quarterly Review* . . . it is said 'we talk now as we did then' [in the reigns of Anne and George 1] 'of Whig and Tory, but the tenets of the two parties have been so completely counterchanged . . . that a Whig of that day resembled a Tory of ours, and *vice versa*'. The reader who contrasts this passage with the authorities cited in the following pages, will be inclined to wonder whether it proceeded from deplorable ignorance in the reviewer, or from his assumption of ignorance in his readers . . .

3.4.10 From Earl Grey, Parliamentary Government *(1864), p. 49.*

Parliamentary government is essentially a government by means of party, since the very condition of its existence is that the Ministers of the Crown should be able in general to guide the decisions of Parliament, and especially of the House of Commons; and all experience proves that no popular assembly can be made to act steadily under recognized leaders except by party organization.

3.4.11 From 'Independent Voting and Party Government', The Saturday Review, *28 February 1857.*

Nothing can be more attractive or plausible at first sight than the theory of independent voting in Parliament. Is our 'distinguished townsman', who bears, like a modern ATLAS, the terrestrial globe upon his shoulders, to become the follower of mortal man, the instrument of faction, the tool of a party? Forbid it, shade of LUCIUS JUNIUS BRUTUS! Forbid it, spirit of the British Constitution! So our borough HAMPDEN enters the Palace of the Legislature, big with the fate of nations and his own importance. He takes his seat below the gangway, with a virtuous resolution to hear both sides of every question, to weigh conflicting arguments, to be open to reason and deaf to eloquence – in short, to be, to present and future generations, the pattern of an 'independent member'. It certainly is impossible not to respect the intentions of such a man. We are almost constrained to exclaim, in the words which JOHNSON addressed to the sanguine freshman –

> Are these thy views? Proceed, ingenuous youth,
> And virtue guard thee to the throne of truth.

In fact, it is not very easy to argue against this view, without either offending the sensibilities of the individual, or affecting to think lightly of principles which no wise or good man will despise. But as, in a complicated calculation, when a man finds that he has arrived at an absurd or impossible result, he is convinced – however little he may be able, at the moment, to discover it – that there must have been some error in the working, so we cannot contemplate the present disorganization of the Parliamentary machine without feeling a conviction that somehow or other, the construction cannot be reasonable which leads to so irrational a conclusion.

The good old practice of Party Government was certainly one which presented many weak points to what Mr CARLYLE calls 'victorious analysis'. Nothing can be easier than to demolish with a crushing logic the partisanship of the Fox Club or the Conservative Association. Orators will find ready listeners when they denounce the servile system under which men follow their leaders like sheep, and act, not as reasonable units, but as a political sum total. In short, it is better to admit at once that, if Party is to be tried by a jury of Benthamites, with the Abbé SIEYES to preside in the Court, the sooner a plea of guilty on all the counts is put in the better. But if it is permitted to us to take the liberty – which, after all, has been an immemorial privilege of illogical and unphilosophical Britons – of beginning altogether at the wrong end, and of testing the system by its fruits instead of reasoning out the result from first principles, we shall perhaps find that this clumsy old machine of party government did its work to the full as well, to say the least, as the logical, symmetrical, and highly reasonable system of independent voting.

The fundamental object of all social organization is, if possible, that the influence of the best and the wisest, who are necessarily the few, should prevail over the weaker and the less wise, who are necessarily the many. This is equally true under all forms of Government, and perhaps it is more forcibly exemplified in the theory of popular than even of monarchical institutions. Now, party Government actually did give practical effect to this elementary requisite of political society, to a degree certainly very different from that which we find realized in the present state of Parliamentary disorganization. The heads of opposing parties were naturally elevated to the positions which they occupied, because they were the best and ablest men to promote the objects and to fight the battles of the 'connexion', as it was appropriately called. Hence the lead of the House of Commons became a species of elective monarchy for which there were but two candidates, each of them distinguished as the choicest champion of the principles which his party represented. The result was, that whichever party prevailed had for its fugleman the strongest and wisest man it could boast, and therefore the policy of the Government was the best which the temper of the people or the patriotism of their representatives admitted; while the Opposition, being also conducted by the ablest of its members, was compelled to pursue a course consistent with the character of persons who might themselves soon be invested with the responsibilities of office.

The opposite principles for which PITT and FOX respectively contended have their source in an antagonism which is as perpetual as the laws of the human mind. But it was an immeasurable advantage that 'stout Sir ANDREW' should vote according to the lights of Mr PITT, and that the 'Friends of the People' should take their constitutional doctrines from Mr FOX. While it was clearly understood that Mr PITT received the implicit support of his party, the convictions of the man became the policy of the Minister, and the government of the country was carried on just as if all the Tories had possessed exactly the same information, intelligence, and ability as Mr PITT; and the Opposition, in like manner, was compelled to conduct itself with the same prudence and patriotism as if each member of it had at stake the same position and reputation as Mr FOX. Thus it came about that the character of Parliament was an impress of the character of the chiefest men who composed it. No man entered the House of Commons as an individual unit, to exercise, independently of all the rest, the inharmonious influence of a second-rate intelligence. He either added the strength of his vote to the superior mind of the leader of his party, or, if capable of greater things, he achieved such a position as to make the rest the auxiliaries of his own more enlightened views. It was by this rude, but effectual method, that Party Government became what all Government should be – that of the best and wisest. It was, in fact, a true kingdom, in the original sense of the word – the Government of the 'knowing' man. Parliament took its character from the few and able, not from the many and weak.

Let us see whether the modern system of each man professing to vote according to his own lights, and not according to those of any leader, does not conduct to an exactly opposite and proportionately disastrous result. It is worthy of consideration how closely the practice of Parliamentary pledges is connected with the doctrine of independent voting. When a man was returned to Parliament as a member of the Tory party in former days, he went to support the policy of Mr PITT. No member was asked to pledge himself to vote in a particular manner on a particular question – the constituency were willing to trust that discretion to Mr PITT, who was probably a much fitter man to exercise it than themselves. And so the result was pretty nearly the same as if the worthy and independent electors of Mudborough had elected Mr PITT himself instead of Mr SMITH. It may be said that, under this system, Mr SMITH was a cypher; but then he was a cypher with the significant digit PITT or FOX, as the case might be, at its head, and so, though nought in himself, he contributed to the magnitude of the Party, and derived significance from its chief. But now that Mr SMITH comes forward, 'pledged to no party, but prepared to exercise his own judgement as an independent member of Parliament, &c., &c.', (in short, the cypher standing alone) it is natural that the Mudburghers, who have no particular knowledge of, or personal confidence in, Mr SMITH, should think themselves entitled to put him through a political Shibboleth. And so Mr SMITH goes into the House of Commons, as he imagines, a free and independent legislator, but in reality more 'cabined, cribbed, confined' by hustings pledges, and altogether much less of a free agent, than any member of the October Club who was brought down mellow to vote for his party. But the mischief does not stop here. If the intelligence of Mr SMITH is bounded by the opinions of the influential grocer, or the energetic class-leader, of Mudborough, the discretion of the Minister is equally limited by the range of Mr SMITH's vision. Having no party, he must have the votes of the independent members. A modern PITT, therefore, must propose, not the measures which seem good to himself, but those which he thinks likely to seem good to SMITH. Hence, it is the intellect of Mr SMITH, and not of a PITT or a FOX, that will, under the system of independent voting, impress its character on the Legislature. And, to pursue the logic of the old woman who begged 'the fire to burn the stick, and the stick to beat the dog, and the dog to bite the pig', we shall find in the end that, under this system, the influential grocer will govern Mr SMITH, and Mr SMITH will govern Mr PITT. And so, after all, it will be the grocer who governs the country – and this because, as an independent member, Mr SMITH thinks it more dignified to pledge himself to the grocer than to Mr PITT.

That this is not a chimerical danger may be easily perceived when we find the financial policy of a Government based on the fact that 'public opinion' – a phrase which will be found, on the whole, to mean the influential grocer and *The Times* newspaper – has expressed its desire that a particular tax should be fixed at a particular sum. We must learn to reverse our old phraseology, and to talk, for the future, not of a Minister who enjoys the confidence of the people, but of a people who enjoy the confidence of a Minister. It can no longer be said that public opinion supports the propositions of Government – Government proposes what public opinion will support. Ministerial responsibility is at an end, in virtue of the doctrine *respondeat superior*; for, at the present day, it is not the Minister who is the superior power. Parliament is demoralized because each independent unit votes with a view to the hustings, and thinks that he can escape the blame of the consequences in the motley herd among which he finds himself. The more prominent men, in losing command over their followers, lose the self-respect which responsibility engenders. It would be easy, were it necessary, to exemplify the fruits of Parliamentary independence. It may suffice if we commend to the consideration of those who have formed a conception of what Government ought to be, the spectacle of a Maynooth division or a Reform debate. They will probably be disposed to acquiesce in the conclusion, that the result of the substitution of independent voting for party Government has been to replace the rule of the few and wise by that of the many and foolish, and to make the lowest instead of the highest intelligence the measure of the Parliamentary standard.

3.4.12   From 'Parliamentary Opposition', The Edinburgh Review (January 1855), pp. 2 and 22.

. . . the distinctive mark of a free government is, not so much the mildness, moderation, or equity of its administration . . . as its permission of a free discussion of its measures . . . It is the legal and acknowledged existence of an organized opposition to the Government which is, in these times, the most salient characteristic of a free country, and its principal distinction from despotisms . . .

A Parliamentary Government is a government of political parties – and wherever it exists, the principal executive offices are filled by the members of the party which is in the ascendant. The criticism of the Government and of its acts is, therefore, carried on by the leaders of the less powerful parties, who are, for the time, excluded from office . . . Ultimately, the public constitutes itself into a jury to try the question at issue between the Government and the Opposition. For this reason, the reporting of the Parliamentary Debates in the daily press exercises a most important influence on the character of the debates themselves, and upon the conduct of the speakers. Though formally addressed to the assembly, they are often in reality spoken to the public at large.

3.4.13 From W. E. Gladstone, 'The Declining Efficiency of Parliament', The Quarterly Review *(June 1856), pp. 521, 550 and 570.*

At the time when Sir Robert Peel's Government was driven from office in 1846, it might upon the whole be justly said, that for a quarter of a century or more the work of legislation for the United Kingdom had been vigorously carried on . . . the condition of the people had undergone a marked improvement, and a general content among the masses . . . had taken the place of a sullen and restless estrangement . . .

Now all this had taken place under a system of party government: a system much maligned, much misunderstood, open no doubt to exception . . . but yet inseparably connected with the government of the country ever since the Crown ceased to be the predominating power in it, and our parliamentary institutions grew into their full development . . .

We now hear grey, or semi-grey politicians . . . descanting, before the admiring babies of the last ten years growth, on the comfort and satisfaction of the good old days of party government, before the great breakup of 1846. Ah! Those were times indeed. What close-running! What whipping-in! . . . it had other aspects. No doubt it was a time, when some men economized the labours of thought by casting wholesale on their leaders the responsibility of their votes . . .

Now, without at all arguing that there are no topics of comfort to be found . . . we very seriously desire to call attention to the disastrous nature of the change which has occurred, in its bearings upon the efficiency of Parliament . . . Given the House of Commons, made up of a party in power and a party out: it is plain that what we should desire on behalf of the country is, stimulus to what is right for the party in, self-restraint and circumspection for the party out. The former is supplied to the Government by the existence of an Opposition, and the Opposition finds the latter in the prospect of power . . . It is not a formal lesson; it is part of the Parliamentary atmosphere, which the British statesman breathes . . . it is high time that . . . we should come to facts, and point out . . . what may be termed as the paralysis of Parliament as the great organ of the constitution for its highest purposes. This is an evil which has been since the year 1846 of almost constantly growing force . . .

[The evil is] the absence of that tension on both sides which is the necessary condition of activity, and which can only result, according to all such experience as our history supplies, from the distribution of the mass of the two Houses of Parliament into parties under the guidance of those in whom confidence is placed . . . A strong Opposition makes a strong Government . . . so with a weak Opposition we have a weak Government, and with no Opposition we have, for the purposes of which we now speak, no Government at all . . .

. . . we must advert to . . . proceedings of the session, particularly in the department of legislation; and we regret to say they are characterized throughout not only by . . . incapacity . . . and [a] combination of levity with ineptness of purpose . . . a ponderous machine sways first in one direction and then in the other . . . sometimes the Minister manifesting his contempt for the House of Commons, and sometimes the House of Commons insisting that the Minister shall eat dirt, and both alike spending in their lateral and tortuous movements the strength, which ought unitedly to propel the legislative body along the path of careful and sedulous improvement . . .

We have already indicated the opinion which we ourselves entertain of the cause to which the evils we have described are principally due . . . It is . . . the dislocation of the old forms of party connection . . . Our complaint therefore is wholly practical, and is founded upon the two glaring facts, first that Parliament has of late years increasingly lost its capacity to make provision for the legislative wants of the country; and secondly, that it does not, under the present circumstances, venture to call the minister to account, when it thinks him wrong, from its ignorance of who is ready to succeed him . . . Want of mutual confidence, want of defined profession of political opinion, the uncertain sound of the trumpet of leaders, the yet more uncertain movement of the followers who should obey . . . seem to be the evils of which we ought to desire the removal.

3.4.14 From Sir John Walsh, M.P., The Practical Results of the Reform Act of 1832 *(1860), pp. 54, 80–1 and 153.*

We may conclude that the Conservatives are a tolerably united party, amounting to three hundred or near it, . . . we may assume that the remaining 350 or 360 members represent three or four divisions of political sects . . . Such a state of things appears to me the normal and permanent condition under the present composition of the House of Commons . . . we . . . have a weak Government, unable to follow out its own views, or to act upon its own convictions, and dragging on a precarious existence by a series of compromises and concessions. The best that can be said for such a state of affairs is that it is favourable to the *status quo* . . . national progress is, in fact, so self-sustained, and so little dependent upon legislative interference, that we may not fare worse for the want of great measures . . . I cannot, however, convince myself that occasions do not arise in which energy, decision, foresight, administrative vigour, are imperatively required; nor can I admit that a hopelessly weak executive is a good form of government . . .

Since the year 1832 the House of Commons has led the Ministry, instead of the Ministry leading the House of Commons. This state of things has become more confirmed since the great disruption of the Conservative Party on the Repeal of the Corn Laws, and the fall of Sir Robert Peel's ministry. It was an unhappy consequence of that great schism that it undid all he had effected in ten years, and extinguished the hope of fashioning the new system into an engine of stable government . . .

If we apply [a] rule of observation to foreign countries, and dismiss for the moment all enquiry into the more remote causes of the disappointments which have attended their efforts to engraft representative institutions upon their ancient systems, we shall find that the obvious and immediate cause of their failure was their inability to organize any . . . constant and steady majority.

Their assemblies, reflecting but too faithfully the confused state of opinions and interests in which the breaking up of old societies left them, represent a chaos of parties.

3.5 PARTY IN THE COUNTRY

3.5.1 From Coningsby *(1844), a novel by Disraeli, 1948 edition, pp. 90–1.*

Taper had his eye on a small constituency which had escaped the fatal schedules [*i.e. of the 1832 Reform Act* – Ed.], and where he had what they called a 'connection'; that is to say, a section of the suffrages who had a lively remembrance of Treasury favours once bestowed by Mr Taper, and who had not been so liberally dealt with by the existing powers . . . Tadpole, on the contrary, who was of a larger grasp of mind than Taper . . . was coquetting with a manufacturing town and a large constituency, where he was to succeed by the aid of the Wesleyans, of which pious body he had suddenly become a fervent admirer . . . The battue and the banquet were over; the ladies had withdrawn; and the butler placed fresh claret on the table.

'And you really think you could give us a majority, Tadpole?' said the Duke.

Mr Tadpole, with some ceremony, took a memo-book out of his pocket, amid the smiles and the faint well-bred merriment of his friends.

'Tadpole is nothing without his book,' whispered Lord Fitz-Booby.
'It is here,' said Mr Tadpole, emphatically patting his volume, 'a clear working majority of twenty-two' . . .
'There is nothing like a good, small majority,' said Mr Taper, 'and a good registration.'
'Ay! register, register, register!' said the Duke. 'Those were immortal words.'

3.5.2 From a letter to Arbuthnot from Peel, 8 November 1838. Printed in C. S. Parker, Sir Robert Peel (1899), Vol. II, p. 368.

Drayton Manor, November 8, 1838.

The Reform Bill has made a change in the position of parties, and in the practical working of public affairs, which the authors of it did not anticipate.

There is a new element of political power – namely the registration of voters, a more powerful one than either the Sovereign or the House of Commons.

That party is the strongest in point of fact which has the existing registration in its favour. It is a dormant instrument, but a most powerful one, in its tacit and preventive operation.

What a check it is at this moment upon the efficiency and influence of the existing government . . . Of what use is the prerogative of dissolution to the Crown, with an unfavourable registry . . . ?

The registration will govern the disposal of offices, and determine the policy of party attacks; and the power of this new element will go on increasing, as its secret strength becomes better known, and is more fully developed. We shall soon have, I have no doubt, a regular systematic organization of it. Where this is to end I know not, but substantial power will be in the Registry Courts, and there the contest will be determined.

3.5.3 From The Liverpool Standard (*April 1835*), *quoted in* The Times, *23 April 1835.*

In the present most unfortunate . . . state of the country, it is the duty of every man who has any regard for the land in which he lives, the church in which he worships, the liberty which he enjoys, to become a member of the Conservative Association formed in his own immediate vicinity. It is with no small degree of pleasure that we perceive that these valuable and important institutions are spreading far and wide, taking for their model the principle, on which the South Lancashire Conservative Association has been established.

3.5.4 From Sir Robert Peel, An Address to the Electors of the Borough of Tamworth (The 'Tamworth Manifesto' (1834).
Peel is seeking re-election under the rule that Members of the House of Commons who were appointed to a Ministry must seek the approval of their constituents.

My acceptance of the First office in the Government terminates for the present my political connection with you. In seeking the renewal of it, . . . I feel it incumbent upon me to enter into a declaration of my views on public policy – as full and unreserved as I can make it, consistently with my duty as a Minister of the Crown.

You are entitled to this from the nature of the trust which I again solicit, from the long habits of friendly intercourse in which we have lived, and from your tried adherence to me in times of difficulty . . . I gladly avail myself of this, a legitimate opportunity, of making a more public appeal – of addressing, through you, to that great and intelligent class of society . . . which is much less interested in the contentions of party than in the maintenance of order – the cause of good government – that frank exposition of general principles and views, which appears to be anxiously expected, and which it ought not to be the inclination, and cannot be the interest, of a Minister of the country to withhold.

3.5.5 From 'The Report from the Select Committee on the Registration of Voters' (1870). Printed in Minutes of Evidence, British Parliamentary Papers, Vol. VI, p. 64.
The chairman is questioning a lawyer in the registry courts on the work of political agents.

Your work in the revision courts is lightened to you by political agents more than by the overseers of parishes, is it not? – Yes, considerably so . . .

If there was no political association to look after the overseers, I suppose you would find the lists very badly kept, and you would have great confusion in your courts? – I should say so . . .

You deal for the most part with the political agents? – Just so; the agents attend me at almost all places and look after the business very well . . .

You think it is quite impossible to find an official in the counties who would do all the work that is now done by the political parties, and do it just as well? – Certainly; I think that the present people do it much more efficiently than any other parties you could possibly meet with.

But then, if the political associations carry on the registration work, do not the voters think that their votes go to the members of those associations who have been at the expense of substantiating their claim? – No, not always; I have known the contrary.

But that is so to a great extent, is it not? – They very often get taken in; but they both work their very hardest for their respective parties.

Do you not think that that is in itself a great evil? – If party spirit is an evil, no doubt it is a great evil; but how can you make it otherwise?

3.5.6 *From Sir Richard Vyvyan,* A Letter from Sir Richard Vyvyan to his Constituents (*1842*), *pp. 32–3 and 42.*

The cabals of the political clubs had no effect upon the elections of 1830; but during the last few years they have extended the influence of party, and brought it to bear upon the hustings of almost every constituency in the United Kingdom . . .

One of the consequences of the Reform Act was the diminution of the oligarchical influence, which previously compelled the Sovereign to select ministers from a limited class of candidates for office; but that influence, which was directed by a few individuals, many of whom were independent noblemen or gentlemen, professing allegiance to no party, has been replaced by the more degrading thraldom of irresponsible juntas . . . who confer with leading persons in almost every constituency in the kingdom. These club-committees regard independence as a parliamentary disqualification; they bring the whole interest of their party to bear upon election contests, and are more inveterate in their hostility against candidates professing independence, than against persons avowing attachment to the opposite party. In this respect, the Reform Act placed the Sovereign and the nation more at the mercy of an exclusive set of public men and their subordinate creatures, than was the case under the old system of nomination; the *bureaucratical* influence has been substituted for that of the aristocracy.

3.5.7 *From 'Tory and Reform Associations',* The Westminster Review (*October 1835*), *pp. 167, 170, 173, 176–8 and 184.*

The country is beset with political clubs and associations. This is an evil no doubt. But the evil is to be imputed much more to the state of the times, – and to the causes which have led to it, than to the associations themselves . . . Before the grave closed on George III . . . The mighty brotherhood of the middle and manufacturing classes, which in 1760 were as nothing, had grown into half the wealth and weight of the nation . . . The time was ripening for change . . . A powerful Parliamentary Opposition responded more and more to the rising voice from without, until political principles, which had been ridiculed on their first announcement, became the test of a party . . . [Clubs are] a sort of instruction which cannot be otherwise than useful in a country where the nomination of the principal governing power of the state resides in the people . . . But . . . we are not blind to the dangers which spring from . . . associations . . . Lord Stanley . . . expressly declares, 'that [your opponents] are those who appeal to the sympathy of the country for the maintenance of the freedom of conscience, and more especially of the deliberative powers of the House of Commons, uncontrolled by any other influence than that of the constituents of each member' . . . the 'Carlton Club' . . . was no mere new club established for the social meeting of gentlemen generally professing the same opinions, as Whites' or Brookes': from the first it was a political association organized for parliamentary and party purposes . . . It extended also to the country . . .

The following circular has fallen into our hands, and we submit it to the public, adding, merely for the sake of general information, that the persons composing the central committee, and whose names appear in the fourth resolution, are carefully elected from all the various classes of society, from the peer to the small tradesman. It is worthy of remark that in this, as in its prototype the Irish Orange Association, all the members of the central committee are recommended to form a chain of subcommittees, over which, each in his sphere presides as chairman. The following is the circular, with the resolutions of the committee:

WESTMINSTER CONSERVATIVE SOCIETY – DISTRICT OF ST JOHN

Sir, – I beg leave to transmit you a Copy of the Resolutions adopted at the General Meeting of the Westminster Conservative Society. In conformity with the sixth of those Resolutions, a Committee has been formed in this District, who request you will allow them to propose you as a Member of the Society. I have the honour to be, Sir, your obedient servant,

April, 1835.

P.S. – The favour of an early reply is requested.

At a Meeting of Electors and Inhabitants of the City of Westminster, interested in the support of Conservative Principles, held on Monday, the 2d day of March, 1835, at Willis's Rooms, King-street, St James's,

Lord Eliot in the Chair,

THE FOLLOWING RESOLUTIONS WERE UNANIMOUSLY PASSED

1. That a CONSERVATIVE SOCIETY having been established for the purpose of securing the fair and independent representation of the city and Liberties of WESTMINSTER in Parliament, and for promoting the Conservative Cause therein; – this Meeting earnestly recommends the Society to the support of such of the Constituency as entertain principles in accordance with their own. And that all persons, now assembled, do hereby enrol themselves as Members of the same.

2. That all Members of this Society do pay an annual Subscription, not exceeding One Guinea, and that the Treasurers be authorized to receive Donations to any amount.

3. That a CENTRAL COMMITTEE be appointed to promote the Election of Conservative Candidates for the City of WESTMINSTER, and to adopt such regulations as they may deem advisable for advancing the purposes of the Society. And that such Committee shall from time to time report to the Society at large.

4. That the following Gentlemen be Members of such Committee, with power to fill up vacancies, and to add to their numbers with the consent of an absolute majority.

Sir Francis Ommanney	Mr Barwise	Mr Eaton
Mr Walford	Mr Spike	Mr Wrangham
Mr Fraser	Mr Shadbolt	Mr Fisher
Mr Freeman	Mr Fincham	The Hon. R. C. Scarlett.
Mr Delwar		

5. That for the future no person shall be admitted, except by the Central Committee, upon the recommendation of two Members of the Society.

6. That Sub-Committees be immediately formed in the several Districts of the City, the Chairman of each of which shall be, ex-officio, a Member of the Central Committee.

7. That Lord ELIOT be appointed President of the Society, who shall be also, ex-officio, a Member of the Central Committee.

8. That the money raised by Subscriptions and Donations be applied to the legitimate expenses incidental to the Registry and the Election, and to the general purposes of the Society, with the approbation of the Central Committee.

9. That the thanks of this Meeting be given to Lord ELIOT for his upright and able conduct in the Chair, and for the part he has taken in establishing the Society.

Here we have the programme for a whole web of affiliated sections and members, from the Carlton Club down to the St John's Union; – the high, the low, and the middle classes, being all artfully dovetailed into a compact and well-disciplined body, ready to receive, transmit, and execute all necessary party instructions, and bidding fair to accumulate and exercise, if not duly checked, a great and irresponsible power in the state. The same system is in progress throughout the country; busily exercising its secret and extensive means of influence and intimidation. The political opinions of friends and dependents, of the smaller farmers, shopkeepers, manufacturers, and innkeepers, etc., are carefully enquired into; and they soon find themselves treated by the members of the association according to the results of those enquiries. The general and local associations keep up a communication with some confidential friend who *happens* to be a member of the Carlton Union. By means of this subterfuge the penalties of a corresponding society are evaded; although the club becomes not the less well acquainted with the political state of every borough and county in the three kingdoms. They learn who are the persons of influence on the spot or in the immediate neighbourhood – what are the prevailing opinions, prejudices, and grievances of the voters – what causes of offence may have been given by the present members – what reasons can be alleged for the failure of unsuccessful candidates. All this, and other more secret information, as touching the price of freemen, etc., when duly recorded, an ample basis on which to found electioneering operations. Lists of candidates are carefully prepared. The question of funds, with the several quotas of contribution from the candidate and the club, are all pre-arranged. Incidental contingencies are provided for; and each embryo candidate is instructed to hold himself in readiness to start, or to declare at a moment's warning. It is thus that all our boroughs and counties are secretly parcelled out, ticketed, labelled, tied up in red tape, and placed in rows on the shelves of the Carlton Union; in order, as Sir Thomas Hesketh pleasantly says, 'that the freedom of the House of Commons may be restored and secured!'

We have now given an outline of those Tory proceedings and attempts at a national organization for the control of elections, which have forced the formation of counteracting societies. We have examined their construction and their measures. We have found nothing dangerous in their proceedings: we have found them in accordance with the principles of their members. We can perceive no attempts at centralization of power; and, above all, we have observed no secrecy in their conduct which should lead to a suspicion of ulterior views. We have, therefore, no hesitation in declaring, that we give them our confidence; and the more so, we repeat, because they are formed in counter-action of clubs, whose construction, and connexions, are attempted to be shrouded in secrecy, and the conduct of whose members is in glaring inconsistency with the political principles and conduct of their lives.

If any Reformers do yet entertain doubts as to the policy which prompted the formation of the Reform Associations, still they must perceive, that the step has been taken, and is now irrevocable. Wherefore, surely it is their duty, as sincere Reformers, to give it the sanction of their names, and the weight of their councils, thereby to enable them to guide and restrict, if need be, the measures of those bodies to wise and useful purposes. In this point of view, we regret the fastidiousness which has kept every member of the Government, as well as every liberal Peer, apart from them. We trust this will speedily be altered; for, if it be be necessary for the Association to exist at all, then every great, good, and substantial Reforming name ought to be inscribed on its roll.

4   1867–1906

Introduction

THE CONSTITUTION

It was during this period that there emerged the conception of party government which was subsequently to dominate the British literature of constitutional interpretation. The acceptance of a cohesive two-party situation as a normal and permanent part of political arrangements combined with a recognition of the existence and importance of a national electorate to produce a view of British politics as involving competition between the two parties for the votes of a mass electorate. Political representation was increasingly seen as a matter of opposition between *parties*, rather than between the ancient institutions of King, Lords and Commons [4.1.1]. If one eighteenth-century view of the constitution could be expressed in terms of a balance of institutions, by the period between the first two Reform Acts this general view had been transformed into that notion of Parliamentary Government enshrined in Bagehot's 'English Constitution'. Opposition was now seen to be directed by the House of Commons against an executive (the Cabinet) *within* the House itself, and since the Cabinet depended upon the support of a majority in the Commons, the view that the Commons as *a whole* exercised the function of opposition to the executive could no longer be maintained. On the other hand, Bagehot's constitution could still be expressed in terms of the authority of the Commons; party labels were not ubiquitous enough, nor were their holders sufficiently cohesive in the lobbies, to prevent the possibility of governmental defeat in the House. When to these facts is added the general desire of the politicians of Palmerstonian England to resist the danger of instruction or domination by the electorate, the persistence of the general emphasis on Parliament as the centre of the constitution is easily explained. Party was important enough to allow older notions of the balance of powers to be confidently refuted, but not so all-important as to lead to a general denial of Parliamentary autonomy or importance.

The period following the 1867 Reform Act saw party developments which led some contemporaries to precisely this denial. The ubiquity of party labels [4.1.2] and the cohesion of party voting made governmental defeat in the Commons after the 1880s seem an abnormal occurrence. Governments were defeated at elections rather than on the floor of the House [4.1.4] and opposition was thus a matter not in any sense for the House as a whole but for that *permanent* minority of members within it who constituted the electorally defeated party [4.3.4]. This *party*, not the House, was the vehicle of opposition. The cumulative effects of this view of politics were seen most clearly in the widespread use of the term 'mandate' – which only made sense on the assumption of a government *capable* of carrying out its electoral promises because of the support provided by a disciplined parliamentary majority – and in the reforms introduced into the procedure of the House. The introduction of 'majority rule' procedures such as the 'guillotine' in the 1880s reflected a tendency to recognize that opposition was no longer an activity that might potentially come from *any* member of the House: it would always come from the same members – the opposition party [4.3.9]. The recognition of the fact that 'the majority of the House' was stable in its composition was also at the heart of Balfour's 1902 reforms in Supply procedure. Balfour described the fact that a majority of members of the House no longer had the function of opposing the executive in the following terms: 'After all, Charles I is not knocking at our door now, and our business now is not to fight with the Crown.'[1]

This substitution of a tension between two parties within the Commons for older views of a tension between three separate institutions as the dominant mode of constitutional interpretation was given added plausibility by the language used by contemporaries in defence of the House of Lords. That the Monarchy was no

[1] *Hansard*, Fourth Series, Vol. 101, c. 1313, 30 January 1902.

137

longer an autonomous political institution was widely accepted, but the position of the House of Lords was less clear. It is of great significance, therefore, that by the end of the nineteenth century the Lords were beginning to defend their legal powers not on the eighteenth-century grounds of institutional balance or the representation of significant interests, but in the language of popular sovereignty. The Lords were to act as a bulwark against the possibility of a government or a Commons majority proceeding without a mandate from the people [4.1.3]. The House of Lords was to be the guardian of electoral choice, and the mechanism by which party competition in elections was to be preserved. Thus was born the doctrine of party government; the two-party system was to replace Parliamentary sovereignty as the dominant category of constitutional thought, and concentration on such formal rules as Ministerial Responsibility was to be eschewed in pursuit of the study of party discipline and the vagaries of 'public opinion'. Party had arrived as a *constitutional* category.

PARTY IN THE COUNTRY

The 1867 Reform Act, by increasing the electorate in England and Wales from approximately one million to nearly two million voters (the increase in the boroughs was of the order of 140 per cent) presented a new stimulus to party organization, as did the further electoral reforms (such as the introduction of the secret ballot in 1872) which followed in its wake. Those who benefited most from the Reform Act were of the skilled tradesman and small shopkeeper sort, and they swelled the ranks of that provincial, urban dissenting opinion which was so important an element of Liberalism in the country by the 1850s.[2]

As had been the case after the 1832 Reform Act, the politicians were aware of the implications of electoral reform. Dissolution as a means of reaping the Parliamentary benefits of electoral popularity (as opposed to resolving a critical question) was evidence of this awareness[3] [4.2.1], and the Conservative appeal over the heads of the Commons after the 1878 Congress of Berlin a clear example. The extent to which elections were subject to party organization

[2] H. J. Hanham, *Elections and Party Management* (1959), p. xiii.
[3] J. P. Mackintosh, *The British Cabinet*, p. 179.

138

was cumulatively apparent: in the election of 1880 all except 39 of the English boroughs had Conservative candidates, the Liberals had only 9 duplicate candidatures, and 'deals' between the parties (involving the 'splitting' of two-member constituencies) were becoming rarer.[4] Gladstone's Midlothian campaigns were yet another example of the importance attached to direct appeals to the voters.

The increasing articulation of party structure in the country after 1867 was an important aspect of the above tendencies and involved changes in the organization of the professional and representative arrangements at both central and local levels. The developments at the central level involved the extension of the parties' capacity for professional electoral management. The Liberal Registration Association (renamed the Liberal Central Association in 1877), which by the 1880s housed the office of the Chief Whip and the principal Party agent, was founded in 1861. Its Conservative counterpart, the Conservative Registration Association (which in 1870 became the Conservative Central Office) was created in 1863–4. Such institutions represented an extension and consolidation of the professional electoral management implicit in the work of Bonham in the 1840s, and the close links with the parliamentary parties (*via* the office of the Whips) were also maintained. The need for political contacts of a more personal and social nature were satisfied by the foundation of such London clubs as the Constitutional and the Reform, which served as meeting-places for metropolitan and provincial politicians, and also undertook some functions of electoral supervision until this latter aspect became the monopoly of the central professional bodies in the 1880s.

Interest in the creation of central bodies which would represent the opinions of local party members and/or form a channel through which these members could be apprised of the policies and strategy of the central party was evident in the foundation of the National Union of Conservative Associations in 1867, and the National Liberal Federation in 1877. The National Union was seen as a body which would promote the formation of new local associations and co-ordinate the activities of existing ones; the idea of the representation of rank and file *opinion*, crucial to the foundation of

[4] B. McGill, '*English Parliamentary Parties, 1868–1885*' (Unpublished Ph.D. thesis, Harvard, 1953), pp. 291–308.

139

the National Liberal Federation, was (with the brief exception of Lord Randolph Churchill's campaign in the 1880s [4.2.12–13]) largely absent in the Conservative case [4.2.11].

These central institutions for the organization and co-ordination of professional electioneering and party membership were paralleled by, and assumed the existence of, local counterparts. By the 1880s professional organization at the constituency level had moved from the hands of the solicitors common to the period before 1867 to those of professional party registration agents in contact with the central professional bodies. Both the National Union and the National Liberal Federation were composed of the local clubs and associations which grew rapidly, especially in the urban areas, after 1867. There were both middle-class clubs and working-men's clubs. In some places the clubs were of a purely social nature, while in others social functions would be combined with electoral organization. In yet other constituencies the local party organization would consist of clubs of a social nature, while the work of electoral organization would be the specialized concern of a constituency association.[5] Until the middle of the 1870s, the Liberal party was less well-organized in the constituencies than were the Conservatives [4.2.4]. The National Union was formed mainly to set up working-men's clubs, and it broadened into a federation of all types of clubs and associations only after 1868. The Liberals, however, often relied for their constituency organization not on 'specialized' bodies of the club or association sort, but upon the great nonconformist interest groups such as the Liberation Society and the United Kingdom Alliance.[6] Not until after the electoral defeat of 1874 did the nonconformists merge their organizations with the formal Liberal organization, a combination which led to the formation of the National Liberal Federation in 1877. This difference between the constituent elements of the two parties and the manner in which the respective rank-and-file party organizations evolved is of great significance in explaining differences in attitudes to the role of the party organization, and the bitterness of the debate which revolved around 'the caucus'.

By the 1880s the main outlines of the structure of modern party organization in the country had been established. There were professional bodies at the centre, working closely with the

[5] Hanham, pp. 103–10.
[6] Ibid., p. 117.

parliamentary parties and with their counterparts in the constituencies, and the National Liberal Federation and the National Union represented the 'popular' aspects of the party: the co-ordination and combination of the constituency clubs and associations to which the rank-and-file party members belonged.

On the other hand, patterns of behaviour prevalent before the Second Reform Act (and limiting the development of articulate central party arrangements) still persisted. Until at least the middle 1870s, party organization was primarily a local matter, with the central institutions playing a limited and co-ordinating part. As late as 1885, the business of professional electioneering was still centred around the registration agent in the constituency, and the early work of the Liberal Registration Association was to organize the registration only in those constituencies which did not possess any local party organization appropriate to this task. Moreover, the local focus of party organization (until the 1880s) reflected the prevalence of localism in attitudes to politics, and the persistence of old habits of deference and patronage. The 1868 election revealed this.[7] Not until well into the 1870s did the formal central party organizations become dominant even in the large towns, and the extension of this organization outside the large urban areas and the general decline of the older political tendencies were provoked mainly by the depression of the 1880s.[8] The appeal to a national opinion explicit in the language of Gladstone and Disraeli between 1867 and 1880 is also to be explained by the prevalence of older habits in Parliament itself; it was to some extent a means of overcoming the unreliability of parliamentary majorities[9] [4.3.14].

The gradual and sporadic extension of a national, formalized, party organization was the product of a variety of tendencies. Legislation on the Secret Ballot and the Elimination of Corrupt Practices in Elections facilitated the participation of newer middle-class groups whose attitudes to party organization were quite different from those of the older types of local leaders, and the redistribution of parliamentary seats in 1884 did much to reduce localism. The railways and the telegraph continued to facilitate communication between province and metropolis, the spread of

[7] McGill, p. 50.
[8] Hanham, p. xv.
[9] Mackintosh, p. 166.

parliamentary party labels (by the election of 1874 it was apparent that electors were thinking of elections much more in terms of a choice between two national party labels)[10] and the development of the Press. Finally, the growth of party organization itself did much to create a national electorate. After 1877 the National Liberal Federation made a conscious attempt to standardize party organization and to promote issues on a national basis (for example, its enthusiastic support of Gladstone's anti-Turkish crusade in 1877–78).

The creation of the National Liberal Federation in 1877 is a reminder that not all the developments in party organization in the later nineteenth century were straightforward matters of the organizing of votes for existing parliamentary parties: party 'machines' could be driven in very different directions by very different kinds of drivers. If it is largely true that the debate about 'the caucus' elevated the Federation to a position of unreal importance, it is equally true that the same debate revealed a great deal about late-nineteenth-century attitudes to politics-at-large. The activities of at least some groups within the Federation represented an attitude to politics, which, while never dominant in the English political tradition, has never been entirely obliterated, and was to be inherited by some sections of the Labour Party. The foundation of the National Liberal Federation in 1877 reflected, in part, the desire of the Radicals for a popular representative organization through which the policies of Hartington and the Whigs could be challenged. The need for such a centralized popular opposition to the party leadership had seemed obvious to Joseph Chamberlain in particular, as a result of his experiences on the Liberal Registration Association. Looked at in another way, the National Liberal Federation was to be the means by which Birmingham principles and men might control the destinies of the Liberal party – both Chamberlain and Frank Schnadhorst (the secretary of the Federation) had been prime movers in the creation of the 'Birmingham Caucus' after 1867[11] [4.2.3].

Thus there was from the beginning in Liberal popular organization at both local and central levels an element of provincial and extra-parliamentary opposition to the existing party leadership and policy which, with the short-lived exception of the activities of

[10] Hanham, p. 209, et seq.
[11] Ibid., p. 38.

Churchill and Gorst in the 1880s, was absent in the Conservative case. While the need for organization as a response to the Second Reform Act was an important element in the creation of both the 'Birmingham 600' and the National Liberal Federation, it did not override the fact of nonconformist concern with issues of policy in general, and their campaign for non-sectarian education in particular. The National Education League (for example) had as much to do with Liberal developments in organization after 1867 as had the intricate voting procedures of the Reform Act itself,[12] and the nonconformist flavour of Liberal organization was manifest in such things as the structure of the Birmingham caucus, with its obvious affinities with Wesleyan church democracy[13] [4.2.8]. None the less, whatever the motives of those who were involved in the reform of party organization, the consequences of reform for the structure of party in the country were plain: the advent of standardization. By the 1880s, party organization in Britain was national in scope, and possessed similar features in both parties:[14] the Conservatives, as well as possessing their own inherited patterns of organization, had learned much from the National Liberal Federation [4.2.2].

The debate which occurred about the activities of 'the caucus' in the late nineteenth century revolved around two questions. First, there was disagreement over the desirability of the electoral control or instruction of Members of Parliament. Second, even where such control or influence was regarded as desirable, it did not necessarily follow that organizations such as the National Union or the National Liberal Federation would be regarded as acceptable means of translating the 'popular will' into political action. The structures of these bodies were viewed in many quarters as leading to the distortion of public opinion, either because local and central arrangements were by no means as democratic as defenders such as Chamberlain tried to show [4.9], or because the interests represented by party members as a whole at both central and local levels were not identical with the interests of the voters themselves [4.2.7–8].

The debate tended to concentrate on the Liberal party, since the positive role assigned to the party in the country by Chamberlain

[12] F. Herrick, 'The Origins of the National Liberal Federation', *Journal of Modern History*, 1945, **27**, *passim*.
[13] McGill, p. 9.
[14] Hanham, p. 133.

and Schnadhorst had no real counterpart on the Conservative side. The relationship between the Federation and the Liberal party in Parliament became a serious consideration after 1880, since the pressure of the organization was then being asserted upon the party when in office, and the attempts to use local organizations to push Members of Parliament in particular directions were a clear challenge to Parliamentary and executive authority.[15] But while the rhetoric of Federation Radicalism caused many to fear for the Parliamentary constitution [4.2.6], the actual threat posed by local and central popular organizations was small. Their sanctions were very few and Members of Parliament were often protected from the pressure of local Radicalism by the existence of divisions within the local associations.[16] Radicalism in the central Federation, moreover, was hamstrung by both the refusal of some local organizations (for example, in Lancashire [4.2.9]) to accept the Federation as much more than a Birmingham bid for unrepresentative hegemony, and by the financial independence of local parties, which for the most part deprived the central party institutions of a potential disciplinary weapon.[17] Nor was the local party's power to withdraw the party label from wayward Members of Parliament a means of certain success. Divisions within the association concerned might do much to mitigate such threats; the acceptance of such a sanction as legitimate was by no means universal;[18] and while voting for the party label rather than the individual candidate was a marked feature of voting by the 1874 and 1880 elections, it too was far from universal. The most careful historian of late-nineteenth-century party organization has concluded that the 'chief characteristic of party organization in the nineteenth century was its impotence'.[19] While the Radical view of politics as a matter of translating the popular will into legislation through the domination of a popular party organization was a somewhat novel view of politics (which the Labour party was to inherit) and one which did much to give Liberal (and, later, Labour) organization a very different flavour from its Conservative counterpart, it never became, in the long run, a major or successful theme in party history [4.2.10].

[15] Ibid., p. 146.
[17] Ibid., p. 369.
[19] Ibid., p. 347.

[16] Ibid., p. 143.
[18] Ibid., p. 290.

PARTY IN PARLIAMENT

It was during this period that a correlation between party label and voting habits was established in both the parliamentary and the electoral spheres. In Parliament, as in the country, neither the fact of party voting nor its widespread acceptance as the normal state of affairs was established before the 1880s [4.3.14]; as late as 1871 Lowe recast his budget after a series of adverse divisions in the House.[20] But by the 1890s, voting cohesion in the House of Commons was widely regarded as one of the facts of life. Spender, writing in 1927, could look back upon the 1890s in the following light:

'It seems a miracle, . . . that the Government of 1892 should have survived for three years. Its chief task, the passing of the Home Rule Bill, was foredoomed to failure; during the second half of its existence it could never reckon on a majority of more than 20; it was rent internally by the personal rivalries which the departure of Mr Gladstone precipitated. Yet never in the subsequent years can I remember such discipline as was imposed on and cheerfully accepted by the rank and file of M.P.s at this period. They lived in the House of Commons, attended every division, and never grumbled or threatened. Yet one heard perpetually of the troubles within, of the 'dreadful day' which Mr Gladstone had had with Queen Victoria, of Harcourt's rising tempers, of the struggles in the Cabinet over this or that detail of the Home Rule Bill, of the incessant battles over Estimates.'[21]

Defences of this state of affairs were offered in abundance, but do not override what is perhaps the most significant characteristic of party voting by the 1890s: the extent to which it was simply taken for granted. As Lowell remarked, 'a member of the House of Commons may be unconscious of party pressure, and of a gradual increase in that pressure, so long as it is natural, continuous, and evenly distributed'.[22]

[20] Mackintosh, p. 166.
[21] J. Spender, *Life, Journalism and Politics* (1927), Vol. I, p. 55.
[22] A. L. Lowell, *Government*, Vol. I I, p. 86.

The general facts about the character of party voting are easily established.[23]

PARTY UNITY 1860-1908

Coefficients of Cohesion

Year		Liberals	Conservatives
1860	All Divisions	59·8	57·3
	Whip Divisions*	58·9	63·0
1871	All Divisions	71·7	76·2
	Whip Divisions	75·5	74·0
1881	All Divisions	82·0	82·9
	Whip Divisions	83·2	87·9
1894	All Divisions	86·9	94·1
	Whip Divisions	89·8	97·9
1899	All Divisions	84·3	94·2
	Whip Divisions	82·5	97·9
1906	All Divisions	93·2	89·8
	Whip Divisions	96·8	91·0
1908	All Divisions	95·0	88·4
	Whip Divisions	94·9	88·3

*i.e. *Divisions where Government whips were issued, irrespective of the actions of the opposition party.*

[23] The following tables are taken from S. H. Beer, *Modern British Politics* (1965), pp. 257–8. Beer calculates the index of party cohesion on the basis that a division in which the members of a party divide 50:50 represents zero cohesion. The index is given by taking the proportion of party members on one side of a division, dividing the result by 50 and converting into a percentage. The figures are based on a sample of 1 in 10 divisions for the relevant years.

The Whipping figures show the proportion of divisions in which *at least one* of the parties issued whips.

Cf. A. L. Lowell, at Section III, f. 60.

Increase in Whipping, 1836-1908

Governing Party

Year	Liberals	Conservatives
1836	48·9	
1850	68·3	
1860	66·9	
1871	82·1	
1881	96·6	
1883	78·2	
1890		79·7
1894	90·2	
1899		85·7
1903		86·5
1906	92·2	
1908	95·7	

An explanation of the emergence, by the 1880s, of a House of Commons in which to vote with one's party was to do the expected thing, must be offered in terms of a variety of contemporary circumstances. First, there was the introduction into the House of Commons of that attitude to party – similar in form (though not in content) to that of Radicalism in the country – represented by the Irish Nationalists [4.3.10–13]. To the Irish, party discipline was a weapon for disruption rather than stability, to be used with regard to its consequences for Irish politics and without regard to its effects on English parliamentary life. By August 1884 the Irish group in the House of Commons had achieved a cohesion in word and deed hitherto unknown in England, based upon those sanctions which English parties lacked – an absence of basic internal differences, payment of M.P.s from a central party fund, and such passionate support from Irish public opinion that effective competition from other local groups was rendered impossible.[24] Though not to be regarded as part of the English party situation in any real sense, the Irish party structure and its potentialities for ends other than mere disruption did not pass unnoticed by English politicians.

Individual factors also played a part. Disraeli's managerial ability and willingness to use party organization as a means of

[24] C. C. O'Brien, *Parnell and his Party* (Oxford, 1957), pp. 142, 148–9, 265.

147

conciliation had been demonstrated in the course of the Reform Bill [4.3.7–8], and were in evidence in the years that followed. Gladstone's concern with principle, and his temperamental preference for 'leadership' rather than 'management' stood in contrast to the Disraelian outlook, and were very much connected with the greater difficulties of cohesion which the Liberals experienced [4.3.15; 4.2.4;3.3.19].

The character of the 'new men' in politics after 1867 constituted a third factor. Impatience with older and aristocratic forms of management was an important element in nineteenth-century provincial opinion, and in this sense the pressure for Civil Service Reform was consistent with the organizational interests of Chamberlain, Schnadhorst and (to a lesser extent) Gorst. To such opinion, party cohesion in the House of Commons represented a manner of conducting business superior to that of an earlier and more easy-going age.[25] Most of the reservations about party cohesion came, significantly enough, from members reared in that earlier age, and to whom the view of Parliament as an efficient machine for manufacturing legislation was singularly distasteful [4.3.16].

The willingness to regard Parliament as a legislative machine which was so important a feature of late-nineteenth-century politics mixed easily enough with a view of party which had grown steadily since the beginning of the century: that the increased legislative activity consequent upon a wider conception of governmental duties and the need for stable government were both, in their different ways, incompatible with 'independent' voting in the House.[26] As in earlier periods, such attitudes to the place of government and legislation were manifested most clearly in changes in parliamentary procedure. The view that such changes in the 1880s were in the main due to Irish obstruction does not easily fit the facts. The Radicals in particular had obvious interests in majority rule in the Commons, and opinion in general saw these reforms as more or less appropriate to changing conceptions of the responsibilities of government[27] [4.2.6; 4.3.2]. Moreover, the view of politics as simply matters of legislation and of deference to popular opinion [4.3.7] effected party cohesion in another, more indirect, way. National election campaigns were implicit in such a view, and while

[25] Mackintosh, p. 188.
[26] Ibid., p. 120.
[27] Redlich, *Procedure*, Vol. I, Part II, Chapters 1 and 2.

the parties might be more or (as in the case of the Liberals) less successful in creating an agreed party 'line', the widespread acceptance of the need for such 'lines' was itself a means by which individual M.P.s came to see themselves as elements within a like-minded party community. Such communal feelings were reinforced by the existence of national party organizations in the country [4.3.6] and the related phenomena of ubiquitous party labels and a party-minded electorate. The knowledge that by the 1880s M.P.s were increasingly being elected because they possessed a national party label was an obvious factor in the growth of a communal party feeling in the House.

It is important to realize, however, that this view of parties as national, articulately-organized and increasingly 'disciplined' groups is not evidence for the view that parties were based on clear differences of principle. The lack of effectiveness on the part of the organizations in the country has already been discussed, and in Parliament itself cohesion was a matter of disciplined voting rather than unanimity of opinion [4.3.15]. This combination of a plurality of opinion with unity in the lobbies is explicit in the remarks of Spender as quoted above, and few contemporaries outside the Radical ranks saw electoral and parliamentary unity as implying any great diminution in the diversity of opinions. Rather, voting cohesion was seen in terms of its constitutional and governmental context [4.3.1]; diversity was not trodden under the boots of the Whips, but was often to be expressed through channels other than the division lobbies [4.3.3]. The recognition of the need for legislation and for increased, consistent governmental activity [4.3.8], together with the obvious advantages of unity in the face of a party-minded electorate, all entailed the emergence of newer forms of expression and the decline of older forms of dissent. Salisbury, along with many other contemporaries, was conscious of the extent to which influence was increasingly exerted in private and party contexts rather than on the floor of the House.[28] The attempt to exert parliamentary influence by defeating particular government measures while keeping the government in office had little of the respectability which it had enjoyed in the 1840s, and in these circumstances a vote which might cause the Government to fall was not to be cast lightheartedly.[29]

[28] Mackintosh, p. 207.
[29] Ibid., p. 177.

The conciliation of opinion, then, was no longer entirely a public activity undertaken on the floor of the House, and division lists could no longer be regarded as a reasonable guide to the diversity of opinion. But that conciliation was involved, and that a sort of self-denial on the part of back-benchers was a vital aspect of this situation, is beyond doubt. Party management has always been a more appropriate description of this situation than party 'discipline', particularly in the late nineteenth century when the sanctions possessed by the parliamentary leaders were even less than in more recent times. The same limitations which applied to the central party organizations in the country applied equally to the leaders in Parliament.[30] To describe the activities of the latter in the language of 'coercion' or 'discipline' is to misunderstand the constitutional and governmental context within which they worked. Opinions about the place of the electorate and the responsibilities of government were, by the late nineteenth century, very different from those general a half-century before. The politicians were both adjusting to such changes and bringing them about, and party cohesion was what emerged from these attempts. What were seen as the necessities of governance are more important than clear divisions of principle or the 'power to discipline' as explanations of party activity in the Parliaments of this and succeeding periods [4.3.1].

The view that politics in the late nineteenth century has its own momentum, not reducible to crude conceptions of 'power' or 'principle', is open, as always, to the argument that it is reducible to considerations of class. That this view is as misleading in this as in any other period can easily be shown: party divisions and party unity are not to be explained in this way. The House of Commons after 1867 was significantly different in composition from the Parliaments which followed the first Reform Act: the Parliaments which sat after 1867 were much more representative of industrialism. The new men and the new opinions were a phenomenon of the 1870s and the 1880s, but their distribution between the parties is significant; the most recent study of the 'class basis' of the parliamentary parties between 1868 and 1880 has revealed that both were cross-sections of the same community.[31] Briefly, the position was that those members whose interests lay solely in the land formed less than a third of the House of Commons, but that

[30] Hanham, p. 147.
[31] McGill, p. 132, et seq.

150

the Tories represented land to a greater extent than did the Liberals. Neither party, however, was without an important landed element, and in both parties members with at least some interests in business or commerce constituted the majority. Further, even if the 'centre of gravity' was nearer to the landed interest in the Conservative Party, the most important instance of internal party division in the late nineteenth century – the Liberal split over Home Rule – cannot be explained in 'class' terms. The Liberals who rebelled against Gladstone's Irish Home Rule proposal in 1886 were a combination of Whig landowners such as Landsdowne, and urban Radicals such as Chamberlain and Goschen. If the net effect of this division and the subsequent merging of the Liberal dissentients with the Conservatives was to increase the extent to which the landed interest was Conservative, it also gave to the Conservatives a number of major middle-class Radical leaders and left both parties 'unrepresentative' (in the 'class' sense) of an electorate in which the working classes were now in a majority. Nor, as is always the case, did class position have any necessary relation to party-political opinion; the new 'middle class' opinions were well represented by Conservatives such as Gorst, Cross and W. H. Smith. The fact that such class divisions were not seen by contemporaries themselves as the basis of political allegiance is shown by the 1886 Liberal split, after which some of the most 'extreme' representatives of the 'new men' went over to the Conservatives on issues which combine the questions of Empire sentiment and national security. If it is true that 'class feeling' is an important aspect of late nineteenth-century politics, it does more to explain differences between the House and the country than between the parties in the House.

PARTY RHETORIC

Political opinion in the country at large was subject to significant changes by the 1880s. It has already been observed[32] that opinion in the country between the first two Reform Acts could be described in terms of a 'popular radical' alliance between the middle and working classes, and that this was not significantly represented in Parliament until after 1867. During the 1870s the views of

[32] See above, e.g. p. 79. and Clark, *The Making, passim.*

provincial urban Dissent came much more into their own, and both parties were affected. The relationship between the National Liberal Federation and such opinion has already been discussed, but the Conservatives were also (though to a lesser extent) involved. The criticisms of Conservative organization after the election defeat of 1880, expressed by Gorst, Churchill and Wolff, reflected the character of 'new opinion', and was accompanied by similar pressure from local associations within the party. This anti-aristocratic criticism of those responsible for the management of the party had its roots in the emergent popular radicalism of the 1840s, and its success in winning greater representation for provincial Conservatism within the National Union in 1886, has been called 'the Conservative Party's 1832'.[33] In this sense, 'Tory Democracy' must be seen as a response to the claims of opinions which had taken on a recognizable form by the 1850s, and a good deal of which Gladstone had succeeded in harnessing to the Liberal party.

But if popular radical opinion was a significant element in Parliament and parties by the 1870s, in the country as a whole a new division of opinion was emerging which, by the beginning of the twentieth century, was to make a popular radical Parliament as 'unrepresentative' of the country as landed Parliaments had been between the first two Reform Acts [4.4.8]. What was involved in this new division of opinion was the development of an identifiable 'class politics', in which the working class increasingly detached itself from its previous alliance with the middle classes, and began to cultivate a sense of political autonomy [4.4.1].

The manifestations of this tendency were many and various. Political rhetoric itself began to use 'working class' in the singular rather than in the plural sense, revealing a novel lack of emphasis on the differences between working-class groups and a concentration on their common characteristics which was manifest in the attempts to form 'general unions'.[34] Such opinion had more in common with the rhetoric of Chartism than with that of the Anti-Corn Law League, and was prepared to think of legislation as a means of social amelioration to an extent which popular radicalism had seldom reached. The creation of a Labour Representation

[33] J. Cornford, 'The Transformation of Conservatism in the Late Nineteenth Century', *Victorian Studies* (September 1963).

[34] A. Briggs, 'The Language of Class in Early Nineteenth Century England' in J. Saville and A. Briggs (eds.), *Essays in Labour History* (1960).

Committee in 1900 was provoked by this emergent class view of politics,[35] and while class politics was at first the prerogative of unskilled sections of the working population, the skilled-labour interest which had been an important element of popular radical support for Liberalism by the 1850s[36] was by the 1880s both more suspicious of Liberalism and increasingly less opposed to some form of independent working-class political representation. These tendencies are also observable in changing voting habits by the 1880s, where the Conservatives appeared increasingly successful in attracting middle-class voters from Liberalism.[37]

It is important, however, to keep a clear perspective on these tendencies. Emergent view of class politics never entirely replaced the older divisions of popular radicalism [4.4.10], and these two divisions taken together by no means account for all political opinion in the late nineteenth century [4.4.5; 4.4.12]. Nor was either kind of division reflected in a clear form in Parliament or in the parties. The middle-class nature of late-nineteenth-century Parliaments makes it impossible to think of party divisions in class terms: not until the Labour Party was well-established in Parliament was it even plausible to explain parties in terms of class politics. It was precisely these cross-currents of opinion which gave variety and confusion to party rhetoric in this period. The rhetoric was fairly uniform, emphasizing programmes and 'party lines' – a consequence of electoral circumstances after 1867 and thus something which had not been characteristic of the politics of the years before the Second Reform Act.[38]

The content of the rhetoric, on the other hand, was not something which easily distinguished one party from another. It is true that Radicalism by the 1880s had become much more concerned with state action and social (as opposed to political) reform than its forebears in the 1840s [4.4.9]; by the beginning of the twentieth century suspicion of government and legislation had become the hallmark of the 'right' rather than, as had been the case since the 1780s, of the 'left' [4.4.7]. But Radicalism of this 'collectivist'

[35] The emergence of labour is discussed in Volume Two.
[36] Vincent, *Formation*, p. 78.
[37] Cornford, op. cit.; R. K. Ensor, 'Some Political and Economic Interactions in later Victorian England', *Transactions of the Royal Historical Society*, 1949, **4** (21), 17.
[38] Lowell, Vol. I, p. 446.

variety was not a dominant factor in the Liberal Party, not wholly to be found within its ranks [4.4.6], and not regarded by all emergent socialists as adequate to the circumstances. The diluted form of 'Manchester School' principles which was characteristic of Gladstonian Liberalism was always highly resistant to collectivist views. Gorst is an example of a Conservative who was as collectivist as many who bore the Radical label,[39] and Keir Hardie and J. R. MacDonald were among many working-class politicians who came up against the unwillingness of ostensibly 'progressive' Liberal associations to adopt candidates of their kind. Even if it is admitted that Radical collectivism received more of a hearing in the Liberal than in the Conservative party, it remains the case that such Radicals and their socialist counterparts formed a minority among party politicians as a whole. As was to be the case in the twentieth century, the political 'left' was often as much at variance with the majority of the party in which it took anchor as with the rival party itself.

The Collectivist rhetoric which accompanied the emergence of class politics is difficult to describe in terms of party labels, and this is equally true of the persistence of the older divisions of popular radicalism. Diluted versions of 'Manchester School' views found an important place in Conservative rhetoric in this period, a fact not unconnected with the Conservative's success in attracting the electoral support of many who had hitherto found a home in the Liberal party. But the description of late-nineteenth- and early twentieth-century Conservatism by a modern historian as 'sceptical of change' and 'frightened of socialism'[40] [4.4.2; 4.4.4] would apply equally well to large numbers of Liberals [4.4.11], and, as the same historian admits, does not exclude a recognition of Conservative views of a more 'interventionist' kind. Tariff Reform was a case in point, as was the pressure for social reform which came from Radicals such as Chamberlain who joined the Conservative ranks after 1886. In short, neither the opinions of popular radicalism, nor those of the class politics which was tending to replace it, could be easily identified with formal divisions between the parties [4.4.3]. The same is true in the (rather different) area of foreign affairs. Irish Home Rule and the Boer War were issues which split the Liberal Party in a serious manner, and in the former case many of

[39] B. B. Gilbert, 'Sir John Gorst: Conservative Rebel', *The Historian* (Spring 1956), especially p. 151.
[40] R. B. MacDowell, *British Conservatism, 1832–1914* (1959), p. 137.

the most bitter opponents of the policy were Radicals. 'Imperialism', like all the other 'isms' of the period, was not a party doctrine,[41] except perhaps in those cases where it could be identified with the question of Tariff Reform; it is yet one more reason for distinguishing clearly between identifiable divisions of opinion, and the formal divisions of party.

The clearest tests of party affiliation in the period – the Tariff Reform question and religion – also provide the clearest evidence for the need to make the above distinctions. Tariff Reform was prosecuted only by Conservatives, and bitterly opposed by the Liberals; yet it was precisely this issue which split the Conservative party after 1903, led some of the Conservative free-traders seriously to consider an electoral alliance with the Liberals,[42] and was a constant source of internal party friction until the early 1930s. The religious issue was clearly an important point of party difference after the 1860s;[43] the issues of the abolition of compulsory church-rates, the disestablishment of the Irish Church and the removal of religious tests in the universities of Oxford and Cambridge, produced clear party divisions in the House of Commons[44] and were ample evidence of the extent to which Liberalism saw itself as the vehicle of popular radicalism, notwithstanding the fact that Gladstone's own religious sympathies lay with High Church Anglicanism. But even this division was to dissolve. Dissent was deeply divided on the questions of Irish Home Rule and the Boer War;[45] and by the time of the Conservative–Liberal disputes over the Education and Licensing Act in the early years of the twentieth century, Dissent was less the conscience of the Liberal party than a convenient source of morale and opposition to the Conservatives which could be invoked by a hard-pressed Liberal leadership in its hour of need. The 'ideological' interpretation of English party divisions in the late nineteenth century is inadequate not only on account of its often-misplaced faith in the role of 'principles' in practical political activity, but also because of the impossibility of translating divisions of principle into divisions of party.

[41] D. Rubinstein, '*The Decline of the Liberal Party, 1880–1900* (Unpublished Ph.D. Thesis, University of London, 1956), p. 240.

[42] H. W. McCreedy, 'The Revolt of the Unionist Free-Fooders', *Parliamentary Affairs*, Spring 1963.

[43] Ensor, p. 20.   [44] McGill, p. 143.

[45] J. F. Glaser, 'English Nonconformity and the Decline of Liberalism', *American Historical Review* (January 1958), p. 355.

4 1867–1906

Documents

THE CONSTITUTION

4.1.1 *From* A. L. Lowell, The Government of England (*1908*). *1920 edition, Vol. 1, p. 437.*

If the predominance of the House of Commons has been lessened by a delegation of authority to the Cabinet, it has also been weakened by the transfer of power directly to the electorate. The two tendencies are not, indeed, disconnected. The transfer of power to the electorate is due in part to the growing influence of the Ministers, to the recognition that policy is mainly directed, not by Parliament, but by them . . . No doubt, the ministry depends for its existence upon the good pleasure of the House of Commons; but it really gets its commission from the country as a result of a General Election. Even if its life should be cut short by the Commons, the new Cabinet would not now rest for support upon that Parliament; but would at once dissolve and seek a fresh majority from the electors. This was by no means true forty years ago. The Parliament elected in 1852, which sat a little more than four years, supported during the first half of that time a coalition Ministry of Liberals and Peelites, and during the second half a ministry of Liberals alone. Nothing of the kind has occurred [since 1868]. Every subsequent change of ministry has either been the immediate consequence of a General Election, or if not, the new Cabinet has kept the old Parliament together only so long as was absolutely necessary to dispose of current business, and has then appealed to the people. Practically, therefore, a change of ministry today is either the result of, or is at once ratified by, a General Election.

4.1.2 From W. S. Gilbert's libretto for Iolanthe *(1882).*

When in the House MPs divide,
If they've a brain and cerebellum, too,
They've got to leave that brain outside,
And vote just as their leaders tell 'em to.
But then the prospect of a lot
Of dull MPs in close proximity,
And thinking for themselves, is what
No man can face with equanimity.
Then let's rejoice with loud Fal-lal-Fal-lal-la!
That nature wisely does contrive – Fal lal la!
That every boy and every gal
That's born into the world alive,
Is either a little Liberal,
Or else a little Conservative!
Fal lal la!

4.1.3 From a speech from The Marquis of Salisbury at Liverpool, *13 April 1882, pp. 4–5*

Undoubtedly, representative institutions . . . occupy a different position
in the present day from what they occupied fifty or even thirty years ago.
This great meeting is a proof of it. The people are taking a more direct
interest in political business and assuming a more direct control over
their representatives . . . [The two Assemblies that sit at Westminster]
. . . are still . . . of the highest importance; but their importance has been
diminished . . . by the fact that the people throughout the country, meeting in meetings like this, can give an impulse to the public policy of the
nation which is, in some degree, independent of the action of its representatives at Westminster. In that sense (and I do not think it is a subject
to be deplored at all) the practical action of the people is superseding the
indirect action of their representatives . . .
     But bear in mind that the House of Commons which we admire, . . .
was a House of Commons freely elected, freely debating, freely checked
by a Second Assembly (Cheers) . . . A House enslaved by the caucus
(Hear, hear) and muzzled by the *clôture* will be a very different body from
that which has hitherto been the glory of English history (Cheers) . . .
Bear in mind that that is the danger to which we are all tending now;
everything points to the increase of power in the hands of one individual,
dictating Minister. The competition of parties is so keen, the power of

applying pressure to individual members is so complete, that every year you will see our representatives, assumed to be independent, more and more exposed to the danger of being forced to fit their convictions into a single mould, provided by the man who happens to be at the head of the dominant party at the time (Hear, hear). This is the justification for a second chamber . . .

4.1.4 From Roundell Palmer (The Earl of Selborne), Memorials (Part II – 'Personal and Political') (1898), Vol. I, p. 470.

Mr Gladstone was occupied, during the autumn of 1879, with his first Midlothian campaign, into which he threw himself like a gladiator in the arena, as no other statesman of similar position had ever done before. As an exhibition of intellectual and oratorical power, it was very remarkable; but it was a precedent tending in its results to the degradation of British politics, by bringing in a system of perpetual canvass, and removing the political centre of gravity from Parliament to the platform.

4.2 PARTY IN THE COUNTRY

4.2.1 From Sir Spencer Walpole, The History of 25 Years (1904), Vol. II, pp. 347–8.
Walpole is discussing the significance of Disraeli's resignation in 1868.

. . . the action of Mr Disraeli, in resigning office without meeting Parliament, however justifiable it may have been, is a mark in the constitutional history of the country. It is the first open recognition in history that the House of Commons itself was of less importance than the electors who formed it, and that a Minister might, and could, defer to public opinion without waiting for its formal expression by a vote in the lower House of Parliament. The House itself was becoming less and less that assembly of wise men who met in earlier times to confer on affairs, and more and more the delegates of the people who sent them to Westminster.

4.2.2 From a letter to Disraeli from J. E. Gorst, 24 February 1881. Disraeli Papers, Hughenden Manor, B/XXI/G/264.

My Dear Lord Beaconsfield,
    Mr W. H. Smith has asked me to send you a Report of what is being done at the Central Conservative Office. I have made it and in two

parts – the first shows what is the ordinary routine work of the office, which has in my opinion been carried on by Mr Stewart and Mr Rose our secretaries with diligence and energy since they have been in charge. I see the one or other of them daily and keep myself informed of all their proceedings – the second shows the special work done since the last session and that which is now engaging our attention.

I have made out the Report in as short and summary a manner as I could in accordance with what I understand to be your wishes: but I can give you more detail upon any point you think necessary. A great deal of time both in correspondence and interviews is taken up by projects for the establishment of Conservative newspapers, both daily and weekly. This arises from persons who form these projects relying rather upon party contributions than upon the commercial merits of their undertakings. These people are treated with civility and attention: but no encouragement is given to their designs on the funds of the party.

Believe me,
Yours faithfully,
J. E. Gorst.

Ordinary Work of Conservative Central Office

Registration

Enquiries are made as to the residence and qualification of the voters of all counties in England and Wales. Forms, instructions, and advice are furnished to both Counties and Boroughs.

Elections

Local leaders are assisted in finding suitable candidates. Forms, instructions and election literature is supplied. County out-voters are canvassed.

Organization

Formation of new associations is promoted and assisted. Model rules etc. are supplied. An annual list of clubs and associations is compiled.

Meetings

The continual holding of small local meetings is advised and encouraged. Speakers and hints for speakers are provided. Special meetings (as for example on the Irish question) are from time to time recommended and promoted.

Publications

Pamphlets and leaflets on current political topics are issued: important speeches are reprinted and circulated.

Press

A weekly publication, called 'The Editor's Handysheet', is issued to provide materials for political articles to the Conservative Provincial Press. Political telegrams are sent from the Lobby to several provincial papers.

Parliamentary

All bills affecting the interests of the party are circulated amongst the local leaders. Petitions are from time to time promoted.

Statistics

Facts respecting Elections Parliamentary and municipal are collected and tabulated. An index of political events during the past ten years is in course of formation.

Correspondence

Enquiries are answered upon such subjects as Finance, Foreign Affairs, Army and Navy administration, Election statistics and procedure, India, Irish affairs, Licensing, Education, Friendly Societies, etc. etc.

Interviews

People of every class call at the office on political business, and every endeavour is made to treat them with courtesy and consideration.

Visits

Constituencies are visited by emissaries from the Central Office of two sorts:

(a) Experienced agents to advise on the legislation and electoral machinery.

(b) Gentlemen to stir up dormant constituencies, and recommend local organization and effort.

Special Work of Conservative Central Office since August 1880.

The Hon. Fitzroy Stewart (our new Secretary) has read up the correspondence of the last 6 years respecting each constituency. He has seen a great number of candidates for Parliament and has made out a list of candidates with their qualifications.

He has also appended to each constituency the names of suitable candidates, amongst whom a selection could be made in case of a vacancy. As the candidates for any constituency become definitely fixed they are of course noted.

A great deal of his time has been taken up by interviews with persons who have schemes for starting every description of newspaper, and who persist in explaining them to somebody who represents the Party.

The National Union which broke out into discord with the Party Managers after the General Election has been brought into concord . . .

4.2.3 From Joseph Chamberlain, 'The Caucus', The Fort-nightly Review (November 1878), pp. 726–7 and 734–41.

A party is a union, more or less temporary in its character, of persons who have important common aims. It does not exclude the ideas of infinite differences and shades of opinion, but it does involve the subord-ination of these to the primary objects of association, so long as the union subsists at all. In a political party, the common aim changes from time to time . . . Who is to decide in the first instance to what efforts the resources of the party are to be directed, and who is to appoint the leaders of the enterprise? . . . the Americans have acted on the opinion that government whether of the nation or of a party within it, rightly belongs to the majority. This rule is too frequently reversed in England, and it is because minorities, and often very small minorities, have had such power in determining the course of English politics, that such a deep hostility is shown by a minority to a system [*i.e. the caucus* – Ed.] which is avowedly designed to relieve majorities of the disabilities under which they have so long laboured . . .

When all the arguments against the caucus are collected and com-pared, it will be found that they resolve themselves into three, repeated with great variety of expression and ingenuity of illustration: (1) It will lead to political corruption; (2) it will disenfranchise minorities and crush out individuality; and (3), somewhat inconsistently, it will misrepresent the real opinion of majorities, and give undue power to an insignificant fraction of the electors. I have dealt with the first two of these objections. I have pointed out that the favourite illustration of America breaks down because of the dissimilarity of the conditions, and that our experience does not give the slightest warrant for the anxiety so loudly expressed. I may add that the bribery which is still so prevalent at many English elections . . . is likely to be less frequent under a system which throws a clear light on the comparative strength of opinions, and which enables a minority without loss of self-respect or sense of injustice to defer to the general sentiment. These results, however, are not, and cannot be ob-tained by the exclusion of minorities or the stifling of independent opinion. The object being to make every man feel a personal interest in government and to widen the basis of representation till it is co-extensive with the whole of the party, would be entirely frustrated by the intoler-ance sometimes attributed to the promoters of organization. It is only when all are assured of a fair hearing and all are convinced of the neces-sity of occasional concession, while at the same time all are seriously and deeply interested in the success of the general policy, that it comes naturally to pass that the decision of the majority is cheerfully accepted ... It cannot be too strongly insisted that *the caucus does not make opinion, it only expresses it*. And in order that it may do this accurately and influentially, not only does it not seek to extinguish shades of feeling, but it accepts, solicits, nay, almost extorts, their manifestation ... It follows from this that the third of the objections which I have named would, if true, be absolutely fatal to the system. If the committees are not really representative, if they only simulate an elective process, and are in fact the nominees of a small section of the party, it must be admitted that the caucus has no more claim to public support than the system of pot-house committees and private coteries which it is designed to supplant, and it will soon shrink into deserved neglect and contempt.

This is the answer to the charges brought against us; for if they were true they would destroy the system ...

Much indignation is expressed at the dictation to which it is assumed Members of Parliament will in future be subjected, and it is confidently asserted that the representatives will sink into the position of mere delegates ... It is of course a nice point of political morality, which every man must decide for himself, how far and how long a Member of Parliament may honourably speak and vote in opposition to the views of those by whom he has been returned. But it may be assumed that something like a general agreement of opinion is tacitly implied in the relation of represented and representative; otherwise, the much-vaunted independence of the one will involve the servile abnegation of all political belief and judgement by the other. More than this general sympathy I doubt if any caucus will ask or any member concede, though the precise limits of independence claimed and allowed must depend on the individual and the circumstances ...

If the new organization succeeds in preventing the waste and division of Liberal strength, it will have accomplished no mean and unimportant work ... But these are not the only results to be hoped for from the spread of political organization. It is part of the great democratic movement of our time, which, not swiftly, ... is still slowly and surely establishing and extending the foundations of liberty.

Every institution which assists the political education of the people, which increases their interest in public affairs, which tempts them to take their share in moulding the destinies of the nation, everything, in short, which helps the people to govern themselves, is a contribution to this great end ... Those ... on whom their convictions do not sit lightly ... will not easily accept inglorious ease. Believing that Liberalism has yet a great mission to accomplish – that it is fraught with incalculable possibilities of good – they will not be slow to make their appeal to the people, whose interest in political affairs and whose share of political power is continually increasing; and they will have good reason to rejoice if organization, with unity and strength, brings also definiteness of aim to the counsels of the Liberal party.

4.2.4 From W. E. Gladstone, 'Electoral Facts', The Nineteenth Century (July–December 1878), pp. 960–1 and 962–3.

It is sometimes surmised that the Liberal party, however sound and honourable, as to the enormous majority of cases, in its personal composition, has nevertheless, when compared with the opposite combination, a larger fraction of adherents whose pursuits and position are to a certain extent unfixed, and who are therefore more open to the fitful influences of personal ambition. And it is a matter not of surmise, but of certainty, that the aggregate energy of the body has been very seriously diminished by what the Scots call the divisive courses of sectional opinion. Without doubt, this loss of collective working power must be in part set down to its superior force of healthy individuality, without which its energy of movement, and its generous love of improving changes, could not be maintained . . . But the sects, which nestle within the party, cannot be treated quite so tenderly . . . Under these sectarian or local influences it happens, more frequently than the Liberals at large are aware, that on the occurrence of parliamentary vacancies, and likewise at General Elections, the party, instead of settling its subaltern differences within itself by a judicious organization, advisedly severs itself into two or more sections, and contends against the political adversary as if with one hand free and the other bound. The consequence is that a majority is broken up into two or three minorities; and Liberal constituencies, because they can only secure agreement with a Liberal candidate on nine points out of ten, make over the seat to a Tory, who in all the ten is against them . . .

Thus it is, that the Liberal party becomes, in too many cases, the laughing-stock of its enemies . . . The question naturally arises, whether this folly is always to be in fashion among us, or whether the malignant elf has been, or can be, effectually exorcized. To expel it, by preliminary arrangements of a popular representative character, is, I apprehend, a main object of what is known as the Birmingham Organization. To prevent its expulsion is the equally natural purpose of the outcry in the Tory camp against that organization.

4.2.5 From Joseph Chamberlain, 'A New Political Organiza-
tion', The Fortnightly Review (*Vol. 22, 1877*), *pp. 126–34.*
Chamberlain is discussing the foundation of the National
Liberal Federation.

. . . there is no reason to conceal the fact that it is the confident expectation of the promoters of the new organization that it will result in greater
definiteness being given to the aims and objects of the party, and that
Mr Gladstone's presence and support has raised the hopes of all who are
interested in its success. The ex-leader of the Liberal party, and the
most popular statesman of our time, has expressed his cordial sympathy
with the efforts of those who are striving to retrieve the fallen fortunes of
the Liberal cause; and he has frankly admitted the claims of the Radicals
– the men who are in earnest – to recognition and fair consideration in
the party councils. After this we may hope at least that the persistent
efforts of some, who call themselves Liberals, to rule out of the party
as rebels and pariahs all who protest against the Fabian policy of inaction
which has so long hindered union and stifled enthusiasm, will be dis-
continued; and that we may be permitted to remind our leaders that we
are tired of marking time, without being accused of mutiny or even of
unreasonable presumption.

It will be admitted that the party is an instrument to achieve some more
definite results than the return to office of a certain number of persons of
undeclared opinions. We have not lost confidence in its efficacy, but we
are anxious to know what are the purposes which those who direct the
machine intend it to serve. At the present moment we are groping
blindly in the dark. Liberals are at a loose end, each advocating some
favourite reform, and producing little impression, because there is no
uniformity or consistency in the agitation. Even Mr Bright, who has just
told us that he hates a programme, has been beating the air like lesser
mortals, and in three successive speeches to his constituents has advocated, one after the other, the completion of National Education, the
Disestablishment of the Church, and the Reform of the Land Laws and
County Administration. If this is not a programme, it is at least a considerable advance towards one; but would it not be better that we should
all know which of these great reforms is the question of the immediate
future, and which should, therefore, receive the concentrated attention
of a united party?

There are times, no doubt, when politicians must be content to test
public opinion without attempting to control it; to feel the pulse of the
nation without committing themselves definitely to what may turn out
to be a Quixotic enterprise. This is the excuse of those Liberals who

justify their inaction by the alleged indifference of the country. The people, they have been repeating for the last four years, are tired of change; complete rest and freedom from agitation is required to restore their healthy appetite. If this view of the position be the correct one, there is nothing for it but to lay up our liberalism *en retraite* for an indefinite period. Our occupation is gone; there is no question of a programme; no need for a leader; all that is required is the service of a political charwoman or two, who will keep the dust from the furniture and the flies from the chandelier.

Unfortunately, however, for this hypothesis, it is contradicted by the facts. The evidence is all the other way. Without a word of guidance or a sign from their official leaders, the Liberals in the constituencies have on three or four occasions spontaneously asserted their influence and have altered the policy of the Government. In the cases of the Merchants' Shipping Bill, the two Slavery Circulars and the Burials Bill, the rank and file have positively dragged their officers into action; and the course of Conservative legislation has been turned by popular agitation. The initiative which the Opposition in Parliament have failed to take has been seized by public meetings. The Assembly has been directed by the Conventions. How long is this to last, and to what length is it desired that it should go?

It will be not the least of the objects of the new Federation to prevent from time to time the possibility of such misconceptions, and to reflect accurately the opinions and the wishes of the majority of Liberals for the information of all who are responsible for party management. By its constitution, membership is restricted to associations based on popular representation, i.e. to those which secure the direct participation of all Liberals in their respective districts in their management and general policy. The Birmingham Liberal Association is the type to which all these organizations approach. The managing committees are elected by *public meetings annually called in each ward, and open to every Liberal resident.* Thus the constituency of the Association is the whole body of Liberals in the borough. The divisions which are so often caused by sectional or personal interests are rendered impossible or harmless by the width of the base on which the association rests, and its thoroughly representative character is so well understood that no imputation of individual dictation or management by clique can possibly be sustained.

The Liberals of Birmingham have fully recognized the altered conditions under which they have to carry on their work. Owing to various causes, and notably to the extension of the suffrage and to the increased interest taken by the mass of the people in general politics, it is not only desirable but absolutely necessary that the whole of the party should be taken into its counsels, and that all its members should share in its control and management. It is no longer safe to attempt to secure the representation of a great constituency for the nominee of a few gentlemen sitting in committee, and basing their claims to dictate the choice of the electors on the fact that they have been willing to subscribe something towards the expenses. The working class, who cannot contribute pecuniarily, though they are often ready to sacrifice a more than proportionate amount of time and labour, are now the majority in most borough constituencies, and no candidate and no policy has a chance of success unless their good will and active support can be first secured. The object of a Liberal association should therefore be to secure a perfect representation of the opinions of the whole party, and to gain their confidence in the absolute fairness and impartiality of the means by which the decision of the majority can be ascertained, in order that the whole force of the organization may afterwards be employed in securing the success of the candidate or the policy adopted.

... the principles on which the Birmingham Association is formed are rapidly commending themselves to Liberals in other towns. Nearly one hundred boroughs were represented at the Conference, and applications are daily received from all parts of the country for information and assistance to enable the local associations to re-form themselves on the Birmingham model. In this way it may be anticipated that local representative bodies will soon exist in every parliamentary constituency, and these will in turn be represented in proportion to the population of their respective districts on the council and committee of the new Federation. A meeting of the central organization will therefore be a meeting of delegates from popularly elected local associations, and will thus collect with unerring certainty the opinions of the majority of the Liberal party in each of the places represented. This collection of opinions from time to time on the questions of the day will be one main object of the Federation, and as the local organizations are intended to ascertain the feelings of their separate districts, the central body will gather this information to a focus, and will be enabled to decide if there be sufficient unanimity and enthusiasm to justify them in recommending further action.

It will be seen that no programme could be imposed on such an organization, as each member will attend its meetings because he is a representative Liberal, and he cannot be asked to produce any other passport. Besides, Liberalism should not be narrowed by any stereotyped creed: it is an open trust, changing and broadening with every advance in intelligence and freedom. Nevertheless, no one who knows the constituencies will doubt that on great questions of principle there will be considerable agreement. When the whole party is represented, the majority will not be for standing still. They belong to what they believe to be the party of progress, and they will not take the trouble of organization on their shoulders without tolerably definite notions of what is to be the outcome of it all.

This matter may be easily tested. Call a public meeting of Liberals in any borough in England or Wales, and ask for its opinion on the question of the extension of the county franchise, or the disestablishment of the English Church. There are many constituencies where the Liberals, so long as these questions are not formally before the country and *faute de mieux*, will accept representatives who candidly express their unwillingness to promote either of these changes. But it is doubtful if there is a single one in which the unbiased opinion of the majority of Liberals would not be given in favour of both. If it be not so, the meetings of the Federation will record the divergence of opinion and justify the inaction of the official leaders; while if, on the contrary, the result should prove that the only people who do not know whither we are going are precisely the persons who have undertaken to direct our advance, and that while party managers have been hesitating public opinion has been ripening and is now formed, it will then be the next duty of the Association to give clear expression and political influence to these opinions, and to secure for them greater attention than they have hitherto enjoyed. It does not follow that the questions named will be the first to attract the consideration of the delegates; they are only used as illustrations of possible differences between the objects which Liberals may have in view, and those which engage the attention of their present representatives in the House of Commons.

The mode of operation is objected to by a hostile critic as an attempt to govern the country by the agency of a gigantic political union. It is not worth while to quarrel about terms. The objects, as stated in the constitution, are the organization of Liberal associations based on popular representation, and the promotion of Liberal principles in the government of the country. To persons to whom Liberal principles still have a definite meaning, these objects do not appear illegitimate nor unworthy of serious effort. The machinery is sufficiently simple. There is to be a council composed of delegated representatives from each Liberal association, appointed in a certain proportion according to population. This council will hold annual meetings in the different towns in succession, and its visit will be made the occasion of a demonstration in favour of Liberal policy. The ordinary work of the Federation is entrusted to a committee, also consisting of delegated representatives elected in proportion to population, but in smaller numbers than the council, and meeting at the call of the chairman and secretary or at the joint request of any three associations.

The functions of this committee are:

1st. To aid in the formation of new Liberal associations based on popular representation, and generally to promote the objects of the Federation.

2nd. To summon the annual meeting of the council, or any other general meeting of council which may be deemed proper.

3rd. To submit to the federated associations political questions and measures upon which united action may be considered desirable.

The last of these is of course the most important, and the nature of the influence exerted may be gathered from a consideration of recent proceedings in connexion with the debate on the Eastern Question, when nearly one hundred and fifty public meetings were held all over the country at a few days' notice in response to a suggestion from the Birmingham Liberal Association alone, and as many more on the recommendation of other political associations.

It must be repeated here that the committee will of course be powerless, if the opinion of the associations represented is adverse, or much divided. But where a feeling in favour of action is unanimous or nearly so, the influence of the Federation will be effectually exerted to secure its concerted expression. It will be seen, therefore, that no interference with the local independence of the federated associations is proposed or contemplated. Each one of these will arrange the details of its own organization and administer its own affairs; but from time to time, and on all occasions of importance, the representatives of all the associations will be summoned to consider the course which will be recommended to their respective organizations. By these means the opinions of Liberals on measures to be supported or resisted will be readily and authoritatively ascertained, and the whole force, strength, and resources of the party may be concentrated on the promotion of reforms found to be generally desired.

Mr Gorst, the member for Chatham, when addressing a meeting of the Metropolitan Alliance of the Conservative Associations, claimed that they had set the example which their opponents were now following. It may be that the idea of the co-operation of independent associations is common to both parties, but the basis of the Liberal Federation is not borrowed from, and cannot be imitated by, any Conservative organization. Conservatism naturally works from above downwards, while Liberalism best fulfils its mission when it works upwards from below. The popular element is not the one in which the Tories are strong, and in their manifestations the leaders are everything and the followers nothing. From their point of view the bulk of their party are a class to be governed and managed, and are not entitled to share freely in the direction of their own affairs. Now, the special merit and characteristic of the new machinery is the principle which must henceforth govern the action of Liberals as a political party – namely, the direct participation of all its members in the direction of its policy and in the selection of those particular measures of reform to which priority shall be given. A fear has been expressed in some quarters that such proceedings may interfere with the proper independence of members of Parliament, and may be used in the coercion of the House of Commons. This theory is surely not complimentary to Liberal members, and it may be asserted in contradiction that, while all of them would resent a French *mandat impératif*, none are unwilling to interchange opinions with their constituents, or to have the advantage of a thorough knowledge of their wishes.

The practical working will be made evident by an illustration. Suppose at a meeting of the committee, at which the delegates from different places are present, that a resolution is carried unanimously in favour of the extension of the county franchise. This would be followed by a recommendation to the separate associations to call public meetings, to obtain petitions, and to take other steps in support of the proposition. The resolution containing these recommendations would then be brought before the local associations at their next meeting. If they approve of the suggestion, they will make the necessary arrangements to carry it out, and will no doubt request their members in Parliament to vote for the motion. But this can only be done if they agree to the recommendations of the central committee. In this case the members will be made acquainted with the desire of their supporters; but it does not follow that any further pressure will be put upon them if they are, on consideration, unable to comply with the request addressed to them. There are two classes of members, in any case, who need fear no coercion: those who are fortunate enough to agree with their constituents, and those who, being in general accord on important principles, occasionally find themselves compelled to differ on a particular question. The constituencies are not so ungenerous nor so unjust as to allow honest differences on certain subjects to outweigh long service and general agreement. Mr John Bright has nearly completed twenty years' service in the representation of Birmingham, the town which it is now sought to describe as a hot-bed of intolerance and the home of a narrow spirit of dictation. During that long period his relations with the borough, honourable alike to the constituency and to its eminent representative, have never been for a moment disturbed, although on some important occasions Mr Bright has found himself obliged to differ from his friends. His right of private judgement has in such cases been uniformly respected, and his seat has always been as safe as that of the most pliant member of the House of Commons. The only persons who can have cause to dread communications from their constituents, are those who have practically ceased to represent the voters by whom they have been elected. Their case is hardly one for commiseration.

An attempt has been made to represent the new Federation as hostile to Lord Hartington and the official leaders. This is really nonsense. It is quite possible that the effect of conference and union will be to show that the Liberal opinion of the country is more advanced than has been hitherto supposed, and it is true that many Liberals think that a somewhat bolder declaration of policy is wanted to give heart and courage to the supporters of the Liberal cause. But what reason is there to believe that the present leaders would resist satisfactory evidence of the wishes of their supporters. If they have been silent and motionless hitherto, they have been justified by the absence of proof that more activity has been desired by the party. With the exception of Mr Gladstone, there is no Liberal leader who would command as much confidence and support as Lord Hartington has secured, and what is sought is not a change of persons, which might be anything but an improvement, but only the formation and the expression of such an amount of public opinion as would encourage our present leaders to move a little quicker and a little farther.

After all there is, perhaps, some reason for the dislike and fear with which what *The Times* calls the new Liberal Caucus is regarded by a certain class of politicians. Those who distrust the people and do not share Burke's faith in their sound political instinct – those who reject the principle, which should be at the bottom of all Liberalism, that the best security for good government is not to be found in *ex cathedra* legislation by the upper classes for the lower, but in consulting those chiefly concerned and giving shape to their aspirations whenever they are not manifestly unfair to others – these all view with natural apprehension a scheme by which the mob, as they are ever ready to term the great bulk of their fellow-countrymen, are for the first time invited and enabled to make their influence felt by means of constitutional machinery.

4.2.6 From H. W. Crosskey, 'The Birmingham Liberal Association and its Assailants', MacMillan's Magazine (November 1878–April 1879), p. 153.

A minority has no right to thwart a majority in determining the course of Liberal policy . . . When the majority have decided that legislation is imperatively demanded in one given direction . . . no member of a minority has the slightest right to demand that he should occupy an office in which he can harass and impede the work the majority have resolved to undertake; . . . a minority in a Liberal Association opposed to

Mr Gladstone's Eastern policy could have no right at such a crisis to select a candidate for a vacant seat in Parliament on the ground that if their views were not represented there would be a 'deplorable loss of variety and fertility in the dominant Liberalism of the day'! There are periods in the history of our country in which the House of Commons cannot be looked upon as a debating club, which fulfils its function when varying 'views' find a fit expression. The happiness of our race hangs largely upon its decisions. It can inflict awful miseries or lighten the grievous burdens under which so many of our people groan. Those Liberals who have political convictions have a higher duty than to devise subtle and intricate methods for the expression of a variety of conflicting opinions. They are bound to select representatives who will support the definite measures they believe to be immediately necessary for the peace and prosperity of the land.

4.2.7 From M. Ostrogorski, Democracy and the Organization of Political Parties *(1902), Vol. I, pp. 594–5.*

... the Caucus, which aimed at hastening the democratic process in English political society, has succeeded only in a superficial, purely apparent fashion. The popular form of the party Organization merely enables the latter to penetrate deeper into the masses for the purpose of capturing them more easily, and not for giving them independence ... The Caucus has in no way helped to raise the tone of public life. Far from liberating it from unwholesome social influences, it has made its Organization, which cleverly superintends the process, an instrument of 'social bribery' practised for the party's benefit. It has not increased material political corruption, but it has encouraged the deterioration of the mind of the electorate. The electioneering impulse is no longer 'spasmodic', it is true; it has no doubt been transformed into steady 'work', but performed by a special contingent of 'workers', who only sow the seed of the 'professional politician' more deeply in English soil; in society as a whole the political pulse does not beat quicker. On the contrary, in preventing the development of a spontaneous political life by its machinery, in offering a permanent obstacle to the free exercise of the judgement, the Caucus tends rather to enfeeble the public mind. It only strengthens political party passion. Blotting out independent thought and enervating the will and the personal responsibility of the voter, the Caucus ends in obliterating the individual, after having undertaken to establish his political autonomy up to the farthest limits of the extra-constitutional sphere. Attacking the old leaders as if they were an impediment to this autonomy, the Caucus has struck a blow at the leadership in general, by disparaging the qualities which constitute leadership in a healthy political community, that is, the personal superiority conferred by knowledge and character, and exalting the conventional and external qualifications enforced by stereotyped methods. In making these qualifications and methods an engine of government, the Caucus bids fair to set up a government by machine instead of a responsible government of human beings.

4.2.8 From J. Marriott, 'The Birmingham Caucus,' The Nineteenth Century (June 1882), pp. 949-51, 954-6 and 960.

To the Liberals of Birmingham belongs the credit of having so managed the electorate of their constituency as to secure to their party the full benefits of the Reform Act of 1867. It was generally supposed by the supporters of Mr Disraeli's Bill that the effect of having three-cornered constituencies would be in some way to check those floodgates of democracy which, according to the old-fashioned Tories, would be opened by its becoming law. If this was the design of the Conservative leader, there is no doubt that Birmingham at once out-manœuvred him. A citizen of that borough, Mr Harris, a Justice of the Peace, and a man of great ability and universally respected by all who knew him, at once recognized the significance of the Act, and adopted means to render its three-cornered clause innocuous to the Liberal party in Birmingham. He, with the aid of some of the most distinguished of his fellow-townsmen, founded the Liberal Association, better known now as the Six Hundred of the Midland capital. Taking as their basis of operation the sixteen wards into which the borough is divided, they formed a committee in each ward, and each of these committees elected thirty-five of their number to be members of a large General Committee of 594. The average number in the Ward Committees is 125, and of the thirty-five selected, thirty are members of the General Committee alone, while five – two of whom must be the chairman and secretary of the Ward Committee – are not only members of this Committee, but are also members of an Executive Committee of the Association, which numbers 114. The 594 of the General Committee are made up of the thirty-five members selected from each of the sixteen wards, with thirty members nominated by the Executive, and four ex-officio members; while the Executive Committee of 114 is made up of the five members selected by each of the sixteen wards, together with thirty members selected by itself, and four officers of the General Committee. There is then another Committee called a Management Sub-Committee, consisting of eleven members, seven of whom are chosen by the Executive Committee from their own number of 114, and the other four are officers of the General Committee.

It was, and probably now is, the boast of the founders of the Association, that its basis was essentially popular, and that the organization was merely a machine by means of which the populace could give articulate expression to their will; and there is no doubt that the primary ward committee of 125 members, or thereabout, is elected at a public meeting of all the Liberals residing in the ward who choose to attend, but here any pretence of consulting the *vox populi Liberalis* ends. To those who are accustomed to public meetings, called together for the purpose of transacting business, this consultation of the people must appear little more than a pretence. Some few Liberals who have a specific object in view summon the meeting of Liberals in the district, and, be the number that attend great or small, it is pretty certain that the majority of them are not prepared for action. The only people prepared will be those who have summoned the meeting, and they certainly will be ready, with a proposal of names for the chairmanship and secretaryship of the Committee, and probably also with the names of a large number of the Committee. The Committee once appointed, the power of the people ceases altogether, and it is filtered through the 594 members of the General Committee and the 114 members of the Executive Committee, till it solidifies in the hands of the Management Sub-Committee of eleven, the four most powerful members of which are probably the four officers of the General Committee. If the president and secretary of the whole Association are decently strong and able men, and they work together, the chances are enormous that the whole power of this intricate organization will rest in their hands, and if the president is wealthy and ambitious as well, he will find in it a most potent instrument for advancing his own ends. Even in clubs and companies, where members and shareholders have generally a far more direct interest in their welfare and management than the average elector has in that of his party, it is well known how, when once a committee or a directorate is formed, all power gravitates toward them, and how they have not only the control for the term for which they are respectively appointed, but how they can influence the re-election of themselves or their own nominees. The members and shareholders are comparatively very weak, and this though the election of their committee or directors is made directly by themselves from their own body. What then must be the measure of the power of the people in an organization like the Birmingham Six Hundred when the people themselves are only consulted once a year, and then only in their particular wards, and when, after their vote is given for the members of their Ward Committee, their voice is silenced for twelve months, and whatever power it may originally have had is not put into force till it has been attenuated by passing through the sieves of the thirty-five, the 594, the 114, till it finally drips through the sieve of the eleven into the expectant palms of the president and the secretary? Associations organized on the pattern of this Birmingham one, so far from being the means of giving adequate expression to the will of the people, are mockeries of the people, and the effect, if not the object, is to make the people convenient tools to place great power in the hands of a few. While the people who attended the primary meeting to elect a Ward Committee are busy all the year with their honest toil, oblivious to a great extent of the existence of the machinery they have started going, the chosen members of the Management Sub-Committee, and especially the president and secretary, are making it the business of their lives to utilize the machine so carefully concocted for some purposes either patriotic or personal.

Had this Association confined its attentions to Birmingham itself it is probable that it might not have attracted much attention. It was Birmingham's business, and no one else's. If the majority liked to domineer, and the minority did not object to, or had not the strength to resist being domineered over, it was not the duty of other towns to interfere. Non-interference with their neighbours' business is the wholesome doctrine our boroughs all act upon. But unfortunately, in the year 1877, the brilliant idea struck their late mayor and then representative in Parliament that what was good for Birmingham must necessarily be good for England, Scotland, and Wales, and probably Ireland too. The idea was probably the natural result of the principle of evolution, and it was soon embodied in a new Association, the object of which was, and still is, to form similar Associations all over the country, and to so connect them that they shall be entirely under the control of the parent one at Birmingham. The new Association was introduced to a wondering, and at first rather bewildered, world amid all the pomp and circumstance becoming the incarnation of a great idea. Its christening, or whatever the rite of inauguration was, took place in the presence of thirty thousand people collected in Bingley Hall, on June 1, 1877, amidst a great flourish of trumpets and repeated salvoes of oratorical artillery. The whole affair was a complete success, and a glowing account of it and its future bearing upon the country was duly chronicled in the July number of the *Fortnightly Review* by the author and originator of its being.

It was only natural that Mr Chamberlain should expect great things from his new Federation. If Mr Harris's Association had been such a success in Birmingham, why should not the new one be equally successful throughout the United Kingdom? The Birmingham Liberal Association was to be the 'type' upon which all other counties and boroughs were to be invited to form organizations. When once formed on this type they were to join the Central Federation, whose headquarters were modest Birmingham itself. The federation was to have a council composed of delegates from all the Federal Associations. A town or district with a population of above 100,000 was to appoint 20 delegates; with a population of above 50,000, 10 delegates; and under 50,000, 5 delegates. The Council was to meet once a year. It was also to have a general committee, consisting of the officers of the Association and delegates from the Federated Associations – a town or district of more than 100,000 sending 5; one of above 50,000, 3; and one under 50,000, 2.

The functions of this Committee were to be:—

1. To aid in the formation of new Liberal Associations based on popular representation, and generally to promote the objects of the Federation.

2. To summon the annual meeting of the Council, or any other general meeting of Council which it may deem proper.

3. To submit to the Federated Associations political questions and measures upon which united action may be considered desirable.

These were, and in the main now are, the rules and objects of the Federation. Its pretension is to express the will of the people, to be founded on a popular basis. It would be an interesting sum to work out the proportion of the power of the people in such associations compared with that of its officers. The result would be to show that the vaunted power of the people was infinitesimal, while that of the officials is enormous. If the unfortunate people consulted once a year in their ward meetings are impotent when their power has been frittered away through the General Committee, the Executive Committee, and the Management Sub-Committee of their own Association, what must its attenuated form be when it has been further frittered away through the Council of Federated Associations till it reaches the General Committee, upon which the strong men are naturally the officers of the Association. The tendency of the Birmingham Liberal Association was to make the president and secretary, and perhaps the treasurer, the most powerful men amongst the Liberals of the borough, and were the National Liberal Federation to be a success, its tendency would be to extend the power of these selfsame men all over England. The boasted 'popular basis' is a mere sham. The real principle of popular government is to bring the representative of the people face to face with the people, and not to have between him and them a complex and intricate machine whose motions will be directed and whose wires will be pulled by paid officials and ambitious politicians. Once create a large body of paid officials acting in unison under one head, and farewell to the purity of political life. It may be taken as an axiom that the more paid officials there are hanging on to any political system, the more chances there are of corruption. Their very livelihood depends upon the places politics have given them, and it is only in the nature of things that at times of political excitement their first thought, like that of the image-makers of Ephesus, should be, not what principles are at stake, but what methods are the best for preserving their places.

That some organization in every county and every borough is necessary for both parties is undoubtedly true, but the simpler it is, and the fewer paid officials it has, the better. Associations for looking after the register, for arranging lectures and meetings for the purposes of spreading political principles, and often for introducing candidates and clubs where those of the same political principles may assemble, are excellent things; but these are very different from an Association which dictates to constituencies who their members shall be, and tries to control the action of their members after the election. This is what associations founded on the type of the Birmingham one do. One of the duties of the General Committee of the typical association is to select Parliamentary candidates. It is an established rule 'that if any person consent to be nominated as a candidate of the Association, in case he is not selected he must submit to the decision of the Committee'. It is clear that if the Association is really a power in its party, no candidate could possibly succeed against the one selected by the General Committee; thus anyone who wishes to have a chance at the ballot-box must first submit to be selected by this Committee, in which the popular power is almost *nil*, and the official power great. When the favoured ones are selected the people have no option but to vote for them or for their political opponents. This is assuredly imposing candidates upon the people, and give them a very little, if any, power in the selection.

Experience has proved that in its grasping after power the Caucus will endeavour to control the actions of members of the Legislature. It is impossible to imagine what greater blow could be aimed at Parliamentary Government than to have a Vigilance Committee outside of it, guided practically by two or three irresponsible individuals, who, whenever important measures were proposed for the consideration of the Legislature, should summon all their federal associations to pronounce upon them before there has been any debate in Parliament, and endeavour to bring pressure upon members to vote as this committee willed, before hearing any argument against or in favour of such measures. The effect would be to transfer all power from Parliament to this self-constituted Vigilance Committee. Yet this is what the Caucus has attempted to do. It considers it part of its duty to 'invite Liberal constituencies to bring legitimate pressure to bear upon their representatives', when those representatives do not vote as the Caucus think they should. Mr Heneage, the member for Grimsby, who first sat in the House in 1864, and has been one of the staunchest and most consistent Liberals both in the dark and in the bright days of the party, had the audacity last year to propose an amendment to the Irish Land Act without first having obtained the approval of Mr Harris, the chairman, Mr Kenrick, the treasurer, Mr Powell Williams, the hon. secretary, and Mr Schnadhorst, the paid secretary, of the Vigilance Committee, and the consequence was that they at once issued a circular soundly rating Mr Heneage for his presumption, including in their scolding 'all the Liberal members who supported his amendment or who intentionally abstained from voting against it'. At the annual meeting held at Liverpool on the 25th of October, when Mr Jesse Collings was chairman, the circular is referred to with considerable self-complacency, and is printed at length in the report of the proceedings.

4.2.9 *From* The Manchester Guardian, *21 December 1882.*

As for local associations, no one who has had anything to do with the machinery of politics in a great town can doubt that they are not merely justifiable but necessary ... But a local association is one thing; an association of such associations, such as is the National Liberal Federation, is another and a very different thing ... representative in any real sense [it] most assuredly is not ... its annual meetings are the least important part of the work of the N.L.F., and the ordinary meetings of its general committee are both far less representative and undertake a far more exalted function. They profess at critical moments to give the cue to the political action of the constituencies all over the Kingdom, and, in fact being made up in an overwhelming proportion of representatives from the immediate neighbourhood of Birmingham, they affect to 'focus' opinion and to pull the strings for the whole country.

4.2.10 *From 'The Nemesis of Party', Anon,* The Fortnightly Review (*January–June 1898*), *p. 11.*

The [National Liberal Federation] came into existence as the organized expression of the strength of a united and triumphant democratic party ...
    [Later] the difference of opinion among Liberal leaders and Liberal voters on the Home Rule question deprived the Liberal party of a very large proportion of the enthusiasm that had up to that point mainly contributed to Liberal victories ... As enthusiasm faded, machinery began to dominate ... it was only natural that, as regard for principles faded out of sight, regard for persons – a weakness to which all political organizations are externally exposed – should gain in strength and importance ...

4.2.11 From a statement by H. C. Raikes, Chairman of the National Union of Conservative and Unionist Associations, in 1873. Report of Proceedings at the Seventh Annual Conference of the N.U.C.U.A. (Leeds 1873), p. 10.

THE CHAIRMAN . . . said . . . that we had now outlived the time of great family influences, and also that period which succeeded the first Reform Bill, which might be called the period of middle class influence in boroughs. We were living in a day in which the people were to be applied to in a much more direct, clear, and positive manner than was the case under the older forms of the Constitution, and, therefore, any party who wished to retain their hold upon the country must ascertain how far their proceedings were in harmony with the wishes of the people. (Hear, Hear.) Having observed what were the functions of the National Union, he said sometimes complaints were made that it did not do all that it ought to do; but he pointed out that it was often suggested that it should do things which did not belong to its peculiar line of duty. The Union had been organized rather as what he might call a handmaid to the party, than to usurp the functions of party leadership.

4.2.12 From Lord Randolph Churchill, 'Elijah's Mantle', The Fortnightly Review (May 1883), pp. 613, 615–16 and 621.

Under a murky sky and amidst splashing rain Sir Stafford Northcote on the 19th April unveiled the statue of Lord Beaconsfield. The occasion was deemed suitable for lamenting the lost glory of the past rather than for anticipating any triumph in the future. Six years ago it was Lord Beaconsfield who unveiled the statue of Lord Derby. At the time, a Conservative government was in office, supported by a majority of 100 in the House of Commons . . . On the 19th of April, 1883, the disagreeable reality present in the minds of those who had collected to honour the occasion, must have been that the majority of 100 in the House of Commons was on the side of the Liberal party . . .

The Liberals can afford better to sustain great disasters than the Conservatives, for there is a recuperative power innate in Liberal principles – the result of the longing of the human mind for progress and for adventure – which enables them to recover rapidly and unexpectedly from misfortunes which would seem to be fatal. The Tories, though possessing many other advantages, fail in this respect. As time goes on their successes will be fewer; . . . unless, indeed, the policy and the principles of the Tory party should undergo a surprising development; unless the secret of Lord Beaconsfield's theory of government is appropriated, understood, believed in . . . broadcast among the people; unless the mantle of Elijah should fall upon someone who is capable enough and fortunate enough, carrying with him a united party, to bring to perfection those schemes of imperial rule, of social reform, which Lord Beaconsfield had only time to dream of, to hint at, and to sketch . . . the 'Tory Democracy' may yet exist; the elements for its composition only require to be collected, and the labour may some day possibly be effected by the man, whoever he may he, upon whom the mantle of Elijah has descended.

4.2.13 From an article by Wolff and Gorst, printed anonymously in The Fortnightly Review *(July–December 1882), pp. 668–72.*

If the Tory party is to continue to exist as a power in the State, it must become a popular party . . . Unfortunately for Conservatism, its leaders belong solely to one class; they are a clique composed of members of the aristocracy, landowners and adherents whose chief merit is subserviency. The party chiefs live in an atmosphere in which a sense of their own importance and of the importance of their class interests is exaggerated, and to which the opinions of the common people can scarcely penetrate . . . After 1868 the aristocratic chiefs for the time retired. They abandoned the cause in despair, and left the Conservative party and Mr Disraeli, whom they anathematized in private, to their own devices. Relieved of the incubus, a new order of things sprang up . . . Between 1868 and 1874 Conservative associations on the Lancashire model grew up in every part of England. They universally complained that they were not patronized by the aristocratic members of the party . . . They were thus driven to devote themselves to registration and the machinery necessary for an election contest. The victory of 1874, which was totally unexpected by the aristocratic section of the party, was the result.

As soon as the success was achieved the men who had stood aloof since 1868 rushed in to share the spoils. A ministry was formed composed almost exclusively of peers and county members. Those by whom the campaign had been planned and fought were forgotten. . . . The defeat of 1880 astonished the aristocratic section as much as the victory of 1874. It was no surprise to those acquainted with the temper of that great section of the party whose voices never reached the leaders' ears . . . the entire organization of the Tory party must undergo a radical reorganization before it can afford grounds for any well-founded satisfaction. In its existing shape it is managed by a committee in London whose names are unknown to the people at large, and who act without any mandate from the constituencies. The Council of the N.U.C.U.A., which is elected annually, has no funds, and is in a chronic position of impotence . . .

Thus the sole present result of the spread of organization . . . is greatly to increase the number of occasions on which the members of the exclusive class exhibit themselves to the multitude . . . If these are the means on which the Conservative leaders rely for bringing themselves back to power, they have a long time to wait.

4.3 PARTY IN PARLIAMENT

4.3.1 From W. E. H. Lecky, The Map of Life *(1900), pp. 12– 14, and 122–4.*

In free countries, party government is the best, if not the only way of conducting public affairs, but it is impossible to conduct it without a large amount of moral compromise; without a frequent surrender of private judgement and will. A good man will choose his party through disinterested motives, and with a firm and honest conviction that it represents the cast of policy most beneficial to the country. He will on grave occasions assert his independence of his party, but in the large majority of cases he must act with his party even if they are pursuing courses in some degree contrary to his own judgement.

Everyone who is actively engaged in politics – everyone especially who is a member of the House of Commons – must soon learn that if the absolute independence of individual judgement were pushed to its extreme, political anarchy would ensue. The complete concurrence of a large number of independent judgements in a complicated measure is impossible. If party government is to be carried on, there must be, both in the Cabinet and in Parliament, perpetual compromise. The first condition of its success is that the Government should have a stable, permanent, disciplined support behind it, and in order that this should be attained the individual member must in most cases vote with his party. Sometimes he must support a measure which he knows to be bad, because its rejection would involve a change of government which he believes would be a still greater evil than its acceptance, and in order to prevent this evil he may have to vote a direct negative to some resolution containing a statement which he believes to be true. At the same time, if he is an honest man, he will not be a mere slave of party. Sometimes a question arises which he considers so supremely important that he will break away from his party and endeavour at all hazards to carry or defeat it. Much more frequently he will either abstain from voting, or will vote against the Government on a particular question, but only when he knows that by taking this course he is simply making a protest which will produce no serious political complication. On most great measures there is a dissentient minority in the Government party, and it often exercises a most useful influence in representing independent opinion, and bringing into the measure modifications and compromises which allay opposition, gratify minorities, and soften differences. But the action of that party will be governed by many motives other than a simple consideration of the merits of the case. It is not sufficient to say that they must vote for every resolution which they believe to be true, for every bill or clause of a bill which they believe to be right, and must vote against every bill, or clause, or resolution about which they form an opposite judgement. Sometimes they will try in private to prevent the introduction of a measure, but when it is introduced they will feel it their duty either positively to support it, or at least to abstain from protesting against it. Sometimes they will either vote against it or abstain from voting at all, but only when the majority is so large that it is sure to be carried. Sometimes their conduct will be the result of a bargain – they will vote for one portion of a bill of which they disapprove because they obtained from the Government a concession on another which they think more important. The nature of their opposition will depend largely upon the strength or weakness of the Government, upon the size of the majority, upon the degree to which a change of ministry would affect the general policy of the country . . .

A Member of Parliament will soon find that he must select a class of subjects which he can himself master, while on many others he must vote blindly with his party . . . The House of Commons is rich in expert knowledge, and few subjects are brought before it which some of its members do not thoroughly understand; but in a vast majority of cases the majority who decide the question are obliged to do so on the most superficial knowledge. Very often it is physically impossible for a member to obtain the knowledge he requires. The most important and detailed investigation has taken place upstairs in a committee to which he did not belong, or he is detained elsewhere on important parliamentary business while the debate is going on. Even when this is not the case, scarcely anyone has the physical and mental power which would enable him to sit intelligently through all the debates. Every Member of Parliament is familiar with the scene, when, after a debate, carried on before nearly empty benches, the division bell rings, and the members stream in to decide the issue. There is a moment of uncertainty. The questions 'which side are we?' 'What is it about?' may be heard again and again. Then the Speaker rises, and with one magical question clears the situation. It is the sentence in which he announces that the tellers for the Ayes or Noes, as the case may be, are the Government whips. It is not argument, it is not eloquence, it is this single sentence which in countless cases determines the result and moulds the legislation of the country . . .

It is a strange process, and to a new member who has been endeavouring through his life to weigh arguments and evidence with scrupulous care, and treat the formation and expression of opinions as a matter of serious duty, it is at first very painful. He finds that he is required again and again to give an effective voice in the great council of the nation, on questions of grave importance, with a levity of conviction upon which he would not act in the most trivial affairs of private life. No doctor would prescribe for the slightest malady; no lawyer would advise in the easiest case; no wise man would act in the simplest transactions of private business, or would even give an opinion to his neighbour at a dinner party without more knowledge of the subject than that on which a Member of Parliament is often obliged to vote. But he soon finds that for good or evil this system is absolutely indispensable to the working of the machine. If no one voted except on matters he really understood and cared for, four-fifths of the questions that are determined by the House of Commons would be determined by mere fractions of its members, and in that case parliamentary government under the party system would be impossible. The stable, disciplined, majorities without which it can never be efficiently conducted would be at an end. Those who refuse to accept the conditions of parliamentary life should abstain from entering into it.

4.3.2 From a speech by Lord Salisbury : an address to a deputa-tation of Conservative associations of England and Wales on his return from the Congress of Berlin. Reported in The Times, *7 August 1878.*

Lord Melbourne used to define a supporter as one who supported him when he was wrong (laughter). I do not ask those in this room to give so extensive a definition to the term; but a supporter must be a man who will support you when your conduct is not understood (cheers) . . . Now, that is the great lesson of the advantages of organizations of this kind, [*i.e. of Conservative associations* – Ed.] not only with respect to the maintenance of those institutions you value, but . . . also for bearing high the name and honour of England in other lands . . . We have just come back from one of the most powerful and enlightened nations of modern times. In that country they have not been particularly successful, perhaps, in defending the freedom of the people against the power of the executive, but they have been still less successful in pushing away from them those subversive theories of which, in this country, we know so little. Look at the returns of these elections – twelve or thirteen parties in the state. That is to say, that those who value order and liberty, which are the common objects of the desire of mankind, cannot sufficiently compress their smaller caprices, whims, and scruples and combine themselves in a great organization to obtain that which they cherish . . . I believe it is only in this country where you will find that affairs are maintained on the support of a thoroughly organized majority depending upon distinctive principles, and therefore it is that the course of our state grows so firm . . . It is not only the institutions of your country that you are defending . . . there cannot be strong and stable government in the face of foreign nations, unless that government is well-supported; . . . it can only be supported by careful organization and by suppressing individual eccentricities (Hear, Hear).

4.3.3 From the Countess of Aberdeen, Edward Marjoribanks, Lord Tweedmouth, Notes and Recollections (*1909*), *pp. 51–2*.

In 1892 came the supreme test of [Marjoribank's] qualities. Mr Gladstone was returned and with a majority of only 40, to carry Home Rule for Ireland. Mr Marjoribanks was appointed chief Whip. Never was there a question which excited more hostility than Home Rule; never was there an Opposition stronger in ability, and the Liberal majority was very small. But on the other hand, never was there a stronger *two* than Mr Gladstone leading and Mr Marjoribanks whipping. The latter set himself resolutely to his task. 'This one thing I do.' His one aim was to give the Party a majority of 40 in every division, and a reference to Hansard will show how well he accomplished the object. He did it by strictness of method and suavity of manner. A story is told, that on one occasion a Junior Whip came into his room to say that Sir So-and-so and Mr So-and-so had left unpaired. 'Then wire for them,' said Mr Marjoribanks. 'What good will *that* do?' said his Junior. 'Then I'll show you what *will* do,' said Mr Marjoribanks, and he wrote something on a sheet of paper. It was 'Sir So-and-so and Mr So-and-so have left for Paris unpaired.' 'Now,' he said, 'wire that to every paper in their respective constituencies, more especially to the Unionist papers. They are sure to insert it.' In a much shorter space of time than the Junior Whip expected, the two defaulters were back in the Lobby and made their way to the Whip's room, fuming and spluttering, 'Who incited these notices in our papers? It is monstrous . . .' But they found they were dashing themselves against a smiling, impenetrable stone wall. 'My dear fellows,' said Mr Marjoribanks, smiling, '. . . I simply can't help myself. If I don't keep our majorities up our courage will disappear, and out we go

183

back to these shaky constituencies of yours, and what will you say then about my good nature? . . .' And so, grumbling and growling, but yet acquiescing, they took up their duties once more.

4.3.4 *From a letter to Goschen from Lord Salisbury, 7 June 1891. Printed in Lady Gwendolyn Cecil,* Life of Salisbury *(1932), Vol. IV, pp. 151–2.*

It has seemed to me several times that the Cabinet does not quite get fair play from the leaders of the Government in the House of Commons, . . . The course in which the Cabinet resolved is something . . . manifestly departed from . . . Of course it is done in perfect good faith, on the plea – the sincere plea – that it is necessary to defer to the opinion of the House of Commons. Of course, it *is* necessary – it is a truism to say so; if by the House of Commons you mean the votes of a majority. But I think resolutions which have been approved in Cabinet are often modified in the House of Commons on account of 'the feeling of the House', which means, *not* the votes of a majority, but the outcry of a small number who are generally almost entirely your opponents . . . Defer to the will of the majority of the House as much as you please – we must all do that. But it is humiliating to be pushed aside on account of 'strong pressure' from Harcourt, Fowler and Trevelyan [*members of the Liberal front bench –* Ed.]. I am afraid that under Dyke's guidance we are allowing this fallacy to conduct us into an *impasse* . . . He is not thinking of the ultimate effect of the measure, or of his chances of obtaining a majority – but of what the people on the other side will say – which is a matter of no importance whatsoever.

4.3.5 *From M. Ostrogorski,* Democracy and the Organization of Political Parties *(1902), Vol. I, pp. 208–9.*

The Liberal majority of 1880 . . . was not homogeneous, and Mr Gladstone's legislative proposals soon created alarm among his moderate followers . . . In these circumstances the Caucus considered that it had an obvious duty to discharge in inviting the local Organizations of the party to bring the refractory members, who did not follow the government with sufficient docility, to their senses. The Committee [*of the National Liberal Federation –* Ed.] sent out a circular [*on 29 June, 1881 –* Ed.] to all the federate Associations, in which it vehemently denounced the lukewarm members of the majority. 'Within a few weeks of their accession to office', ran the document, 'it became apparent that among the members of the House of Commons who had secured Liberal seats, there were some who were not heartily loyal to their leaders . . . During the present session the same disloyalty has reappeared and has threatened the Government with very serious embarrassments . . . Liberal members recently supported an amendment hostile to the Irish Bill of the Government or intentionally abstained from voting against it.' Declaring such a state of things to be intolerable, the Committee of the Federation called on the Associations to take the measures required by the situation.

'This circular produced the effect which the Committee hoped to secure' it soon announced with satisfaction. Telegrams or letters from the local Associations poured in on the members . . . At Birmingham, in a formal meeting of the '600', notice was given that all the disloyal Liberal members would be turned out of their seats . . .

4.3.6 From C. Ilbert, Legislative Methods and Forms *(Oxford, 1901), pp. 211, 212 and 213.*

The eighteenth century and the first two decades of the nineteenth century were indeed prolific of legislation, though mostly of an ephemeral character. The Parliament of the eighteenth century passed many laws, which would now be classed as local Acts, for authorizing the construction of railways [*sic* – Ed.], canals, and bridges . . . and the relief of the poor. But it created no new institutions. The Justice of the Peace was the Alpha and the Omega of its simple system of local government, and most matters of rural importance could be settled in Squire Allworthy's justice-room.

Take up a volume of the eighteenth-century statutes, and compare it with a volume of the Victorian period, and you will find yourself in a new world. In the eighteenth century there was no Local Government Board, no Board of Education, no Board of Agriculture, and the duties of the Board of Trade were almost nominal. Nor were there county councils, district councils, or parish councils . . . The functions, both of the central, and of local authorities, were comparatively few and simple. There were no railways, and no limited companies. Gas and Electricity had not been utilized. Parliament concerned itself little or not at all with educational or sanitary questions, and factory legislation was a thing of the future. Industry was indeed regulated, but mainly in a paternal fashion by Justices of the Peace. In a great part of the country such local administration as was required was exercised by the justices, and the numerous laws which were passed in the eighteenth century for conferring on them additional powers, though often intolerably prolix, were comparatively simple.

The shifting centre of political gravity after the Reform Act of 1832, the enormous strides of scientific discovery, commercial enterprise, and industrial activity, the new problems presented by the massing of great numbers in towns and factories under artificial conditions . . . all these causes have materially altered the character and increased the volume of Victorian legislation. New authorities have been created with new duties, new powers, and new areas. And care has not always been taken to fit the new system into the old . . . Hence the chaos of rates, areas and authorities with which we are all familiar . . . The net result of the legislative activity which has characterized, though with different degrees of intensity, the period since 1832, has been the building up piecemeal of an administrative machine of great complexity, which stands in as constant need of repair, renewal, reconstruction, and adaptation to new requirements as the plant of a modern factory. The legislation required for this purpose is enough, and more than enough, to absorb the whole legislative time of the House of Commons, and the problem of finding the requisite time for this class of legislation increases in difficulty every year, and taxes to the utmost, if it does not baffle, the ingenuity of those who are responsible for the arrangement of parliamentary business.

4.3.7 From Sir Henry Maine, Popular Government (1885), 1890 edition, pp. 118–20, 147 and 151.

The power of the House of Commons over legislation, including constitutional legislation, might seem at first sight to be complete and unqualified. Nevertheless . . . it some time ago surrendered the initiative in legislation, and it is now more and more surrendering the conduct of it, to the so-called Ministers of the Crown. It may be further observed from the language of those who, on the whole, contend for the widest extension of its powers, that a new theory has made its appearance, which raises a number of embarrassing questions as to the authority of the House of Commons in constitutional legislation. This is the theory of the Mandate. It seems to be conceded that the electoral body must supply the House of Commons with a mandate to alter the constitution . . . What is a Mandate? . . . I conjecture that it is a fragment of a French phrase, *mandat impératif,* which means an express direction from a constituency which its representative is not permitted to disobey, and I imagine the mutilation to imply that the direction may be given in some loose and general manner. But in what manner? Is it meant that, if a candidate in an election address declares that he is in favour of household suffrage or woman suffrage, and is afterwards elected, he has a mandate to vote for it, but not otherwise? And, if so, how many election addresses, containing such references, and how many returns, constitute a Mandate to the entire House of Commons? Again, assuming the Mandate to have been obtained, how long is it in force? . . . These unsettled questions form the staple of the controversy which raged among us for months, but the prominence which they obtained is not in the very least arbitrary or accidental . . . all these questions belong to the very essence of constitutional doctrine. There is no one of them which is peculiar to this country; what is peculiar to this country is the extreme vagueness with which all of them are conceived and stated . . . it would seem that the discussion of British constitutional legislation is distinguished from the discussion of all other legislation by having no fixed points to turn upon, and therefore by its irrational violence. Is it therefore idle to hope that at some calmer moment – now that the creation of two or three million more voters has been accomplished – we may borrow a few of the American securities against surprise and irreflection in constitutional legislation, and express them with something like the American precision? . . . We are drifting towards a type of government associated with terrible events – a single Assembly, armed with full powers over the constitution, which it may exercise at pleasure . . . legislation is one of the activities of popular government; and the keenest interest in these activities is felt by all the popularly-governed communities. It is one great advantage of popular government over government of the older type, that it is so intensely interesting . . . The English Parliament . . . legislated against little since fifty years since, when it fell under the influence of Bentham and his disciples. Ever since the first Reform Act, however, the volume of legislation has been increasing, and this has been very much owing to the unlooked-for operation of a venerable constitutional form, the Royal Speech at the commencement of each Session. Once it was the King who spoke, now it is the Cabinet as the organ of the party who supports it; and it is rapidly becoming the practice of parties to outbid one another in the length of the tale of legislation to which they pledge themselves in successive Royal Speeches.

There is undoubted danger in looking upon politics as a deeply-interesting game, a never-ending cricket match between Blue and Yellow. The practice is yet more dangerous when the ever-accumulating stakes are legislative and the danger is peculiarly great under a constitutional system which does not provide for measures reforming the constitution any different or more solemn procedure than that which is followed in ordinary legislation. Neither experience nor probability affords any ground for thinking that there may be an infinity of legislative innovation, at once safe and beneficent . . . I do not think it likely to be denied, that the activity of popular government is more and more tending to exhibit itself in legislation, or that the materials for legislation are being constantly supplied for in ever-increasing abundance through the competition of parties, or lastly, that the keen interest which the community takes in looking on, as a body of spectators, at the various activities of popular government, is the chief reason of the general impression that ours is an Age of Progress, to be indefinitely continued.

4.3.8 From C. Ilbert, Legislative Methods and Forms (Oxford, 1901), p. 82.

It must be borne in mind that the share of the Executive government in, and their responsibility for, the work of current legislation, has enormously increased during recent years. Many measures which at the present day could not be carried except as Government measures, were, in the last century, and in the earlier part of this century, introduced and carried by private members.

4.3.9 From a circular to Associations from the officers of the National Liberal Federation, printed in The National Liberal Federation, Fifth Annual Report, Presented at a Meeting of the Council held in Ashton-Under-Lyme, 19 December 1882, (Birmingham, 1883), pp. 10–11.

Atlas Chambers,
  Paradia Street,
    Birmingham
      February 11th, 1882.
Dear Sir,
    We feel it to be an urgent duty to call your immediate attention to the opposition with which the Government are threatened, from various quarters, in respect to their proposals for a reform of the Rules of Procedure in the House of Commons. The Government have been placed in office by the Liberal Party in order that they may carry a series of measures for which the country has long been reacting. It is only necessary to refer to the Reform of County Government, a Revision of the Land Laws, and an Extension of the Franchise in Counties – to all of which Mr Gladstone's administration stands pledged – in order to show how essential it is that the power to obstruct public business in the House, which has of late years been so flagrantly abused, should be effectively checked. The Government have, accordingly, put into definite shape, and propose to give the force of authority to Rules of Procedure by which, in the main, the House has, by the common consent of its

members, been actually governed for many years past, which, until a recent period, have been honourably observed, and without which the business of a deliberative assembly cannot be carried on. Unless license in debate be prevented, representation becomes of no effect; for, as we have seen, a small number of Members, by persistently prolonging debate, can stop the progress of every important bill.

Under these circumstances, and bearing in mind how largely the hope of Liberal legislation is centred in Mr Gladstone, and in his colleagues in the Government, we ask you to consider the desirability of at once offering Her Majesty's Ministers the support of your Association in passing the Rules which, after anxious and mature deliberation, they have submitted to Parliament as absolutely necessary for the purpose in view. The Tories are of course opposing these Rules, inasmuch as it cannot be the interest of their party that the great measures which the Government are prepared to bring in should pass into law . . .

We believe that the Government must receive the united support of the Liberal party in taking effectual steps to restore the dignity of the House of Commons, as well as to enable them to give effect to the will of the constituencies as expressed in the last general election, and to redeem their own pledges then given to the country. Unless obstruction can be stopped, there is no hope of obtaining these results; and unless the Rules which the Government declare to be absolutely necessary to the conduct of public business are accepted, obstruction cannot be stopped, and consequently the legislative reforms upon which the Liberal party have set their hearts must be infinitely delayed . . .

We are,
Yours faithfully,
William Harris, Chairman of the Council.
William Kenrick, Treasurer.
J. Powell Williams, Hon. Sec.
F. Schnadhorst, Secretary.

4.3.10 From The Annual Register (*1877*), *pp. 45–6.*

The sitting which began at 4 o'clock on Tuesday, July 31, will be memorable in the History of the House of Commons. We say began, because it was not until after 6 on the next evening that it ended, having lasted twenty-six hours and a half. It was the crisis in a strange plot, developed for the first time in the walls of St Stephen's by a little band of Irish members, who made themselves known as the Obstructives, and endeavoured through an abuse of the rules of the House to clog altogether the wheels of legislation. The students of our political history know that the rules and standing orders of the House of Commons are framed with great elasticity, upon the principle of mutual forbearance, with a view to securing as far as possible the rights of minorities, and on the assumption of fairness and courtesy on all sides. Freedom of action is the basis of the English principle, which has secured for us an amount of order and regularity of procedure which the many legislative assemblies founded upon its pattern have failed to attain in anything like the same degree . . .

Nothing worse need be feared, it was thought, than that minorities would do in future what they had done in the past . . . a few stubborn dissentients would now and again waste the time of the House in attempting to impede the passage of some bill obnoxious to them; but after all the bill would pass, and in the meantime the determined obstructors of one measure on one night would become the rational debaters of another on the following night, and perhaps do as much to facilitate business on the latter occasion as they had done to delay it on the former . . . No one had as yet even framed the conception of a group of members who should . . . obstruct the progress of legislation, not as an occasional exertion of the inflexibility of their principles, but as the regular business of their parliamentary lives.

Among the impracticable ranks of the Home Rulers were to be found this session a small knot of members who for the first time converted these recognized privileges into an engine of systematic obstruction . . . Mr Parnell . . . developed the practice of obstruction in a new direction, and inaugurated a systematic policy of interference with every measure introduced under the charge of Government officials.

4.3.11 From Lord George Hamilton, Parliamentary Reminiscences and Reflections, 1868–1885 (1917), Vol. I, pp. 188–9.

The Session of 1881 raised momentous and far-reaching issues . . . Eminent Irish Home-Rulers . . . have been credited with the prediction that the compulsory retention of Irishmen in the House of Commons would 'play the devil' with that institution. I use this slang phrase, as it best expresses the process of abasement which must occur where the main object of a large number of the members is to humiliate and degrade the status and spirit of the institution to which they belong. In a Parliament where such factiousness prevails, its sinister effect can only be counteracted by giving to the majority an inflexible and indisputable procedure; but these epithets are the reverse of the easy-going, slopperty rules of debate and interrogation in the House of Commons. In the opinion of many Members, their latitude and tolerance are considered to tend to the exaltation and glory of the House of Commons, the theory being that all Members of Parliament are gentlemen, and that if they do not behave as such in Parliament they will lose their influence. To put it plainly, the Irish Members of Parliament, under Parnell's guidance, were specially selected that they might upset this tradition, and they all did so, some with regret, some with delight.

4.3.12 *From* The Irish Times (*Dublin*), *2 October 1885.*

All the preparations have been made for the Conventions which are to begin in Wicklow next Monday under the auspices of the [Irish] Parliamentary Party. It is understood that these meetings are not to take place with any object of determining on a programme or adopting what might be called a policy. The programme and policy have been defined already by the leader of the party ... Now is the time, according to the guiding spirit, when the Irish members, raised in number at least to 80, and acting as one man at the bidding of one man, will be able to extract what they demand from one party or the other, whichever may triumph in the English elections ... It is to select candidates who will believe this, and pledge themselves to absolute obedience, that the Conventions will be held ... This process of finding a Parliamentary representative is unique. There has not been anything like it even in Birmingham, the region of the caucus.

4.3.13 *From the Irish Parliamentary Pledge, drawn up by T. M. Healy, 1884. Printed in E. Curtis and R. B. MacDowell (editors),* Irish Historical Documents, 1172–1922 (1943).

I pledge myself, that in the event of my election to Parliament, I will sit, act, and vote with the Irish parliamentary party; and if at a meeting of the party, convened upon due notice, specially to consider the question, it be determined by resolution, supported by a majority of the Irish party, that I have not fulfilled the above pledges, I hereby undertake to resign my seat.

4.3.14 *From* The Earl of Oxford and Asquith, *Fifty Years of Parliament (1926), Vol. I, p. 5.*

As late as 1872, Brand, an old and experienced Whip, who had just completed his first session in the Speaker's Chair, records his opinion that 'of the two leading men in the House, Gladstone and Disraeli, neither has a strong hold on his followers'. They were in their different

H

ways, two of the greatest Parliamentarians in our history; but when they became, as each did in turn, the idol of the nation, it was not by reason of their ascendancy in the House of Commons, but through their capacity to touch and capture, the one the imagination, the other the conscience, of their countrymen outside.

4.3.15 From T. E. Kebbel, 'The Spirit of Party', The Nineteenth Century (January–June 1882), pp. 385–6.

Let us now turn for a moment to the effect likely to be produced by the disintegration of Parliamentary parties on the political creeds which they represent. It seems to me that this would be far more unfavourable to Liberalism than to Conservatism, and that because of a difference between the two of which Liberals are accustomed to boast. Conservatism is homogeneous, Liberalism is not. Organization and discipline are natural and spontaneous in the former. They are artificial and compulsory in the latter, and, but for the external bond which is woven out of the obligations and traditions of party, could hardly be maintained at all . . . Conservatism is a positive creed which no man professes who has not something to lose, either material or moral, by the triumph of the opposite creed. Here we have a guarantee for discipline stronger even than party spirit. And closely connected with this feature of Conservatism is another which strengthens my arguments still further. If we exclude the enthusiastic minority . . ., the Liberal party is much less acted upon by moral considerations than the Conservative. I mean the Conservatism appeals to the affections more strongly than the rival creed. Liberalism is intellectual, utilitarian, progressive. Of the power of association and prescription, of the romantic, the picturesque and the venerable, all of which speaks to the heart rather than to the head, it takes comparatively small account.

4.3.16 From a letter to W. S. Caine from John Bright, 22 June 1886. Printed in J. Newton, W. S. Caine (1907), p. 167.

One Ash,
Rochdale,
June 22, 1886,

Dear Mr Caine,

I see you are engaged in a fight at Barrow. I much hope you will win. It is not pleasant to see how unforgiving some of our heretofore Liberal friends are if their representatives refuse to surrender judgement and conscience to their demands or the sudden changes of their political leader.

The action of our clubs and associations is rapidly engaged in making delegates of their members, and in insisting on their forgetting all principles when the interests of a party, or the leader of a party, are supposed to be at stake. What will be the value of a party when its whole power is laid at the disposal of a leader from whose authority no appeal is allowed? At the moment it is notorious that scores of members of the House of Commons have voted with the Government, who, in private, have condemned the Irish Bills. Is it wise for a Liberal elector or constituency to prefer such a member, abject at the feet of a Minister, to one who takes the course dictated by his conscience and his sense of honour?

4.4 PARTY RHETORIC

4.4.1 From G. Lowes-Dickinson, A Modern Symposium *(1905), pp. 14–37.*
The speakers who figure in these extracts are Lord Cantilupe, a Tory (based upon Lord Salisbury); Reuben Mendoza, a Conservative (based upon Disraeli); Alfred Remenham, a Liberal (based upon Gladstone); and George Allison, a Socialist (probably based upon Sidney Webb).

[Cantilupe]: 'Why I went into politics? Why did I? I'm sure I don't know. Certainly I wasn't intended for it. I was intended for a country gentleman, and I hope for the rest of my life to be one; which, perhaps, if I were candid, is the real reason of my retirement. But I was pushed into politics when I was young, as a kind of family duty; and once in it's very hard to get out again. I'm coming out now because, among other things, there's no longer any place for me. Toryism is dead. And I, as you justly describe me, am a Tory. But you want to know why? Well, I don't know that I can tell you. Perhaps I ought to be able to. Remenham, I know, can and will give you the clearest possible account of why he is a Liberal. But then Remenham has principles; and I have only prejudices. I am a Tory because I was born one, just as another man is a Radical because he was born one. But Remenham, I really believe, is a Liberal, because he has convinced himself that he ought to be one. I admire him for it, but I am quite unable to understand him. And, for my own part, if I am to defend, or rather to explain myself, I can only do so by explaining my prejudices. And really I am glad to have the opportunity of doing

193

so, if only because it is a satisfaction occasionally to say what one thinks; a thing which has become impossible in public life.

'The first of my prejudices is that I believe in inequality. I'm not at all sure that that is a prejudice confined to myself – most people seem to act upon it in practice, even in America. But I not only recognize the fact, I approve the ideal of inequality. I don't want, myself, to be the equal of Darwin or of the German Emperor; and I don't see why anybody should want to be my equal. I like a society properly ordered in ranks and classes. I like my butcher or my gardener to take off his hat to me, and I like, myself, to stand bareheaded in the presence of the Queen. I don't know that I'm better or worse than the village carpenter; but I'm different; and I like him to recognize that fact, and to recognize it myself. In America, I am told, everyone is always informing you, in everything they do and say, directly or indirectly, that they are as good as you are. That isn't true, and if it were, it isn't good manners to keep saying it. I prefer a society where people have places and know them. They always do have places in any possible society; only, in a democratic society, they refuse to recognize them; and, consequently, social relations are much ruder, more unpleasant and less humane than they are, or used to be, in England. That is my first prejudice; and it follows, of course, that I hate the whole democratic movement. I see no sense in pretending to make people equal politically when they're unequal in every other respect. Do what you may, it will always be a few people that will govern. And the only real result of the extension of the franchise has been to transfer political power from the landlords to the trading classes and the wire-pullers. Well, I don't think the change is a good one. And that brings me to my second prejudice, a prejudice against trade. I don't mean, of course, that we can do without it. A country must have wealth, though I think we were a much better country when we had less than we have now. Nor do I dispute that there are to be found excellent, honourable, and capable men of business. But I believe that the pursuit of wealth tends to unfit men for the service of the state. And I sympathize with the somewhat extreme view of the ancient world that those who are engaged in trade ought to be excluded from public functions. I believe in government by gentlemen; and the world gentleman I understand in the proper, old-fashioned English sense, as a man of independent means, brought up from his boyhood in the atmosphere of public life, and destined either for the army, the navy, the Church, or Parliament. It was that kind of man that made Rome great, and that made England great in the past; and I don't believe that a country will ever be great which is governed by merchants and shopkeepers and artisans. Not because they are not, or may not be, estimable people; but because their occupations and manner of life unfit them for public service.

'Well, that is the kind of feeling – I won't call it a principle – which determined my conduct in public life. And you will remember that it seemed to be far more possible to give expression to it when first I entered politics than it is now. Even after the first Reform Act – which, in my opinion was conceived upon the wrong lines – the landed gentry still governed England; and if I could have had my way they would have continued to do so. It wasn't really parliamentary reform that was wanted; it was better and more intelligent government. And such government the then ruling class was capable of supplying, as is shown by the series of measures passed in the thirties and forties, the new Poor Law and the Public Health Acts and the rest. Even the repeal of the Corn Laws shows at least how capable they were of sacrificing their own interests to the nation; though otherwise I consider that measure the greatest of their blunders. I don't profess to be a political economist, and I am ready to take it from those whose business it is to know that our wealth has been increased by Free Trade. But no one has ever convinced me, though many people have tried, that the increase of wealth ought to be the sole object of a nation's policy. And it is surely as clear as day that the policy of Free Trade has dislocated the whole structure of our society. It has substituted a miserable city-proletariat for healthy labourers on the soil; it has transferred the great bulk of wealth from the country-gentleman to the traders; and in so doing it has more and more transferred power from those who had the tradition of using it to those who have no tradition at all except that of accumulation. The very thing which I should have thought must be the main business of a statesman – the determination of the proper relations of classes to one another – we have handed over to the chances of competition. We have abandoned the problem in despair, instead of attempting to solve it; with the result, that our population – so it seems to me – is daily degenerating before our eyes, in physique, in morals, in taste, in everything that matters; while we console ourselves with the increasing aggregate of our wealth. Free Trade, in my opinion, was the first great betrayal by the governing class of the country and themselves, and the second was the extension of the franchise. I do not say that I would not have made any change at all in the parliamentary system that had been handed down to us. But I would never have admitted, even implicitly, that every man has a right to vote, still less that all have an equal right. For society, say what we may, is not composed of individuals but of classes; and by classes it ought to be represented. I would have enfranchised peasants, artisans, merchants, manufacturers, as such, taking as my unit the interest, not the individual, and assigning to each so much weight as would enable its influence to be felt, while preserving to the landed gentry their preponderance. That would have been difficult, no doubt, but it would have been worth doing;

whereas it was, to my mind, as foolish as it was easy simply to add new batches of electors, till we shall arrive, I do not doubt, at what, in effect, is universal suffrage, without having ever admitted to ourselves that we wanted to have it.

'But what has been done is final and irremediable. Henceforth, numbers, or rather those who control numbers, will dominate England; and they will not be the men under whom hitherto she has grown great. For people like myself there is no longer a place in politics. And really, so far as I am personally concerned, I am rather glad to know it. Those who have got us into the mess must get us out of it. Probably they will do so, in their own way; but they will make, in the process, a very different England from the one I have known and understood and loved. We shall have a population of city people, better fed and housed, I hope, than they are now, clever and quick and smart, living entirely by their heads, ready to turn out in a moment for use everything they know, but knowing really very little, and not knowing it very well. There will be fewer of the kind of people in whom I take pleasure, whom I like to regard as peculiarly English, and who are the products of the countryside; fellows who grow like vegetables, and, without knowing how, put on sense as they put on flesh by an unconscious process of assimilation; who will stand for an hour at a time watching a horse or a pig, with stolid moon-faces as motionless as a pond; the sort of men that visitors from town imagine to be stupid because they take five minutes to answer a question, and then probably answer by asking another; but who have stored up in them a wealth of experience far too extensive and complicated for them ever to have taken account of it. They live by their instincts not their brains; but their instincts are the slow deposit of long years of practical dealings with nature. That is the kind of man I like. And I like to live among them in the way I do – in a traditional relation which it never occurs to them to resent, any more than it does to me to abuse it. That sort of relation you can't create; it has to grow, and to be handed down from father to son. The new men who come on to the land never manage to establish it. They bring with them the isolation which is the product of cities. They have no idea of any tie except that of wages; the notion of neighbour-liness they do not understand. And that reminds me of a curious thing. People go to town for society; but I have always found that there is no real society except in the country. We may be stupid there, but we belong to a scheme of things which embodies the wisdom of generations. We meet not in drawing-rooms, but in the hunting-field, on the county-bench, at dinners of tenants or farmers' associations. Our private business is intermixed with our public. Our occupation does not involve competition; and the daily performance of its duties we feel to be itself a kind of national service. That is an order of things which I understand

and admire, as my fathers understood and admired it before me. And that is why I am a Tory; not because of any opinions I hold, but because that is my character. I stood for Toryism while it meant something; and now that it means nothing, though I stand for it no longer, still I can't help *being* it. The England that is will last my time; the England that is to be does not interest me; and it is as well that I should have nothing to do with directing it.

'I don't know whether that is a sufficient account of the question I was told to answer; but it's the best I can make, and I think it ought to be sufficient. I always imagine myself saying to God, if He asks me to give an account of myself: "Here I am, as you made me. You can take me or leave me. If I had to live again I would live just so. And if you want me to live differently, you must make me different." I have championed a losing cause, and I am sorry it has lost. But I do not break my heart about it. I can still live for the rest of my days the life I respect and enjoy. And I am content to leave the nation in the hands of Remenham, who, as I see, is all impatience to reply to my heresies.'

I cannot even accept the theory, to which he [Cantilupe] gave expression, of a fixed and stable representation of interests. It is indeed true that society, by the mysterious dispensation of the Divine Being, is wonderfully compounded of the most diverse elements and classes, corresponding to the various needs and requirements of human life. And it is an ancient theory, supported by the authority of great names, by Plato, my revered master, the poet-philosopher, by Aristotle, the founder of political science, that the problem of a statesman is so to adjust these otherwise discordant elements as to form once for all in the body-politic a perfect, a final and immutable harmony. There is, according to this view, one simple chord and one only, which the great organ of society is adapted to play; and the business of the legislator is merely to tune the instrument so that it shall play it correctly. Thus, if Plato could have had his way, his great common chord, his harmony of producers, soldiers and philosophers, would still have been droning monotonously down the ages, wherever men were assembled to dwell together. Doubtless the concord he conceived was beautiful. But the dissonances he would have silenced, but which, with ever-augmenting force, peal and crash, from his day to ours, through the echoing vault of time, embody, as I am apt to think, a harmony more august than any which even he was able to imagine, and in their intricate succession weave the plan of a world-symphony too high to be apprehended save in part by our grosser sense, but perceived with delight by the pure intelligence of immortal spirits. It is indeed the fundamental defect of all imaginary polities – and how much more of such as fossilize, without even idealizing, the actual! – that even though they be perfect, their perfection is relative only to a

197

single set of conditions; and that could they perpetuate themselves they would also perpetuate these, which should have been but brief and transitory phases in the history of the race. Had it been possible for Plato to establish over the habitable globe his golden chain of philosophic cities, he would have riveted upon the world for ever the institutions of slavery and caste, would have sealed at the source the springs of science and invention, and imprisoned in perennial impotence that mighty genius of empire which alone has been able to co-ordinate to a common and beneficent end the stubborn and rebellious members of this growing creature Man. And if the imagination of a Plato, permitted to work its will, would thus have sterilized the germs of progress, what shall we say of such men as ourselves imposing on the fecundity of nature the limits and rules of our imperfect mensuration! Rather should we, in humility, submit ourselves to her guidance, and so adapt our institutions that they shall hamper as little as may be the movements and forces operating within them. For it is by conflict, as we have now learnt, that the higher emerges from the lower, and nature herself, it would almost seem, does not direct but looks on, as her world emerges in painful toil from chaos. We do not find her with precipitate zeal intervening to arrest at a given point the ferment of creation; stretching her hand when she sees the gleam of the halcyon or the rose to bid the process cease that would destroy them; and sacrificing to the completeness of those lower forms the nobler imperfection of man and of what may lie beyond him. She looks always to the end; and so in our statesmanship should we, striving to express, not to limit, by our institutions the forces with which we have to deal. Our polity should grow, like a skin, upon the living tissue of society. For who are we that we should say to this man or that, go plough, keep shop, or govern the state? That we should say to the merchant, "thus much power shall be yours", and to the farmer, "thus much yours?" No! rather let us say to each and to all, Take the place you can, enjoy the authority you can win! Let our constitution express the balance of forces in our society, and as they change let the disposition of power change with them! That is the creed of liberalism, supported by nature herself, and sanctioned, I would add with reverence, by the Almighty Power, in the disposition and order of His stupendous creation.

'But it is not a creed that levels, nor one that destroys. None can have more regard than I – not Cantilupe himself – for our ancient crown, our hereditary aristocracy. These, while they deserve it – and long may they do so! – will retain their honoured place in the hearts and affections of the people. Only, alongside of them, I would make room for all elements and interests that may come into being in the natural course of the play of social forces. But these will be far too numerous, far too inextricably interwoven, too rapidly changing in relative weight and importance, for the intelligence of man to attempt, by any artificial scheme, to balance and adjust their conflicting claims. Open to all men equally, within the limits of prudence, the avenue to political influence, and let them use, as they can and will, in combined or isolated action, the opportunities thus liberally bestowed. That is the keynote of the policy which I have consistently adopted from my entrance into public life, and which I am prepared to prosecute to the end, though that end should be the universal suffrage so dreaded by the last speaker. He tells me it is a policy of reckless abandonment. But abandonment to what? Abandonment to the people! And the question is, Do we trust the people? I do; he does not! There, I venture to think, is the real difference between us.

'Yes, I am not ashamed to say it, I trust the People! What should I trust, if I could not trust them? What else is a nation but an assemblage of the talents, the capacities, the virtues of the citizens of whom it is composed? To utilize those talents, to evoke those capacities, to offer scope and opportunity to those virtues, must be the end and purpose of every great and generous policy; and to that end, up to the measure of my powers, I have striven to minister, not rashly, I hope, nor with impatience, but in the spirit of a sober and assured faith.

'Such is my conception of liberalism. But if liberalism has its mission at home, not less important are its principles in the region of international relations. I will not now embark on the troubled sea of foreign policy. But on one point I will touch, since it was raised by the last speaker, and that is the question of our foreign trade. In no department of human activity, I will venture to say, are the intentions of the Almighty more plainly indicated, than in this of the interchange of the products of labour. To each part of the habitable globe have been assigned its special gifts for the use and delectation of Man; to every nation its peculiar skill, its appropriate opportunities. As the world was created for labour, so it was created for exchange. Across the ocean, bridged at last by the indomitable pertinacity of art, the granaries of the new world call, in their inexhaustible fecundity for the iron and steel, the implements and engines of the old. The shepherd-kings of the limitless plains of Australia, the Indian ryot, the now happily emancipated negro of Georgia and Carolina, feed and are fed by the factories and looms of Manchester and Bradford. Pall Mall is made glad with the produce of the vineyards of France and Spain; and the Italian peasant goes clad in the labours of the Leicester artisan. The golden chain revolves, the silver buckets rise and fall; and one to the other passes on, as it fills and overflows, the stream that pours from Nature's cornucopia! Such is the law ordained by the Power that presides over the destinies of the world; and not all the interferences of man with His beneficent purposes can avail altogether to check and frustrate their happy operation. Yet have the blind cupidity, the ignorant apprehensions of national zeal dislocated, so far as was possible, the wheels and cogs of the great machine, hampered its working and limited its uses. And if there be anything of which this great nation may justly boast, it is that she has been the first to tear down the barriers and dams of a perverted ingenuity, and to admit in unrestricted plenitude to every channel of her verdant meadows the limpid and fertilizing stream of trade.

'Verily she has had her reward! Search the records of history, and you will seek in vain for a prosperity so immense, so continuous, so progressive, as that which has blessed this country in the last half-century of her annals. This access of wealth was admitted indeed by the speaker who preceded me. But he complained that we had taken no account of the changes which the new system was introducing into the character and occupations of the people. It is true; and he would be a rash man who should venture to forecast and to determine the remoter results of such a policy; or should shrink from the consequences of liberty on the ground that he cannot anticipate their character. Which of us would have the courage, even if he had the power, to impose upon a nation for all time the form of its economic life, the type of its character, the direction of its enterprise? The possibilities that lie in the womb of Nature are greater than we can gauge; we can but facilitate their birth, we may not prescribe their anatomy. The evils of the day call for the remedies of the day; but none can anticipate with advantage the necessities of the future. And meantime what cause is there for misgiving? I confess that I see none. The policy of freedom has been justified, I contend, by its results. And so confident am I of this, that the time, I believe, is not far distant, when other countries will awake at last to their own true interests and emulate, not more to their advantage than to ours, our fiscal legislation. I see the time approaching when the nations of the world, laying aside their political animosities, will be knitted together in the peaceful rivalry of trade; when those barriers of nationality which belong to the infancy of the race will melt and dissolve in the sunshine of science and art; when the roar of the cannon will yield to the softer murmur of the loom, and the apron of the artisan, the blouse of the peasant, be more honourable than the scarlet of the soldier; when the cosmopolitan armies of trade will replace the militia of death; when that which God has joined together will no longer be sundered by the ignorance, the folly, the wickedness of man; when the labour and the invention of one will become the heritage of all; and the peoples of the earth meet no longer on the field of battle, but by their chosen delegates, as in the vision of our greatest poet, in the "Parliament of Man, the Federation of the World".'

'[Mendoza]: One who has not the privilege of immediate access to the counsels of the Divine Being cannot but feel himself at a disadvantage in following a man so favoured as my distinguished friend. The disadvantage, however, is one to which I have had, perforce, to grow accustomed during long years of parliamentary strife, I have resigned myself to creeping where he soars, to guessing where he prophesies. But there is compensation everywhere. And, perhaps, there are certain points which may be revealed to babes and sucklings, while they are concealed from beings more august. The worm, I suppose, must be aware of excrescences and roughnesses of the soil which escape the more comprehensive vision of the eagle; and to the worm, at least, these are of more importance than mountain ranges and oceans which he will never reach. It is from that humble point of view that I shall offer a few remarks supplementary to, perhaps even critical of, the eloquent apostrophe we have been permitted to enjoy.

'The keynote of my friend's address was liberty. There is no British heart which does not beat higher at the sound of that word. But while I listened to his impassioned plea, I could not help wondering why he did not propose to dispense to us in even larger and more liberal measure the supreme and precious gift of freedom. True, he has done much to remove the barriers that separated nation from nation, and man from man. But how much remains to be accomplished before we can be truly said to have brought ourselves into line with Nature! Consider, for example, the policeman! Has my friend ever reflected on all that is implied in that solemn figure; on all that it symbolizes of interference with the purposes of a beneficent Creator? The policeman is a permanent public defiance of Nature. Through him the weak rule the strong, the few the many, the intelligent the fools. Through him survive those whom the struggle for existence should have eliminated. He substitutes the unfit for the fit. He dislocates the economy of the universe. Under his shelter take root and thrive all monstrous and parasitic growths. Marriage clings to his skirts, property nestles in his bosom. And while these flourish, where is liberty? The law of Nature we all know:

> The good old rule, the ancient plan
> That he should take who has the power,
> And he should keep who can!

'But this, by the witchcraft of property, we have set aside. Our walls of brick and stone we have manned with invisible guards. We have thronged with fiery faces and arms the fences of our gardens and parks. The plate-glass of our windows we have made more impenetrable than adamant. To our very infants we have given the strength of giants. Babies surfeit, while strong men starve; and the foetus in the womb stretches out unformed hands to annex a principality. Is this liberty? Is this Nature? No! It is a Merlin's prison! Yet, monstrous, it subsists! Has our friend, then, no power to dissolve the charm? Or, can it be that he has not the will?

'Again, can we be said to be free, can we be said to be in harmony with Nature, while we endure the bonds of matrimony? While we fetter the happy promiscuity of instinct, and subject our roving fancy to the dominion of "one unchanging wife?" Here, indeed, I frankly admit, Nature has her revenges; and an actual polygamy flourishes even under the aegis of our law. But the law exists; it is the warp on which, by the woof of property, we fashion that Nessus-shirt, the Family, in which, we have swathed the giant energies of mankind. But while that shirt clings close to every limb, what avails it, in the name of liberty, to snap, here and there, a button or a lace? A more heroic work is required of the great protagonist, if, indeed, he will follow his mistress to the end. He shakes his head. What! Is his service, then, but half-hearted after all? Or, can it be, that behind the mask of the goddess he begins to divine the teeth and claws of the brute? But if nature be no goddess, how can we accept her as sponsor for liberty? And if liberty be taken on its own merits, how is it to be distinguished from anarchy? How, but by the due admixture of coercion? And, that admitted, must we not descend from the mountaintop of prophecy to the dreary plains of political compromise?'

Up to this point Mendoza had preserved that tone of elaborate irony which, it will be remembered, was so disconcerting to English audiences, and stood so much in the way of his popularity. But now his manner changed. Becoming more serious, and I fear I must add, more dull than I had ever heard him before, he gave us what I suppose to be the most intimate exposition he had ever permitted himself to offer of the Conservative point of view, as he understood it.

'These,' he resumed, 'are questions which I must leave my friend to answer for himself. The ground is too high for me. I have no skill in the flights of speculation. I take no pleasure in the enunciation of principles. To my restricted vision, placed as I am upon the earth, isolated facts obtrude themselves with a capricious particularity which defies my powers of generalization. And that, perhaps, is the reason why I attached myself to the party to which I have the honour to belong. For it is, I think, the party which sees things as they are; as they are, that is, to mere human vision. Remenham, in his haste, has called us the party of reaction. I would rather say, we are the party of realism. We have in view, not Man, but Englishmen; not ideal polities, but the British Constitution; not Political Economy, but the actual course of our trade. Through this great forest of fact, this tangle of old and new, these secular oaks, sturdy shrubs, beautiful parasitic creepers, we move with a prudent diffidence, following the old tracks, endeavouring to keep them open, but hesitating to cut new routes till we are clear as to the goal for which we are asked to sacrifice our finest timber. Fundamental changes we regard as exceptional and pathological. Yet, being bound by no theories, when we are convinced of their necessity, we inaugurate them boldly and carry them through to the end. And thus it is that having decided that the time had come to call the people to the councils of the nation, we struck boldly and once for all by a measure which I will never admit – and here I regret that Cantilupe is not with me – which I will never admit to be at variance with the best and soundest traditions of conservatism.

'But such measures are exceptional, and we hope they will be final. We take no delight in tinkering the constitution. The mechanism of government we recognize to be only a means; the test of the statesman is his power to govern. And remaining as we do, inaccessible to that gospel of liberty of which our opponents have had a special revelation, we find in the existing state of England much that appears to us to need control. We are unable to share the optimism which animates Remenham and his friends as to the direction and effects of the new forces of industry. Above the whirr of the spindle and the shaft we hear the cry of the poor. Behind our flourishing warehouses and shops we see the hovels of the artisan. We watch along our highroads the long procession of labourers deserting their ancestral villages for the cities; we trace them to the slum and the sweater's den; we follow them to the poorhouse and the prison; we see them disappear engulfed in the abyss, while others press at their heels to take their place and share their destiny. And in face of all this we do not think it to be our duty to fold our arms and invoke the principle of liberty. We feel that we owe it to the nation to preserve intact its human heritage, the only source of its greatness and its wealth; and we are pre- pared, with such wisdom as we have, to legislate to that end, undeterred by the fear of incurring the charge of socialism.

'But while we thus concern ourselves with the condition of these islands, we have not forgotten that we have relations to the world outside. If, indeed, we could share the views to which Remenham has given such eloquent expression, this is a matter which would give us little anxiety. He beholds, as in a vision, the era of peace and goodwill ushered in by the genius of commerce. By a mysterious dispensation of Providence he sees cupidity and competition furthering the ends of charity and peace. But here once more I am unable to follow his audacious flight. Confined to the sphere of observation, I cannot but note that in the long and sanguinary course of history there has been no cause so fruitful of war as the rivalries of trade. Our own annals at every point are eloquent of this truth; nor do I see anything in the conditions of the modern world that should limit its application. We have been told that all nations will adopt our fiscal policy. Why should they, unless it is to their interest? We adopted it because we thought it was to ours; and we shall abandon it if we ever change our opinion. And when I say "interest" I would not be understood to mean economic interest in the narrower sense. A nation, like an individual, I conceive, has a personality to maintain. It must be its object not to accumulate wealth at all costs, but to develop and maintain capacity, to be powerful, energetic, many-sided, and above all independent. Whether the policy we have adopted will continue to guarantee this result, I am not prophet enough to venture to affirm. But if it does not, I cannot doubt that we shall be driven to revise it. Nor can I believe that other nations, not even our own colonies, will follow us in our present policy, if to do so would be to jeopardy their rising industries and unduly to narrow the scope of their economic energies. I do not, then, I confess, look forward with enthusiasm or with hope to the Crystal Palace millennium that inspired the eloquence of Remenham. I see the future pregnant with wars and rumours of wars. And in particular I see this nation, by virtue of its wealth, its power, its unparalleled success, the target for the envy, the hatred, the cupidity of all the peoples of Europe. I see them looking abroad for outlets for their expanding population, only to find every corner of the habitable globe preoccupied by the English race and overshadowed by the English flag. But from this, which is our main danger, I conjure my main hope for the future. England is more than England. She has grown in her sleep. She has stretched over every continent huge embryo limbs which wait only for the beat of her heart, the motion of her spirit, to assume their form and function as members of one great body of empire. The spirit, I think, begins to stir, the blood to circulate. Our colonies, I believe, are not destined to drop from us like ripe fruit; our dependencies will not fall to other masters. The nation sooner or later will wake to its imperial mission. The hearts of Englishmen beyond the seas will beat in unison with ours. And the federation I foresee is not the federation of Mankind, but that of the British race throughout the world.'

He paused, and in the stillness that followed we became aware of the gathering dusk. The first stars were appearing, and the young moon was low in the west. From the shadow below we heard the murmur of a fountain, and the call of a nightingale sounded in the wood. Something in the time and the place must have worked on Mendoza's mood; for when he resumed it was in a different key.

'Such,' he began, 'is my vision, if I permit myself to dream. But who shall say whether it is more than a dream? There is something in the air tonight which compels candour. And if I am to tell my inmost thought, I must confess on what a flood of nescience we, who seem to direct the affairs of nations, are borne along together with those whom we appear to control. We are permitted, like children, to lay our hands upon the reins; but it is a dark and unknown genius who drives. We are his creatures; and it is his ends, not ours, that are furthered by our contests, our efforts, our ideals. In the arena Remenham and I must play our part, combat bravely, and be ready to die when the crowd turn down their thumbs. But here in a moment of withdrawal, I at least cannot fail to recognize behind the issues that divide us the tie of a common destiny. We shall pass and a new generation will succeed us; a generation to whom our ideals will be irrelevant, our catchwords empty, our controversies unintelligible.

Hi motus animorum atque haec certamina tanta
Pulveris exigui jactu compressa quiescunt.

'The dust of oblivion will bury our debates. Something we shall have achieved, but not what we intended. My dream may, perhaps, be furthered by Remenham, and his by me, or, it may be, neither his nor mine by either. The Providence whose purposes he so readily divines is dark to me. And perhaps, for that reason, I am able to regard him with more charity than he has always been willing, I suspect, to extend to me. This, at any rate, is the moment of truce. The great arena is empty, the silent benches vanish into the night. Under the glimmer of the moon figures more than mortal haunt the scene of our ephemeral contests. It is they which stand behind us and deal the blows which seem to be ours. When we are laid in the dust they will animate other combatants; when our names are forgotten they will blazon others in perishable gold. Why, then, should we strive and cry, even now in the twilight hour? The same sky encompasses us, the same stars are above us. What are my opinions, what are Remenham's? Froth on the surface! The current bears all alike along to the destined end. For a moment let us meet and feel its silent, irresistible force; and in this moment reach across the table the hand of peace.'

[Allison]: 'This is all very touching,' he began, 'but Mendoza is shaking hands with the wrong person. He's much nearer to me than he is to Remenham, and I don't at all despair of converting him. For he does at least understand that the character of every society depends upon its law of property; and he even seems to have a suspicion that the law, as we have it, is not what you would call absolute perfection. It's true that he shows no particular inclination to alter it. But that may come; and I'm not without hope of seeing, before I die, a Tory-Socialist party. Remenham's is a different case, and I fear there's nothing to be made of him. He does, I believe, really think that in some extraordinary way the law of

205

property, like the Anglican Church, is one of the dispensations of Providence; and that if he removes all other restrictions, leaving that, he will have what he calls a natural society. But Nature, as Mendoza has pointed out, is anarchy. Civilization means restriction; and so does socialism. So far from being anarchy, it is the very antithesis of it. Anarchy is the goal of liberalism, if liberalism could ever be persuaded to be logical. So the scarecrow of anarchy, at least, need not frighten away any would-be convert to socialism. There remains, it is true, the other scarecrow, revolution; and that, I admit, has more life in it. Socialism *is* revolutionary; but so is liberalism, or was, while it was anything. Revolution does not imply violence. On the contrary, violence is the abortion of revolution. Do I, for instance, look like a Marat or a Danton? I ask you, candidly!'

He certainly did not. On the contrary, with his short squat figure, pointed beard and spectacles, he presented a curious blend of the middle-class Englishman and the German savant. There was a burst of laughter at his question, in which he joined himself. But when he resumed it was in a more serious tone and somewhat in the manner of a lecturer. It was indeed, at that time, very largely by lectures that he carried on his propaganda.

'No,' he said, 'socialism may roar; but, in England at any rate, it roars as gently as any sucking-dove. Revolution I admit is the goal; but the process is substitution. We propose to transform society almost without anyone knowing it; to work from the foundation upwards without unduly disturbing the superstructure. By a mere adjustment of rates and taxes we shall redistribute property; by an extension of the powers of local bodies we shall nationalize industry. But in all this there need be no shock, no abrupt transition. On the contrary, it is essential to our scheme that there should not be. We are men of science and we realize that the whole structure of society rests upon habit. With the new organization must therefore grow the new habit that is to support it. To precipitate organic change is merely to court reaction. That is the lesson of all revolution; and it is one which English socialists, at any rate, have learnt. We think, moreover, that capitalist society is, by its own momentum, travelling towards the goal which we desire. Every consolidation of business upon a grand scale implies the development of precisely those talents of organization without which the socialistic state could not come into being or maintain itself; while at the same time the substitution of monopoly for competition removes the only check upon the power of capital to exploit society, and brings home to every citizen in his tenderest point – his pocket – the necessity for that public control from which he might otherwise be inclined to shrink. Capitalist society is thus preparing its own euthanasia; and we socialists ought to be regarded not as assassins of the old order, but as midwives to deliver it of the child with which it is in travail.

'That child will be a society not of liberty but of regulation. It is here that we join issue not only with doctrinaire liberals, but with that large body of ordinary commonsense Englishmen who feel a general and instinctive distrust of all state interference. That distrust, I would point out, is really an anachronism. It dates from a time when the state was at once incompetent and unpopular, from the days of monarchic or aristocratic government carried on frankly in the interests of particular classes or persons. But the democratic revolution and the introduction of bureaucracy has swept all that away; and governments in every civilized country are now moving towards the ideal of an expert administration controlled by an alert and intelligent public opinion. Much, it is true, has yet to be done before that ideal will be realized. In some countries, notably in the United States, the necessity of the expert has hardly made itself felt. In others, such as Germany, popular control is very inadequately provided for. But the tendency is clear; and nowhere clearer than in this country. Here at any rate we may hopefully look forward to a continual extension both of the activity and of the intelligence of public officials; while at the same time, by an appropriate development of the representative machinery, we may guard ourselves against the danger of an irresponsible bureaucracy. The problem of reconciling administrative efficiency with popular control is no doubt a difficult one; but I feel confident that it can be solved. This perhaps is hardly the place to develop my favourite idea of the professional representative; but I may be permitted to refer to it in passing. By a professional representative I mean one trained in a scientific and systematic way to elicit the real opinion of his constituents and to embody it in practicable proposals. He will have to study what they really want, not what they think they want, and to discover for himself in what way it can be obtained. Such men need not be elected; Indeed I am inclined to think that the plan of popular election has had its day. The essential is that they should be selected by some test of efficiency, such as examination or previous record, and that they should keep themselves in constant touch with their constituents. But I must not dwell upon details. My main object is to show that when government is in the hands of expert administrators, controlled by expert representatives, there need be no anxiety felt in extending indefinitely the sphere of the state.

'This extension will of course be primarily economic, for, as is now generally recognized, the whole character of a society depends upon its economic organization. Revolution, if it is to be profound, must begin with the organization of industry; but it does not follow that it will end there. It is a libel on the socialist ideal to call it materialistic, to say that it is indifferent or hostile to the higher activities. No one, to begin with, is more conscious than a true socialist of the importance of science. Not only is the sociology on which his position is based a branch of science; but it is a fundamental part of his creed that the progress of man depends upon his mastery of Nature, and that for acquiring that mastery science is his only weapon. Again, it is absurd to accuse us of indifference to ethics. Our standards, indeed, may not be the same as those of bourgeois society; if they were, that would be their condemnation; for a new economic régime necessarily postulates a new ethic. But every régime requires and produces its appropriate standards; and the socialist régime will be no exception. Our feeling upon that subject is simply that we need not trouble about the ethic because it will follow of itself upon the economic revolution. For, as we read history, the economic factor determines all the others. "Man ist was er isst," as the German said; and morals, art, religion, all the so-called "ideal activities", are just allotropic forms of bread and meat. They will come by themselves if they are wanted; and in the socialist state they will be better not worse provided for than under the present competitive system. For here again the principle of the expert will come in. It will be the business of the state, if it determines that such activities ought to be encouraged, to devise a machinery for selecting and educating men of genius, in proportion to the demand, and assigning to them their appropriate sphere of activity and their sufficient wage. This will apply, I conceive, equally to the minister of religion as to the professors of the various branches of art. Nor would I suggest that the socialist community should establish any one form of religion, seeing that we are not in a position to determine scientifically which, or whether any, are true. I would give encouragement to all and several, of course under the necessary restrictions, in the hope that, in course of time, by a process of natural selection, that one will survive which is the best adapted to the new environment. But meantime the advantage of the new over the old organization is apparent. We shall hear no more of genius starving in a garret; of ill paid or overpaid ministers of the gospel; of privileged and unprivileged sects. All will be orderly, regular, and secure, as it should be in a civilized state; and for the first time in history society will be in a position to extract the maximum of good from those strange and irregular human organizations whose subsistence hitherto has been so precarious and whose output so capricious and uncertain. A socialist state, if I may say so, will pigeon-hole religion, literature and art; and if these are really normal and fruitful functions they cannot fail, like other functions, to profit by such treatment.

'I have thus indicated in outline the main features of the socialist scheme – an economic revolution accomplished by a gradual and peaceful transition and issuing in a system of collectivism so complete as to include all the human activities that are really valuable. But what I should find it hard to convey, except to an audience prepared by years of study, is the enthusiasm, or rather the grounds for the enthusiasm, that animates us. Whereas all other political parties are groping in the dark, relying upon partial and outworn formulae, in which even they themselves have ceased to believe, we alone advance in the broad daylight, along a road whose course we clearly trace backward and forward, towards a goal distinctly seen on the horizon. History and analysis are our guides; history for the first time comprehended, analysis for the first time scientifically applied. Unlike all the resolutionists of the past, we derive our inspiration not from our own intuitions or ideals, but from the ascertained course of the world. We co-operate with the universe; and hence at once our confidence and our patience. We can afford to wait because the force of events is bearing us on of its own accord to the end we desire. Even if we rest on our oars, none the less we are drifting onwards; or if we are checked for a moment the eddy in which we are caught is merely local. Alone among all politicians we have faith; but our faith is built upon science, and it is therefore a faith which will endure.'

4.4.2 From W. H. Mallock, Social Equality (1882), pp. 13–16.

When [Conservatives] criticize, for instance, any scheme that seems to tamper with property – and such essentially are the special schemes they contend against – they have practically but one way of condemning it; they call it a scheme of theft; and if they can justify this description of it, they seem to think that the last word has been said. And once no doubt they would have been perfectly right in thinking so. Once *theft* was a word weighted with common odium . . . But this is precisely the point at which the great change has occurred . . . it is now maintained deliberately that the key to all social progress is some redistribution of property, and some violation of rights that have been hitherto held sacred. Thus to call the democrats a set of thieves and confiscators, is merely to apply names to them which they have no wish to repudiate . . . [Conservatives] must prove that property is a thing which should be respected, before they can secure a verdict against those who do not respect it. The whole situation is really contained in that. Property in our day is theoretically in a new position. It is the defendant now. If property is to be defended at all, it must be defended on wider grounds . . . It must be shown that an attack on it would not injure the few only, but that it would equally bring ruin on the many; – this can be done only by an accurate and scientific demonstration of either or both of two distinct positions. One is, that however desirable it might be to equalize property, it would be impossible to do so for more than a single moment; that the equality of such a moment would be one of want, horror, and consternation, not of property . . .

The other is, that, even supposing that permanent equality were not thus unobtainable, but that it could really be established as a stable social condition, its establishment would not be to the interest of even the poorest classes: in other words, that the inequality now surrounding us is not an accidental defect which we must minimize as far as possible; but that it is, on the contrary, an efficient cause of civilization – that it is the cause of plenty, but not the cause of want.

4.4.3 From a speech by Lord Randolph Churchill at Birmingham in October 1883. Printed in W. S. Churchill, Lord Randolph Churchill (1906), Vol. I, p. 309.

The great bulk of the Tory party throughout the country is composed of the artisans and labouring classes . . . the Conservative party will never exercise power until it has gained the confidence of the working classes: and the working classes are quite determined to govern themselves, and will not be either driven or hoodwinked by any class or class interests. Our interests are perfectly safe if we trust them fully, frankly and freely; but if we oppose them, and endeavour to drive them and hoodwink them, our interests, our Constitution, and all we love and revere will go down.

4.4.4 From Lord Salisbury, 'The Commune and the Internationale', The Quarterly Review (October 1871), pp. 549, 565, 572–3 and 580.

. . . municipal liberties, if you come to count them, are not the things for which people get themselves and their neighbours shot. They mean, with us, the power of looking to the drains, keeping the pavement in good order, regulating the dustman and the water-cart . . ., and, moreover, of exercising all these cherished privileges without interference from the central government . . . Men do not die upon the barricades for prerogatives of this sort . . . The Commune was doing battle for something more attractive than any vestry or common council powers. The liberties it claimed, like many of the liberties for which men cry the loudest, meant the liberty of doing as it liked with the lives and property of other people . . .

The conflict has left far behind it the boundaries of ordinary political discussion. Forms of government, rights of franchise, are questions simply trivial compared to the vast issues which this new alliance between fanaticism and ruffianism has raised. A new sect, claiming to number millions in its ranks, powerful enough to hunt out a Government and set its heel on a great city for two months, wielding for the time a force of 150,000 armed men, schemes to eradicate from among human institutions at once marriage, property and religion. Are the representatives of the French nation to be blamed for thinking that with such an enemy there can be neither truce nor compromise? They give no quarter to all that humanity values most: and when once they have commenced the shedding of blood they must look for the measure they have meted out to others. The usages of war are for adversaries who recognize the possibility of adjusting their hostile claims, and have not extinguished the hope of living someday side by side in peace. The conflict between Socialism and existing civilization must be a death struggle. If the combat is once commenced, one or other of the combatants must perish. It is idle to plead that the schemes of these men are their religion. There are religions so hostile to morality, so poisonous to the life-springs of society, that they are outside the pale of human tolerance . . .

It is impossible to study the forces which are driving our brilliant neighbours through such appalling trials to an unknown goal without a passing reflection upon our own dangers and the future that lies before us . . . Shall we ever be seeking in theoretic constitutions, for some new principle of political cohesion to reconstruct a society shattered by revolution . . . ?

There is nothing in the attitude of English workmen, as a body, to give cause for apprehensions of this kind . . . The workmen of this country have been active of late years, but it has usually been with the very practical object of raising the rate of wages . . .

[But] there is no belief to which this age . . . more passionately clings than the belief in progress . . . ; the optimism of politicians in recent times has been something more serious than amiable weakness . . . the assurance that constant future progress is a certainty, and that there must be within reach of legislation some remedy for every evil, has been their intellectual datum-line. This conviction explains the apparent recklessness with which changes have been advocated, without any effort to ascertain their real operation, either by experiment or at least by tentative advance . . . we all know that to be ruled by the Liberal party is the *sine qua non* of political well-being . . . It is a party which does not aim at any definite objects . . . There is no particular political change, or set of political changes which will satisfy its ambition. The only result of achieving them will be to stimulate it to plan a new campaign, of which fresh and farther-reaching changes shall be the aim . . . Radicals have improved upon all previous reformers by making change an institution. They honour the process of subversion and replacement abstractedly, without reference to the objects on which it is exercised . . .

It is obvious that as the party of resistance rests upon the satisfaction which the nation feels, or is presumed to feel, with its present institutions, the party of movement, on the other hand, lives upon discontent . . . As each successive cause of discontent is removed, by the complete triumph of the discontented class or section, the party of movement, in order to sustain its existence, must find some new subject of complaint.

4.4.5 From a speech by Disraeli to the National Union of Conservative and Unionist Associations at the Crystal Palace, 24 June 1872. Reported in The Times, 25 June 1872.

Far be it from me for a moment to intimate that a country like England should not profit by the political experience and science of Continental nations of not inferior civilisation . . . But the tone and tendency of Liberalism cannot be concealed. It is to attack the institutions of the country under the name of Reform (Cheers) and to make war on the manners and customs of the people of this country under the pretext of Progress (Cheers) . . . Gentlemen, the Tory party, unless it is a national party, is nothing (Cheers). It is not a confederacy of nobles, it is not a democratic multitude; it is a party formed from all the numerous classes of the realm – classes alike and equal before the law, but whose different conditions and different aims give vigour and variety to our national life . . . I have always been of the opinion that the Tory party has three great objects. The first is to maintain the institutions of the country – not from any sentiment of political superstition, but because we believe that the principles of liberty, of order, of law, and of religion (Cheers) – ought not to be intrusted to the caprice and passion of multitudes, but should be embodied in a form of permanence and power. We associate with the monarchy the ideas which it represents – the majesty of law, the administration of justice, the fountain of mercy and honour. We know that the Estates of the realm, by the privileges they enjoy, are the best security for public liberty and good government. We believe that a national profession of faith can only be attained by maintaining an established church (Cheers) . . . Well, it is a curious circumstance that during 40 years of triumphant Liberalism, every one of these institutions has been attacked and assailed . . . Well, gentlemen, as far as the institutions of the country – the Monarchy and the Lords spiritual and temporal – are concerned, I think we may fairly say . . . that public opinion is in favour of those institutions . . .

[The 1867 Reform Act] was founded on a confidence that the great body of this country were 'Conservative' – I use the word in its purest and loftiest sense. I mean that the people of England, and especially the working classes of England, are proud of belonging to a great country, and are resolved to maintain, if they can, the Empire of England . . . I venture to express my opinion, long entertained . . . that that is the conviction and disposition of the great mass of our people . . .

If the first great object of the Tory party is to maintain the institutions of the country, the second is, in my opinion, to maintain the Empire of England (Hear, Hear) . . . Another great object of the Tory party, and one not inferior to the maintenance of the Empire, or the upholding of our institutions is, the elevation of the condition of the people . . . Consider the condition of the great body of the working classes of this country. They are in possession of personal privileges – of personal rights and liberties – which are not enjoyed by the aristocrats of any other country. Recently they have obtained – and wisely obtained – a great enjoyment of political right; and when the people of England see that under the constitution of this country . . . they possess every personal right of freedom . . . is it at all wonderful that they should wish to elevate and improve their condition, and is it unreasonable that they should ask the Legislature to assist them in that behest as far as it is consistent with the general welfare of the realm? (Cheers). Why, the people of England would be greater idiots than the Jacobinical leaders of London even suppose, if, with their experience and acuteness, they had not long seen that the time had arrived when social, and not political improvement is the object at which they should aim (Cheers).

4.4.6 From A. B. Forwood, 'Democratic Toryism', The Contemporary Review (January–June 1883), pp. 299–300.

My official duties have brought me into constant and close connection with Conservatives of every class and position in life, and I have no hesitation in stating that if, as a party, Conservatism is simply to be the brake on the wheel of legislation, having no enlightened or progressive policy of its own, it will soon cease, and deservedly so, to exercise any political power in the city of Liverpool. Birmingham has taken the lead in the country of the party aiming at revolutionary changes; in like manner, the Conservatives of Liverpool aspire to head that phalanx of men who, whilst sound upon Constitutional principles, are yet alive to the necessity for such national progress as the growing intelligence of the age demands. I will venture to give a summary of the political opinions I expressed during the election . . . I defined Conservatism to mean a firm determination to uphold the principles of a Constitutional Monarchy, with the Houses of Lords and Commons as independent branches of the legislature; the maintenance of the connection between Church and State; and I urged that every effort should be exerted to foster and strengthen the bonds of union between the mother country and her colonies and dependencies . . . While Conservatism means a firm resistance to all movements subversive of our cherished institutions, it is far from asserting that changes and modifications may not be required from time to time . . .

A local Radical newspaper described me as a 'democratic Tory'. In reply to that statement I said 'If this term means that I have a firm reliance upon and belief in the Conservative instincts of the people, then I am a democratic Tory' . . . I have not a word to retract. My conviction is that the working classes must, from the necessity of their position, have a leaning to Conservatism. In the event of social disorder or disturbance they are the first to feel any ill effects; capital quickly shuts its portals, and employment soon diminishes. As political intelligence spreads amongst the people, so must Conservatism extend. The worst policy the Conservative party can adopt is to exhibit a want of confidence on the people. Trust them, and they will reciprocate the sentiment. My experience of the feelings of the working classes is that they are far from sympathizing with the Radical shibboleth for abolishing class distinctions, nor are they advocates of the doctrine of equality and fraternity in a Republican sense . . . They are . . . alive to the necessity of Government being conducted by the better-educated people and those who have leisure to devote to the work . . . Whilst we in the abstract evince a sympathy with the labouring classes, we must not let our sentiments stop at this point, but let them take a concrete form. No selfish class legislation must mark our policy; we must pay as much regard to measures 'conceived in the interests of the working classes' as we do to the wants of any other body in the community. In past years the Conservatives have shown their sympathy with the people by supporting such measures as the Factory Acts and the Reform Act of 1867. Let a similar policy activate us today. . . .

4. 4. 7 *From A. V. Dicey,* Lectures on the Relation between Law and Public Opinion in the Nineteenth Century (*1905*), *p. 258.*
The passage occurs in the Lecture entitled 'The Period of Collectivism (1865–1900)'.

The fundamental principle which is accepted by every man who leans towards any form of socialism or collectivism, is faith in the benefits to be derived by the mass of the people from the action or intervention of the State even in matters which might be, and often are, left to the uncontrolled management of the persons involved.

This doctrine involves two assumptions: the one is the denial that laissez-faire is in most cases, or even in many cases, a principle of sound legislation; the second is a belief in the benefit of governmental guidance or interference, even when it greatly limits the sphere of individual choice or liberty.

4.4.8 From G. Lowes-Dickinson, The Development of Parliament during the Nineteenth Century (*1895*), *pp. 125–6, 151–2 and 159.*

... it was never the deliberate intention of the governing class, either before or after the first Reform Bill, to accomplish the transition to democracy that has actually taken place. They continued to lower the franchise because, having once begun, there was no particular reason why they should stop; and they seem hardly yet to be aware that in pursuing this apparently continuous course they have been leading society to the verge of a critical transformation. But when we turn from the debates in Parliament and the rhetoric of the National Liberal Federation, to examine the course of opinion among the masses who have been gradually admitted to power, we find that, on the one hand, so far as they have come to political consciousness at all, they have adopted from the beginning the democratic programme; on the other, that their object, in desiring political power, has been primarily to better their economic state, and more particularly, not only in the last ten years but also in the earlier decades of the century, has been conceived, with more or less distinctness, as a fundamental modification of the existing tenure of property.

Such an attitude was the natural and intelligible result of the position to which the working classes were reduced by the new methods of industry ... the more the dependence of the labourer on the capitalist increased, the more persistently the theory began to emerge and define itself, that his only hope of deliverance was in acquiring the control of the means of production. And though it is only in the last decade that this theory has taken the field as a vigorous and consistent collectivist propaganda, yet it was active, obscurely and confusedly, in the earlier revolutionary movements of the century, and gave a social significance to what appears on the surface to be a purely political agitation. From the very beginning, in fact, the movement for parliamentary reform presented a phase, though no doubt a subordinate one, which in a certain

215

vague sense may be called socialistic – that is to say, which proposed to benefit the poor at the expense of the rich . . .

Adult suffrage (including women and paupers), payment of members and of election expenses, short parliaments, and the abolition of the House of Lords are included in the programme of the Fabian Society, no less than in that of the Social Democratic Federation; and in both cases these proposals are only the means to the establishment of a socialistic state . . . this new movement is not merely an academic propaganda, which has not had, and is not likely to have, any effects on the actual course of events . . . if the resolutions of the Trade Union Congress are any indication of working class opinion, they have completely abandoned the individualistic standpoint which they adopted between 1850 and 1880. The nationalization of land . . . has never ceased to find support among them; and in 1882 it was formally adopted by the Congress. The further extension of the principle to all the means of production was rejected in 1890 and 1892, but in 1894 the Congress passed, by a majority of 219 to 61, the following resolution: 'That, in the opinion of this Congress, it is essential to the maintenance of British industries to nationalize the land and the whole means of production, distribution and exchange, and that the Parliamentary Committee be instructed to promote and support legislation with the above object' . . .

The working class is ranging itself against the owners of land and capital. The nation is dividing into two antagonistic sections, and it is to one of these sections, that which is numerically the larger, that must fall, according to the democratic theory of government, the absolute monopoly of power.

4.4.9 *From a speech by Joseph Chamberlain to the Birmingham Artisans' Association, 5 January 1885. Printed in* The New Democracy (*National Liberal Federation, Birmingham 1885*).

The Franchise Bill has been passed (great cheering), and the pistol of which Lord Salisbury spoke so emphatically has been loaded, and it is in our hands. (Renewed cheers.) Next year two millions of men will enter for the first time into the full enjoyment of their political rights. These men are, for the most part, your fellow workmen in factory and in field, and for the first time the toilers and spinners (loud cheers) will have a majority of votes, and the control if they desire it, of the Government of the country . . . The centre of power has been shifted, and the old order is giving place to the new (Hear, Hear) . . .

These changed conditions will require novel combinations to meet them . . . The organization of the party and the programme of the party must be alike enlarged to meet the necessities of the situation . . . There will be more need than ever for organization if you are to gain the full advantage of the new conditions. Vested interests, special crotchets, and personal claims have a natural tendency to combine. They are on their defence; they are bound together by common ties and by common fears; and if the public good, if the interest of the great majority is without discipline and without recognized leaders, it will be like a mob that disperses before the steady tread of a few policemen . . . I want to impress upon you that our free, open, creative Liberal associations are the essential conditions of success in the future, as they have mainly contributed to our success in the past (Hear, Hear) . . .

But when your organization is perfected, when in due proportion to their numbers every class and every district sends up its member to the great council of the nation, which for the first time will be truly representative, what will this assembly do with the powers entrusted to it? What effect will the change we have been considering have upon the future policy of the country? . . . There are two branches of the subject on which . . . I wish to make a few observations. In the first place, I think that, on the whole, the extension of popular authority will make for peace . . . I do not think that the democracy will have any love for a policy of intervention and aggression, nor any ambition for conquest and universal dominion . . .

What is to be the nature of the domestic legislation of the future? (Hear, Hear). I cannot help thinking that it will be more directed to what are called social subjects than has hitherto been the case. How to promote the greater happiness of the masses of the people (Hear, Hear), how to increase their enjoyment of life (cheers), that is the problem of the future – You must look for the cure in legislation laying the heaviest burdens on the shoulders best able to bear them (cheers) – Legislation which will, in some degree, at any rate, replace the labourer on the soil and find employment for him without forcing him into competition with the artisans of the towns (Hear, Hear) – Legislation which will give a free education to every child in the land, and which will thus enable everyone, even the poorest, to make the best use of the faculties with which he may be gifted . . . In the era which is now commencing we shall see many experiments intended to lessen the evils which poverty brings in its train, to increase the rewards of labour, to bring hope to the miserable, to give courage to the weak, and in this way to advance the aim and end of all our Liberal policy – the greatest happiness of the greatest number. (Loud and continued cheers.)

4.4.10 From 'The National Liberal Federation', by 'A Moderate Radical', The Contemporary Review *(February 1898), p. 300.*

Liberalism is not merely the patching-up of this or that hole, the removal of this or that abuse; these are its details, its incidents, its regular tasks: Liberalism is the steady and gradual cultivation of higher ideals for political and social life, the growing intolerance of wrongs which before were not perceived; the eagerness for new and more widespread advantages which were not seen or were deemed impossible; the resolution to 'do good and to distribute' . . . Liberals are always, in and out of season, discussing reforms. To do so is their constant preoccupation. The reform of mankind is their business in life. The world would be intolerable to them but for the hope of progress. To sit still and amuse themselves is in a moving world a folly, and in a naughty and selfish world a crime.

4.4.11 From Robert Lowe, Primary and Classical Education *(1867), pp. 31–2.*

The time has gone past evidently when the higher classes can hope by any indirect influence, either of property or of coercion of any kind, to direct the course of public affairs. Power has passed out of their hands, and what they do must be done by the influence of superior education and superior cultivation; by the influence of mind over mind . . . Well, then, gentlemen, how is this likely to be done? Is it by confining the attention of the sons of the wealthier classes of the country to the history of . . . old languages and . . . Pagan republics, of which working men never heard, with which they are never brought in contact and of which, from the necessity of the case, they know nothing? Is it not better that gentlemen should know the things which the working men know, only know them infinitely better in their principles and in their details, so that they may be able, in their intercourse and their commerce with them, to assert the superiority over them which greater intelligence and leisure is sure to give . . . ?

The lower classes ought to be educated to discharge the duties cast upon them. They should also be educated that they may appreciate and defer to a higher cultivation when they meet it; and the higher class ought to be educated in a very different manner, in order that they may exhibit to the lower classes that higher education to which, if it were shown to them, they would bow down and defer.

4.4.12 From Lord Cowper, 'Desultory Reflections of a Whig'
The Nineteenth Century (*May 1883*), pp. 729–30.

I was born of a family which has professed Whig principles for more than two hundred years: in fact, ever since the word Whig was first invented ... [but] ... I very soon resolved that my deliberately formed opinions should determine what party I should belong to ...

I endeavoured, therefore, to approach the subject in an impartial spirit, and in this I was greatly assisted by a study of history ... It was brought home to me with irresistible force that if our past history has on the whole been great and glorious, it is owing to the men in each generation who were in favour of moderate innovation ... All the reading and all the observation and reasoning which I was capable of resulted eventually in my taking up the same position in politics which I should have taken up if I had blindly followed the hereditary opinions of my family ...

Whig principles, then, as I understand them, are based upon a study of the history of England. The man who holds them must begin by admiring that history and being proud of that country ... my object is not to establish the fact that the condition of England is superior to that of other countries, and that our history is glorious ... It is to those who hold this belief that I address myself. Let them consider how it was that we arrived at such a state of things. It was by the leading men of each generation feeling their way carefully, remedying as far as they could those evils that appeared most prominent, overcoming Conservative obstruction on the one hand, and restraining impetuous Radicalism on the other.